Studies in

AFRICAN AMERICAN HISTORY AND CULTURE

edited by

GRAHAM HODGES
COLGATE UNIVERSITY

A GARLAND SERIES

THE
OF THE
NEW-YORK
HISTORY

AFRICAN FREE-SCHOOLS,

FROM THEIR ESTABLISHMENT IN 1787,

TO THE PRESENT TIME;

EMBRACING A PERIOD OF MORE THAN

FORTY YEARS:

ALSO

A BRIEF ACCOUNT

OF THE

SUCCESSFUL LABORS,

OF THE

NEW-YORK MANUMISSION SOCIETY:

WITH

AN APPENDIX,

Containing Specimens of Original Composition, both in prose and verse, by several of the pupils; Pieces spoken at public examinations; an interesting Dialogue between Doctor Samuel L. Mitchill, of New-York, and a little black boy of ten years old; and Lines illustrative of the Lancasterian system of instruction

BY CHARLES C. ANDREWS,

TEACHER OF THE MALE SCHOOL.

New-York:

PRINTED BY MAHLON DAY.

NO. 376, PEARL-STREET.

1830.

NEW-YORK AFRICAN FREE-SCHOOL, No. 2.

Engraved from a drawing taken by P. Reason, a pupil, aged 13 years.

The Afro-American in New York City 1827–1860

George E. Walker

GARLAND PUBLISHING, INC.
NEW YORK & LONDON 1993

Library of Congress Cataloging-in-Publication Data

Walker, George E. (George Elizur), 1947–
    The Afro-American in New York City, 1827–1860 / George E. Walker.
        p.   cm. — (Studies in African American history and culture)
    Includes bibliographical references and index.
    ISBN 0–8153–1010–2 (alk. paper)
    1. Afro-Americans—New York (N.Y.)—History—19th century. 2. New York
(N.Y.)—History—1775–1865.   I. Title   II. Series.
F130.N4W34   1993
974.7'100496073—dc20   92-46183
                                                                    CIP

Printed on acid-free, 250-year-life paper
Manufactured in the United States of America

This book is dedicated to Robert M. Alexander, Esq.,a great friend, mentor, and advisor.

Contents

Preface

Until recently, the historiography of African-Americans in New York City was limited mainly to the period after the Civil War. While there have been three studies of slavery in New York[1], it was not until the appearance in 1966 of Rhoda G. Freeman's doctoral dissertation[2] that a thorough and systematic attempt was made to trace various aspects of the life of the free black in New York City. While Freeman's work has remained unpublished, it did supersede two earlier published articles written by A.A. Payne and Leo H. Hirsh, Jr.[3]

Freeman drew several major conclusions from her study. She correctly noted for example that the African-American in New York City was only nominally free since American society, influenced greatly by the existence of slavery, rejected the notion of extending an equal status to anyone of African descent, even where such a person was "free" within the letter of the law.

In addition to this, she observed that owing to lack of capital, few skills, and intense immigrant competition, the black man "all but lost the battle for economic security."[4] These disabilities, coupled with

---

[1] Edwin Olson, "Negro Slavery in New York, 1626-1827" (unpublished Ph.D. dissertation), New York University, 1938; Edgar J. McManus, "Negro Slavery in New York" (unpublished Ph.D. dissertation), Columbia University, 1959; Thomas J. Davis, "Slavery in Colonial New York City," (unpublished Ph.D. dissertation), Columbia University, 1974.

[2] Rhoda G. Freeman, "The Free Negro in New York City in the Era Before the Civil War," (unpublished Ph.D. dissertation), Columbia University, 1966. (Hereafter cited as Freeman, "The Free Negro in New York City.")

[3] A.A. Payne, "The Negro in New York Prior to 1860," *The Howard Review,* 1 (June, 1923):1-64; Leo H. Hirsch, Jr., *Negro History,* 16 (October, 1931):382-473.

[4] Freeman, "The Free Negro in New York City," 435.

severe legal and political proscriptions, all but relegated the African-American to a position of second-class citizenship.[5]

Freeman's most insightful study served as a springboard for this author's 1975 study which appeared originally as my Columbia University doctoral dissertation. Unlike Freeman, who categorically disclaimed the notion of black life in New York City as constituting a "community" except in the limited sense of an "aggregate," I endeavored, after an exhaustive search of the sources to establish the existence of a "self-conscious community" that largely accounted for the intense agitation, racial awareness, and unity characteristics of the African-American in New York City.

In addition to the platform and pulpit, two of the most effective instrumentalities employed by African-Americans in New York City to call attention to their plight, the press would, after 1827, play an increasingly pivotal role in rallying the community around a program of action.

This study traces the complex social, economic, religious, and political forces which affected African-Americans and their overall response to them. It more specifically illustrates how the prevailing views and actions of the dominant society serve to limit the aspirations of African-Americans in rising above their supposed "place" within American life.

As Phyllis F. Field very perceptively observed in her masterful study, *The Politics of Race in New York: the Struggle for Black Suffrage in the Civil War Era* (Ithaca, NY, 1982), 24-25, free African-Americans lived in a society with "such a powerful and pervasive prejudice" against them that it was "bound to have practical implications for the way whites and blacks lived together in America." No spokesperson captured more graphically and with such inimitable eloquence the dilemma of free African-Americans in New York City as elsewhere in the United States than Frederick Douglass. Speaking at the National Convention of Colored People held at Rochester, New York in July 1853, he declared:

> As a people, we feel ourselves to be not only deeply injured, but grossly misunderstood. Our white fellow-countrymen do not know us. They are strangers to our character, ignorant of our capacity, oblivious of our history and progress, and are

---

[5] *Ibid.*, 436.

misinformed as to the principles and ideas that control and guide us as a people. The great mass of American citizens estimate us as being a characterless and purposeless people; and hence we hold up our heads, if at all, against the withering influences of a nation's scorn and contempt.

It will not be surprising that we are so misunderstood and misused when the motives for misrepresenting us and for degrading us are duly considered. Indeed, it will seem strange, upon such consideration, (and in view of the ten thousand channels through which malign feelings find utterance and influence,) that we have not fallen in public estimation than we have done. For, with the single exception of the Jews, under the whole heavens, there is not to be found a people pursued with a more relentless prejudice and persecution than are the Free Colored people of the United States.

Like Frederick Douglass, black Americans understood the reality of their predicament in this country but never surrendered willingly to the idea of caste and permanent inequality. Thus, inherent in this analysis will be an examination of the many-sided struggle waged by this group for full freedom and equality within American society and the important role played by black leaders in giving voice and direction to this struggle.

Since this study first appeared in 1975, two major works, focusing on the status of black life in major northern cities have been published. They are respectively, Gary B. Nash, *Forging Freedom: The Formation of Philadelphia's Black Community*, 1720-1840 (Cambridge, MA: Harvard University Press, 1988); Shane White, *Somewhat More Independent: The End of Slavery in New York City, 1770-1810* (Athens, GA: The University of Georgia Press, 1991). Both these books are first-rate.

New York City was chosen for this study because historically, it was a major center and springboard in the organization of the nation's blacks. The activities of blacks emanating from this metropolis have exerted a profound influence upon our larger American life. In addition, there existed then, as there undoubtedly exists now, a unique grouping of social, cultural and racial (or ethnic) variants which can be found in no other American city.

In 1860, the black population of the City was second only to that of Philadelphia. And it was here that the three major newspapers of the race were published.

I have emphasized the years 1827-1860 because the former date marks the beginning of General Emancipation in the State. It was also the year in which the first known newspaper edited by African-Americans was published in the City.

One distinct limitation of this study has to do with the question of black suffrage. Unfortunately, specific data are not available concerning the exact number of blacks who voted in the various wards of the municipality in any given election. Wile information respecting those blacks qualified to vote does exist, no categorical conclusions regarding the influence and leverage of these voters will be drawn.

In general, throughout this study, I shall seek to show how a proscribed and persecuted group of people managed to survive and build a community which sought to achieve if not for themselves, at least for their children, those basic rights and decencies to which every white native American was considered heir.

In the preparation of this book I have had the generous assistance and co-operation of the following: the libraries and personnel of the Columbia University Library, the Library of Congress, New-York Historical Society, New York Public Library, Schomburg Collection of Black History and Culture, Moorland-Spingarn Research Center (Howard University), Library Company of Philadelphia, Langston Hughes Memorial Library (Lincoln University, Pennsylvania) and the George Mason University Library.

I also wish to thank the late Professor Dwight C. Miner of Columbia University, a gracious friend and mentor, for his tireless assistance and encouragement and proof-reading of the entire manuscript. Professors Eric Foner, James P. Shenton, and Charles V. Hamilton, all of Columbia University, provided invaluable assistance throughout the research and writing of the manuscript. My good friend, Dr. Philip S. Foner, also read the manuscript and provided much useful advice. Finally I wish to thank Robert Hayward, a student of mine, for his desktop publishing abilities, and Ms. Claudia Hirsch, Assistant Editor of Garland Publishing Company, for their patience and understanding as the manuscript was readied for publication.

George E. Walker

George Mason University
Department of History
Fairfax, Virginia 22030

Anthony Benezet instructing black students

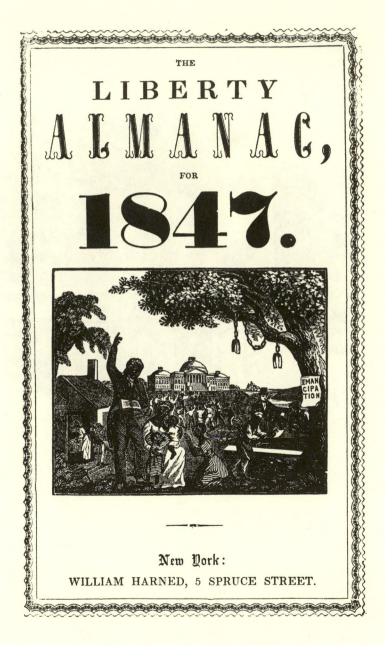

THE
LIBERTY
ALMANAC,
FOR
1847.

New York:
WILLIAM HARNED, 5 SPRUCE STREET.

The Liberty Almanac for 1847

DECLARATION OF THE ANTI-SLAVERY CONVENTION.

ASSEMBLED IN PHILADELPHIA, DECEMBER 4, 1833.

Declaration of Sentiments, American Anti-Slavery Society

Henry Highland Garnett

Charles L. Reason

Lincoln University, Pennsylvania, the first black college founded
in the United States, 1854

The Afro-American in New York City
1827–1860

Social Conditions

July 4, 1827 was a truly memorable day in the history of New York City. For in addition to the grand celebrations held in commemoration of the nation's independence, it also marked the complete freedom from chattel slavery of that state's bond population.

On that occasion, William Hamilton, one of the most prominent blacks in New York City, and active in its life for over three decades, mounted the pulpit of the African Zion Church and proclaimed in ringing tones:

> My brethren and fellow-citizens, I hail you all. This day we stand redeemed from a bitter thralldom. Of us it may be truly said, "the last agony is o'er." THE AFRICANS ARE RESTORED! No more shall the accursed name of *slave* be attached to us— no more shall negro and slave be synonimous [*sic*].

> Fellow citizens, I come to felicitate you on the victory obtained. . . .This day has the state of New York regenerated herself—this day has she been cleansed of a most foul, poisonous and damnable stain.[1]

Yet amid the sounds of fife and drum and the wafting of banners and pennants, some blacks were moved to bitter reflection. Even in a state of supposed freedom they could hardly fail to note the disparity between their condition and that of their white brethren. For while slavery did end in New York, the legacy of that experience would still shadow the African-American in virtually every facet of his daily life. Like his counterpart in other northern cities, the status of the black man would be merely one of quasi-freedom. And nowhere was his

---

[1] William Hamilton, *An Oration Delivered in the African Zion Church, on the fourth of July, 1827 in commemoration of the abolition of domestic slavery in the State* (New York, 1827), 5-6.

unequal position in society more pointed and obvious than in his social condition.

Considerable insight can be gained into the African-American's peculiar station in society by tracing the population movement and understanding the general living standards of this group. For while there is general agreement that blacks represented an oppressed and debased portion of the community, their constant efforts to rise within the scales of society cannot be minimized. Even though daily confronted with prejudice and discrimination they did not too easily dismiss the premises implicit within the American dream.

New York City in 1830 was a bustling metropolis with a total population of 197,112 inhabitants.[2] Of this number there were 14,083 free blacks.[3] Five years later the general population increased to 268,098[4] of which 15,127 were blacks.[5]

At this time the city consisted merely of Manhattan proper, although some blacks took up residence in Brooklyn and Williamsburg, both of which were separate municipalities.[6] New York, as was true of nearly all other major American cities, was divided into wards, political subdivisions for purposes of administration and representation. In 1825 there were 15 wards in New York City; of these blacks were domiciled in wards One to Twelve.[7] By 1830 they had spread out to the Fourteenth Ward.[8] Twenty-five years later, when ward divisions had increased to 22,

---

[2]   U.S. Census Office, *Fifth Census or Enumeration of the Inhabitants of the United States, 1830* . . . (Washington, D.C., 1832), 51. Hereafter cited as U.S.C.

[3]   *Ibid.*

[4]   New York State, *Census for 1835* (Albany, 1836), Double Leaf, No. 26.

[5]   *Ibid.*, Double Leaf, No. 26. See also Appendix.

[6]   Brooklyn and Williamsburg will be included in this study since they contained a sizable black population.

[7]   *The Colored American*, March 25, 1837. See also Appendix.

[8]   U.S.C., *Fifth Census or Enumeration of the Inhabitants of the United States, 1830* . . . , 51.

blacks were to be found in each of them.[9]   The federal census took note of this fact five years later.[10]

The manner in which the African-American population shifted from ward to ward is a phenomenon worth noting. Between the years 1825 and 1860, some wards would gain in percentages of blacks while others would lose considerable numbers. The first federal census showed that the free African-American was not limited to any particular division within the country but it was scattered throughout.[11] Yet during the first decades of the Nineteenth Century a perceptible shift in the population occurred, with the greatest concentration moving slowly westward and northward. Rhoda G. Freeman found that the "area north of Chambers up to Houston Street and west of the Bowery, but particularly west of Broadway became, by the period of general emancipation, the area where the greatest number of Negroes lived."[12]

Between 1825 and 1835 the largest proportion of blacks lived in the Sixth Ward, spreading from Five Points north and west to the Hudson River.[13] In 1827, the northern part of the Sixth Ward became part of the Fourteenth Ward. The Fifth and Eight Wards remained the most populous, although the Fourteenth Ward continued to attract blacks. A well-known African-American newspaper, published in New York City, noted this changed by reporting the following data:

---

[9] New York State, *Census for 1855* (Albany, N.Y., 1857), 8.

[10] U.S.C., *Population of the United States in 1860* (Washington, D.C., 1864), 337.

[11] U.S.C., *Heads of Families at the First Census of the United States in the Year 1790* (Washington, D.C., 1908), 116-137.

[12] Rhoda G. Freeman, "The Free Negro in New York City in the Era Before the Civil War," (unpublished Ph.D. dissertation), Columbia University, 1966, 218-219. (Hereafter cited as Freeman, "The Free Negro in New York City.")

[13] Robert Ernst, *Immigrant Life in New York City, 1825-1863* (New York, 1949), 41. (Hereafter cited as Ernst, *Immigrant Life in New York City.*)

Colored population of the City of New York
(Comparative view for the years 1825, 1830, 1835)

Ward	1825	1830	1835
First	1,035	830	583
Second	598	426	312
Third	881	631	602
Fourth	603	609	210
Fifth	1,719	2,097	1,203
Sixth	2,843	1,878	1,799
Seventh	752	682	820
Eighth	1,547	1,818	2,776
Ninth	640	864	296
Tenth	1,006	1,140	1,000
Eleventh	172	641	798
Twelfth	779	998	1,276
Thirteenth	—	565?	699
Fourteenth	—	899	1,009
Fifteenth	—	—	940
Total	**12,575**	**14,953**	**15,120**

(Source: *Colored American*, March 25, 1837)

While the general population of Manhattan steadily increased throughout this period (1825-1860), the African-American population showed an expansion only until 1840. In that year, the total city population stood at 312,710, of which 16,358 were black.[14] By 1845 however, the general population totaled 371,223, while the number of blacks decreased to 13,004.[15] In 1860, with a total city population of

---

[14] U.S.C., *Sixth Census or Enumeration of the Inhabitants of the United States . . . 1840* (Washington, D.C., 1841), 114.

[15] New York State, *Census for 1845* (Albany, 1846), New York County. There were some African-Americans, however, who took exception to the accuracy of the new York State Census of 1845, particularly with regard to the decrease of the City's black population. Said the *Anglo-African Magazine:* "The State Census of the City of New York taken in 1845, gave only 11,831 colored population. It showed at that time that there had been only 2,445 deaths since 1840 and no marked emigration, and hence supposing there had not been a

813,669, blacks were down to 12,574.[16] Robert Ernst has attributed this decline in part to the "aroused hostility to Negroes during these years of abolitionist activity."[17] Even if this should be conceded, the decline was not as all-pervasive as it appears, for the African-American population of Brooklyn increased from 2,000 in 1840 to 5,000 in 1860.[18]

This very decline in the African-American population did have one perceptible effect: it made possible a greater concentration of the remaining blacks within certain limits. For, as a student of this period discovered, "as businesses took over the Fifth Ward between Chambers and Canal Streets, west of Broadway, the displaced colored population moved above Houston until by 1860 nearly 1,500 of the 12,574 Negroes in the city lived between Twenty-Third and Fortieth Streets, west of Sixth Avenue."[19]

Within the confines of his limited environment the free African-American sought to survive and adjust his life-styles to the larger society. The task, to say the least, would not be easy, for though nominally free, the fact of his *blackness* would *limit* and *define* his options. Moreover, the varying attitudes of whites towards him would act as a barometer in measuring his progress.

"These poor people," observed an English traveler, "feel that they live by sufferance—their humility is quite touching in reference to white persons—and their position is so calculated to debilitate the mind, to teach them submission and dependence rather than anything like forethought and providence that it is not surprising to see them continue under the cloud and rarely break out from it."[20] Mary Lundie Duncan, who wrote these words, was only one in a score of British travelers who took the time and trouble to observe America close-up.

---

single birth, the population should then have been 13,913 or 2,032 more than the Census." The *Anglo-African Magazine*, 1:No. 5, May, 1859, 142-143. See also New York *Tribune*, November 30, 1845.

[16] U.S.C., *Population of the United States in 1860* (Washington, D.C., 1864), 337.

[17] Ernst, *Immigrant Life in New York City*, 235.

[18] George E. Haynes, *The Negro at Work in New York City: A Study in Economic Progress* (New York, 1912), 46-46.

[19] Freeman, "The Free Negro in New York City," 219.

[20] Mary Lundie Duncan, *America as I Found It* (New York, 1852), 257.

And nearly all of them who subsequently wrote about their experiences were deeply moved by the spirit-crushing effects of caste.

Yet even though race operated as a formidable barrier to black aspirations, as we shall see later in this chapter, one should not fail to emphasize the viability of the free Negro community in spite of these social obstacles. In at least two areas, that of housing and health, the overall condition of blacks was generally below that of the larger white community. But, in the control of vice and crime, the African-American did not lag too far behind others. Indeed, in some cases, his progress in this area was marked.

Free blacks during this period had generally large households. Wards Five and Six for example, were the largest in relationship to heads of families.[21] Although the average number of persons in a household was about three, some wards had considerably more persons than others. In Ward One for example, Stacy Stiles of Water Street, who was listed as between 24 and 36 years of age, had three persons in his household.[22] But on New Street in the same ward, Richard Augustus, listed by the Federal census of 1830 as 100 years and over, had 14 persons in his household.[23] In Ward Five on Church Street, Henry Collins, aged between 36 and 55 years, headed a household of 22. But on Chapel Street in the same ward, Ann Woodward, listed also as 36-55, had three in her household.[24]

Wards Five and Six were the largest in terms of persons listed as heads of households. Wards Nine to Fourteen reported the lowest number as heads of households.[25]

The unusual size of some of these households can be attributed in part to boarders or to other members not part of the immediate family. Some of these outside individuals were even white, for the manuscript records of the state census of 1855 reveal that on a house-by-house and family-by-family basis, blacks and whites resided in the same

---

[21] Carter G. Woodson, *Free Negro Heads of Families in the United States in 1830 together with a Brief Treatment of the Free Negro* (Washington, D.C., 1925), 92-95.

[22] *Ibid.*, 91.

[23] *Ibid.*, 92.

[24] *Ibid.*, 92.

[25] *Ibid.*, 97-100.

houses even in areas of the greatest concentration of the African-American population and often as boarders in the same apartment.[26]

During the period of general emancipation some blacks found themselves relegated to the least desirable housing of the city. This was to be expected since their rather depressed economic condition limited access to better housing. They were not alone in this respect, however, for many poor whites, notably the Irish, shared the same predicament.

The housing conditions of blacks became exacerbated somewhat with the influx of Irish immigrants in the period after 1830. To meet the demand for more housing, owners and agents converted old homes into tenements by erecting partitions for the accommodation of three or more families.[27] While the Irish became the principal occupants of these dwellings, blacks too were often crowded into them.[28]

Charles Dickens, an astute observer of the American scene, visited the United States in 1842, on a grand tour. While in New York City, he had occasion to see the Five Points area,[29] a district notorious for its criminality and widespread poverty, in which most of the inhabitants led wretched lives in cellars and garrets.[30]

Even though very few blacks lived in the Five Points, those who did existed in stark contrast to their more fortunate brethren. The housing and general living conditions were simply appalling. Dickens discovered that in one room the air was stale and the floor cold and dank; in the corner of the room lay a pile of filthy rags which served to cover the men, women, and children there. Going about, he observed that from "every corner . . . in these dark retreats, some figure crawls half-awakened, as if the judgment hour were near at hand, and every

---

[26] Rhoda G. Freeman, "The Free Negro in New York City," 219.

[27] Ernst, *Immigrant Life in New York City*, 48.

[28] "Report of the Select Committee Appointed to Examine into the Condition of Tenant Houses in New York and Brooklyn," New York State Assembly, *Documents*, 80th Sess., 1857, 3, No. 205, 22. (Hereafter cited as New York State Assembly, "Report of the Select Committee Appointed to Examine into the Condition of Tenant Houses . . .")

[29] The Five Points district was located in the old Sixth Ward of New York City. It was largely an Irish area with a sprinkling of some blacks.

[30] Ernst, *Immigrant Life in New York City*, 39.

obscene grave were giving up its dead." "Where dogs would howl to lie," he added, "women and men, and boys slink off to sleep, forcing the dislodged rats to move away in quest of better lodgings."[31]

To remedy some of the grosser abuses perpetrated by the landlords of these dwellings, a special committee was appointed by the New York State Assembly to make recommendations.[32] The five-member committee made what was described as a *"thorough, personal* inspection of tenant houses in every ward of the city." While the group was harshly critical of the situation existing in Five Points and in other depressed sections of the city, it has some praise for the general living habits of African-Americans. One member of the committee noted:

> I am not an Abolitionist; but I tell you what it is, gentlemen. If I were to build tenement houses in New York, I should get coloured tenants, if I could. They are more cleanly in their habits than the Irish, or a majority of the poorer class of Americans. I have found very few, in the course of our investigations, who were not neat. It matters not how poor they are, they are generally clean.

---

[31] Charles Dickens, *American Notes for General Circulation* (Boston, 1892), 128-129.

[32] In the Preamble of the resolution (passed March 3, 1856) creating this committee it was said: *"Whereas,* Complaints have been made as to the manner in which buildings known as 'tenant houses,' in the city of New York, have been and are being constructed; that the same are often carried to a great height, without proper regard to the strength of the foundation walls; that said buildings are cut up into small apartments, which have very little ventilation; that the halls or passage-ways through said buildings are unproportionately narrow, and not constructed with proper care to the safety and lives of tenants; that these houses are mostly filled with the poorer class of persons, hundreds of whom are often crowded into a single building, without any means of egress in case of fire or sudden alarm, except through a single narrow passage . . . therefore, *Resolved* . . . etc." New York State Assembly, "Report of the Select Committee Appointed to Examine into the Condition of Tenant Houses," 1-2.

The other members of the committee who were present supported these remarks.[33] In concluding its investigation the committee made a number of recommendations, one of which asked for the enactment of a law against permitting the renting of underground apartments or cellars as tenements. Another urged that rooms be properly divided into separate apartments to prevent prostitution and incest. It insisted that subletting be permanently prohibited, and lastly, asked for the prevention of drunkenness, by providing for every man "a clean and comfortable home."[34]

While housing conditions played a crucial role in the day to day well-being of blacks and foreign immigrants, no problem was fraught with seemingly greater significance than that of health. Both blacks and whites showed a marked tendency to succumb to the ravages of various maladies and their susceptibility to disease appeared to be in direct proportion to their exposure to an unwholesome environment.[35]

---

[33] *National Anti-Slavery Standard,* April 12, 1856. In a letter to the editor of the *Anti-Slavery Standard,* a writer styling himself, "Open Eye" followed up the Committee's observations, by saying in reference to them that "if this is true—and we have no reason to question it—it speaks volumes in favour of the coloured people in this city. Despised and trampled upon as they are," he continued, "and generally very poor, wouldn't it be strange [not] to find them living in filth? Indeed, is it not generally supposed that, instead of being the most cleanly, they are the most filthy of tenants? This opinion, which, we think, generally prevails is not founded upon actual knowledge, but is an inference drawn from the fact that the coloured people are the most despised and oppressed class among us. This being known, people at once come to the conclusion that filth and degradation must, of course, go hand in hand with poverty." *Ibid.,* April 12, 1856.

[34] New York State Assembly, "Report of the Select Committee Appointed to Examine into the Condition of Tenant Houses," 3.

[35] It was said, for example, that "in the damp, dark and chilly cellars, fevers, rheumatism, contagious and inflammatory disorders, affection of the lungs, skin and eyes, and numerous others, are rife, and too often successfully combat the skill of the physician and the benevolence of strangers." New York City, City Inspector, *Annual Report* (1842), 165.

In the summer and autumn of 1820, a bilious typhus fever, known
as the "Bank-Street Fever" prevailed in much of New York City. One
Dr. Pennel, in an essay published the following year, observed:

> Out of the whole number of blacks in this district, viz. 562,
> 119 lived in cellars, of whom 54 were sick of the prevailing
> fever, 24 of whom died at their homes; while of the remaining
> number of black inhabitants, viz. 443, 101 were sick, of
> whom 46 died at their homes. From which it appears that out
> of 443 who were better lodged, only 101 were sick of this
> disease; while out of 119 living in unwholesome cellars, that
> *nearly one half were taken down with disease*, and that nearly
> one half died at their places of dwelling.

He concluded with a significant observation:

> Out of 48 blacks, living in ten cellars, 33 were sick, of whom
> 14 died; while out of 120 whites, living *immediately over
> their heads, in the apartments of the same houses, not one
> even had the fever.*[36]

Consumption, or tuberculosis, was a common disease among the
poor living in New York. In some areas of the city, it was a veritable
scourge. While it exacted a considerable toll in white lives, it took a
disproportionate number of blacks. For example, in 1826, there were
117 African-Americans out of a total of 820 who died from this
ailment, or fourteen percent. The following year the number of 100
Negro deaths of a total of 729, and in 1828, 99 blacks of a total of 906
died from this cause.[37]

By 1857 the City Inspector could report that, as compared with
1,078 natives, 1,734 immigrants died of tuberculosis. But this disease
was nearly twice as fatal to blacks as to whites, again reflecting the

---

[36] *Ibid.*, 165 (Italics in the original).

[37] Freeman, "The Free Negro in New York City," 230. But by
1839, the *Colored American* could report that the "natives of Great
Britain and Ireland, resident in this city, are a poor and laboring class.
So are the people of color. . . .Yet we find by the City's Inspector's
Report (491) that only three colored, to four of this class of white
citizens, fall victim to consumption." *Ibid.*, January 26, 1839.

disparity in the living conditions of the former which were comparable to those of the foreign born.[38]

In addition to tuberculosis, pneumonia and bronchitis were common, while scrofula was a dreaded affliction among the pauper population. The ravages of these diseases affected more immigrants than those of the native population. Robert Ernst found that "during the ten years from 1849 to 1859 of all persons admitted to Bellevue Hospital, a public institution, 83.9 percent were foreign born." Moreover, Ernst discovered that "deaths from all causes were always proportionally higher among the foreign population than among the natives."[39]

Still, in view of all this evidence, the question remains: What was the percentage of deaths of blacks to that of the total population? One student of this period estimated it at approximately four percent.[40] For the white community it was only two percent in 1835, and "even the enormous immigrant population, coming as it did sick, weak and diseased, did not raise the mortality rate to more than three percent."[41] Thus the decline in the absolute number of blacks in the city may be attributed to this higher mortality rate as well as to other factors.

Another problem that vexed New York's free black population concerned the extent to which members of this group engaged in vice and crime. The subject came in for particular attention because one of the most unfortunate assumptions or, should one say, stereotypes associated with the African-American at the time, even by some of his avowed "friends," revolved around the belief in his natural propensity in these areas.

Although this feeling has not entirely died out, even in our own day, it was truly widespread in the 19th Century American. Buttressing the idea was the African-American's supposed prominence in vice-ridden areas and in penal institutions. Even if this be

---

[38] New York City, City Inspector, *Annual Report* (1857), 185.

[39] Ernst, *Immigrant Life in New York City*, 53.

[40] Freeman, "The Free Negro in New York City," 230. But at a Convention of blacks held in Albany, New York, in February, 1852, it was found that the proportion of deaths among blacks in New York City had decreased gradually from 1 in 22 in 1821 to 1 in 41 in 1845. See *Frederick Douglass Paper*, February 5, 1852.

[41] *Ibid.*, 230.

conceded, the abject condition of many blacks, along with the blatant inequalities of the laws, operated to hustle them down the road to complete degradation and thus by a perverse logic reinforce this negative image in the minds of whites.

In a society which exalted the almighty dollar and whose underlying social values put a premium on the man who succeeded in life, however questionably, blacks received a chorus of advice to avoid unseemly behavior and to lead lives of industry and honesty. In 1834, for example, the Executive Committee of the American Anti-Slavery Society observed in an address to the people of color in New York City:

> It cannot be denied that a vast amount of ignorance, vice and misery, exists in this city; and although we are not of the number who underrate the virtues of colored people, and magnify their faults, but on the contrary would repel the constant slanders brought against them, it would be folly in us to deny that there are numbers of colored persons who are helping to swell the amount of degradation, infamy and ruin, which so fearfully abounds in this great city.[42]

The Executive Committee outlined these views in a matter of fact manner. It found intemperance among blacks to be particularly unfortunate since numerous dram shops operating in the city were kept by "colored persons" and often frequented by youths and other individuals of questionable morals. It noted with sorrow those blacks who seemed "situated to do much good," and argued that, since gambling "strikes at the very vitals of society," the laboring class should not waste their time and energies in that manner. Finally, it exhorted blacks to labor honorably and avoid dram selling and "other iniquity for support" and branded those who continued these practices no better than common robbers and manstealers since "to rob our neighbors of property, cannot, certainly, be more heinous, than to rob him of reputation, health and life by tempting him to the indulgence of ruinous passions and appetites."[43]

---

[42] *Address to the People of Color, in the City of New York, by Members of the Executive Committee of the American Anti-Slavery Society* (New York, 1834), 4.

[43] *Ibid.,* 4-5.

As for intemperance, the portrait drawn by the Executive Committee was somewhat misleading. It seemed to imply at least an unconcern by the Negro community with respect to this problem. Blacks themselves spoke out against the excesses of intemperance and the evils which it spawned and launched a crusade to focus attention upon it. A subscriber wrote to Samuel Cornish, editor of the *Colored American*, that intemperance was as prevalent among whites as blacks, but that the latter came in for more criticism due to their lowly status in society. "We know," said the writer, "that the charge of sensuality and degradation has been heaped without measure upon the colored race. This has been used as an argument against any efforts for their elevation." He continued by making this interesting but incisive observation:

> Suppose that I am walking through the streets of this city with an opposer of colored people, and we find two men, one colored and one white, lying drunk on the walk. There, says the opposer, I told you they were a drunken set, and do all you can, you cannot elevate them. But I turn his attention to the white drunkard and apply his reasoning to him. Ah! says the opposer, he is only an *exception* to the class to which he belongs, many of whom have reached the top of refinement and education—have become great in the world.[44]

He concluded that in the mind of the opposer the white drunkard was "an exception, not the general rule. . . . Hence he draws an argument from this circumstance, which, however unjust, in his mind outweighs every consideration to the contrary."[45]

It was largely to dispel such an image on the part of whites that blacks organized to fight intemperance. They had earlier formed, in 1831, a Society for Temperance in New York City, the Colored Presbyterian Congregation in Duane Street being most active in this effort. In August 1831, 29 members were added to their Temperance Society.[46] The effort continued unabated, for in a latter to Gerrit Smith, the noted New York abolitionist and philanthropist, Dr. James

---

[44] *The Colored American*, February 23, 1839 (Italics added).

[45] *Ibid.*, February 23, 1839. The writer signs himself F.A.S. See also *Ibid.*, March 2, 1839.

[46] New York *Evangelist*, August 27, 1831.

McCune Smith, a prominent black physician, complained that within one year three "rum places" had been opened for African-Americans, and he himself was threatened with lawsuits for declaiming against them.[47] But the work of Smith and others was silently bearing fruit, so that by 1853, the *National Anti-Slavery Standard* could report:

> We do not remember to have seen a drunken coloured man in the streets of New York. We had, therefore, an idea that the coloured people have no special weakness toward the alcoholic. It appears, however, there is a stir among them at present on the subject of total abstinence. Meetings are held, societies are formed, pledges are taken, and the 'cause' generally is prosperous.[48]

The issue of crime also provoked considerable discussion in both the white community and the black. This subject was layered with so many deep-seated preconceptions that it became frequently difficult to deal with it in a calm and rational manner. One of these uncritical assumptions, entertained especially by the disparagers of the African-American, viewed every member of that group as a potential criminal. This feeling was undoubtedly nurtured by the unfortunate social conditions of many blacks, i.e., their ignorance, poverty, and general precarious position within society. James McCune Smith, for example, pointed out that, in judging the free African-American population of New York, some social commentators who were ignorant of the actual conditions of blacks "and hindered by their prejudices, from inquiring thereinto, gather their opinions of us from specimens visible in the Five Points . . . satisfied by a single glance as the 'deformed leg.'"[49]

While some blacks indeed were prone to criminality, it would be highly inaccurate to take the wrongdoings of a few as a gauge of the

---

47   Dr. James McCune Smith to Gerrit Smith, July 7, 1848. Quoted in U.S. W.P.A., *Calendar of the Gerrit Smith Papers in Syracuse University Library*, 2 vols. (Albany, 1941), 2:44. (Hereafter cited as U.S. W.P.A., *Calendar of the Gerrit Smith Papers*).

48   *National Anti-Slavery Standard*, November 26, 1853.

49   Carter G. Woodson, *The Mind of the Negro as Reflected in Letters Written during the Crisis, 1800-1860* (Washington, D.C., 1926), 279. (Hereafter cited as Woodson, *The Mind of the Negro*.)

whole community. This nevertheless was done again and again. In 1827, for example, a white Newark, New Jersey, minister, in commenting upon the possible advantages of emancipation while blacks remained in this country, was emphatic in his insistence that none existed. "Visit our jails and penitentiaries," he declared, "and you will find them crowded with coloured convicts. Beyond a doubt their moral character is far more debased than any part of the white population."[50]

This reference to blacks being frequently committed to penal institutions was often resorted to by the maligners of that race. Some even went so far as to assert, often without corroboration, that the black population of these prisons exceeded that of whites. Actually, at no time during the period of general emancipation was this the case.

In 1843 the Commissioners of the Alms House issued their report on the penal population. They found that at Blackwell's Island there were 109 white male convicts, and 41 black, making a total of 150. Of those persons who had been committed as vagrants, 156 were white males, while only 21 were black. Similarly, among the female prisoners at Blackwell's, there were 18 whites and only 3 blacks. Of those females committed as vagrants, 334 were whites, and 39 were black.[51] In the City Prison the same figures generally held.[52]

---

[50] *Freedom's Journal*, March 30, 1827. While it is generally true during this period that in *proportion to their numbers*, the rate of black crime was higher than that of whites, a fact which even the editors of *Freedom's Journal* conceded, that the same paper nevertheless qualified this by saying: " . . . take the white man in its aggregate; also the coloured man's, and see if the scales does not *preponderate to our advantage*, notwithstanding instances of crime are in greater proportion among us. . . .The coloured man's offence, three times out of four, grows out of the *circumstances of his condition*, while the white man's, most generally, is *premeditated and vicious*. Therefore, if more of our people, in proportion, have happily become the tenants of jails and penitentiaries, it does not prove them more subject to crime, or their characters more debased." *Ibid.*, March 30, 1827 (Italics added).

[51] New York City, *Report of the Commissioners of the Alms House in Answer to Certain Resolutions of Enquiry, Adopted by the Board of Aldermen*, Doc. No. 23 (1843), 254-255.

By the 1850's, with the gradual but perceptible decline in the African-American population of New York City, the incidence of crime and arrests among them also decreased. Commenting on the Annual Report of the New York Metropolitan Police Department for the year ending 1859, William Goodell, a prominent political abolitionist and reformer, found that the total number of arrests in that city for the previous year was 60,885 and "among these were 566 colored persons." Goodell then went on to show that blacks were in 1850, by actual enumeration, about 2.68 percent of the whole population, so that the amount of crime disclosed among them was little more than one-third as great according to their numbers, as that among whites.[53]

Social discrimination against free blacks in New York City was another phenomenon that had far-ranging effects on the daily lives of these people. In a larger sense, the difference in treatment meted out to the African-American was merely a reflection of the pervasive racism which tainted nearly every aspect of northern society and dogged the black man from the cradle to the grave. Discrimination was the rule, not the exception, in schools, workshops, churches, homes and in the Courts of Law.[54] Blacks also found it increasingly difficult to attend theaters, inns, and zoos, without being insulted or molested. They were often barred from traveling on streetcars and securing first-class passage on steamboats. Finally the revolting spirit of caste saluted them at man's last abode. Even in cemeteries they could not find surcease from invidious distinctions.

During the 1830's and 1840's blacks avoided use of public vehicles because of the widespread discriminatory practices. When it was necessary to travel to other areas of the country they met with

---

[52] In the City Prison were 87 white males and 12 black males making the total number of male prisoners 99. There were also confined 34 white females and 14 black females making the whole number of female prisoners 48. *Ibid.*, 255-256.

[53] *American Anti-Slavery Society, Twenty-Sixth Annual Report* (New York, 1859), 76-77. See also *National Anti-Slavery Standard*, December 4, 1858.

[54] Discrimination against blacks as it manifested itself in the schools, workshops, churches and Courts of Law will be discussed in subsequent chapters.

even sharper discrimination. The "conduct of officers of steamboats and packets to coloured people has been cruel in the extreme," wrote the editors of *Freedom's Journal* in 1827.[55] The fight against discrimination took a heavy personal toll with respect to the Reverend Theodore S. Wright, distinguished black clergyman and pastor of the First Colored Presbyterian Church in New York City. In a speech delivered by him, and printed in the *Emancipator*, October 26, 1837, he charged that his wife had been refused proper accommodations on a steamboat and a dirty, chill area was assigned to her. She caught cold and subsequently died of the illness.[56]

The Reverend Peter Williams, Jr. of New York City, a black Episcopal clergyman,[57] was refused a passage on an American packet bound for Europe. He embarked from New York City on board an English vessel, whose captain treated him with "distinguished kindness and attention." Later, on leaving London, he again attempted to obtain passage on an American ship but was refused. He returned on an English one.[58]

The disheartening part of most of this discrimination was that it made no distinction as to worth and respectability. Blacks who were highly cultured and had achieved considerable wealth and standing in the community found themselves treated as brutally and crudely as the most common laborer. Thomas Van Rensselaer, a black man who was active in the early Negro Convention Movement, and who later edited a paper known as the *Ram's Horn*, found himself on many occasions denied admittance to theaters, restaurants, hotels and other places of

---

[55] *Freedom's Journal*, March 23, 1827.

[56] *Emancipator*, October 26, 1837. The *Emancipator* was for a time the official organ of the American Anti-Slavery Society.

[57] ' Peter Williams, Jr., was the first rector of St. Philip's Church. The son of a prominent black Methodist, he began his career as a lay reader and was ordained a deacon in October, 1820. Almost six years later he was ordained a priest, the first of his race to be so elevated. He served at St. Philip's until his death in 1840 at the age of forty-three. He was, according to the editor of the *Colored American*, "universally beloved."

[58] American Anti-Slavery Society, *Fourth Annual Report* (New York, 1837), 110.

public resort.[59]   Thomas Downing, one of the wealthiest blacks in New York City, whose oyster-house was patronized by whites, was beaten by agents of the Harlem Railroad when he attempted to ride on that line.[60] In the 1830's, when blacks sought to visit the menagerie, the New York Zoological Institute warned them:

> The proprietors wish to it be understood, that PEOPLE OF COLOR are *not permitted to enter*, EXCEPT WHEN IN ATTENDANCE UPON CHILDREN AND FAMILIES.[61]

In the 1850's there was a step-up in the nature of this discrimination.   African-Americans found it increasingly difficult to ride the public streetcars, for example, and some of the most outrageous incidents involving this form of discrimination centered around the use of public conveyances.

Miss Elizabeth Jenkins, described as a "highly-respectable female," was brutally insulted and dragged off the Third Avenue City cars by a conductor when she attempted to take a seat. Blacks were not legally forbidden to ride the public cars, but if objections were made by the white riders, they were generally refused admittance. The incident involving Miss Jenkins took place on the afternoon of Sunday, July 16, 1854. Miss Jenkins, a teacher in the male department of the public schools, was on her way to he First Colored Congregation Church, on Sixth Street, near the Bowery, where she

---

[59] On one occasion Gerrit Smith said: "Is it an innocent feeling, which led the keeper of a place of public resort in this city to strike with his cane an esteemed friend, Mr. Thomas Van Rensselaer, simply because Mr. Van Rensselaer had the presumption, notwithstanding his skin color, to propose to enter that resort?" See American Anti-Slavery Society, *Fifth Annual Report* (New York, 1838) 35.

[60] *Colored American*, January 16, 1841; February 20, 1841.

[61] American Anti-Slavery Society, Fourth Annual Report, 109. Said a well-known anti-slavery newspaper in rebuking this discrimination: "'People of color!' Indeed! Wonder if these savage proprietors and managers, for savages and worse than savages they are, to make such an arrangement—wonder if they allow *animals* of color in their institute! Sordid knaves—why one [would] think they supposed the good people of this city and strangers visiting it, as sordid and mean as themselves." *Emancipator*, March 9, 1837.

was an organist. The injuries she sustained as a result of this attack, prevented her from attending the church, but prompted the pastor of that congregation to call a meeting to deal with the issue.[62] The Reverend L. Tilman, pastor of the church and chairman of the meeting, introduced the resolutions which were unanimously adopted. One resolution stated that "we regard such conduct as intolerant, in a civil and religious point of view, and that it calls for the reprehension of respectable portion of the community." Another asked that there be "a committee of five appointed to ascertain all the facts in the case, and if possible bring the whole affair before the legal authorities, and that we demand at the hands of the proprietors as colored citizens, the equal right to accommodation of transit in the cars, so long as we possess the regular qualifications." Before the meeting adjourned, a motion was adopted asking that the resolutions passed be forwarded and printed in the *New York Tribune* and *Frederick Douglass Paper*.[63]

Perhaps one of the most celebrated of these cases was that involving the Reverend James W. C. Pennington, who for a time was Moderator of the Fourth Presbytery, composed chiefly of white ministers, was frequently refused service when he attempted to ride the omnibuses of the city.[64] In 1851, the American and Foreign Anti-Slavery Society, taking note of this discrimination, attacked it unequivocally and asserted that "loafers, blacklegs, robbers, thieves, and drunkards of all descriptions provided their complexion are white, are freely allowed the use of those vehicles, but a colored skin, though on a doctor of divinity, is a complete bar of exclusion."[65]

---

[62] *Frederick Douglass Paper*, June 28, 1854. See also case of Elizabeth Jenkins vs. Third Avenue Railroad Company in the *National Anti-Slavery Standard*, March 3, 1855.

[63] *Ibid.*, June 28, 1854.

[64] The Reverend James William Charles Pennington was a prominent New York Clergyman and pastor of the Shiloh Presbyterian Congregational Church of that city from 1848 to 1855. Pennington, whose original name was Pembroke, was born a slave in Maryland. Trained at first as a blacksmith, he later escaped and went to New York. The degree of Doctor of Divinity was conferred upon him by Heidelberg University in 1851. A prolific writer, he was the author of several works. See his autobiography, *The Fugitive Blacksmith*.

[65] American and Foreign Anti-Slavery Society, *Eleventh Annual Report* (New York, 1851), 153.

But words of condemnation however sincere and indignant proved to no avail, for two years later (1853), in a letter to the editor of the New York *Evangelist*, the Reverend Pennington complained:

> You are aware that I am pastor of the Presbyterian church on the corner of Prince and Marion streets, in this city. My congregation extends from No. 1 Pearl street to 65th street, and from Hoboken to Brooklyn and Williamsburg; so that in the discharge of my pastoral duties, I am constantly called to different points and from one extremity to the other of this immense field. And yet sir, according to usage in this community, I cannot avail myself of the use of any of the lines of omnibuses or any of the multiplying lines of railways in the city.[66]

Finally in June 1855, the situation involving Reverend Pennington reached a critical stage. The Sixth Avenue Street Car was a case in point. It had a long history of insulting and intimidating blacks. Although there was no specific legal ordinance barring their admittance, still it was generally understood that People of Color were not welcomed. When therefore Reverend Pennington had occasion to use the line, he was immediately assaulted and thrown off. The incident provoked nationwide attention. Said the *Frederick Douglass Paper*:

> Our readers are aware that the Rev. Dr. Pennington, of New York City, a gentleman of high intellectual and moral worth, was recently ejected from a public car, in Sixth Avenue, by the Conductor, in a worse than brutal manner. It seems that the Dr., shortly after taking his seat, was notified by the Conductor that he must leave the car, as the regulation of the Company strictly prohibited colored people from riding in any of their cars save those provided for their especial *accommodation*. The Rev. gentleman very properly refused to accede to the Conductor's wishes, whereupon the

---

[66] The New York *Evangelist*, reprinted in the *African Repository*, 29 (March 1853):82. Reverend Pennington wrote an amusing article on the exclusion of colored persons from public conveyances. See *National Anti-Slavery Standard*, November 25, 1852.

Conductor and the driver pounced upon him, and forcibly ejected him He, however, knowing his rights and resolving, like a man, to maintain them, still held on to the car, behind which he ran as far as the lower depot, where, finding a policeman, demanded the arrest of the cowardly assailants. The policeman endeavored to dissuade the Dr. from taking any legal course to punish the offenders; but he very wisely resolved to have the question settled at once, whether or not, a man can be thus assaulted by his fellow man in the public conveyance of the city of New York with impunity?[67]

Pennington took the matter before the Superior Court. There was no question that blacks could ride the cars, since the lower courts had already decided the issue in the affirmative. But Pennington and his friend sought a definitive ruling from a higher tribunal. The Legal Rights Association was organized in 1855 shortly after the incident. Its object was to assist blacks in obtaining redress in cases involving similar kinds of discrimination.[68] Nothing seemed to have come of the litigation for the Sixth Avenue Line continued these practices for years.

---

[67] *Frederick Douglass Paper*, June 8, 1855. Pennington's experience was quite different from that which William H. Day had undergone almost two years earlier. In the December 1853, Day, editor of the *Aliened American*, a black newspaper published in Cleveland, Ohio, gave an interesting account of a visit he had recently made to New York City. A person whom the *National Anti-Slavery Standard* described as "an educated gentleman of refined manners and winning address," Day along with his wife rode uptown on the Sixth Avenue Railroad without being molested. He noted that "no white person in the car seemed to be at all astonished, and of course *we* were not." Quoted in the *National Anti-Slavery Standard*, December 31, 1853. (Italics in the original).

[68] New York *Tribune*, May 25, 1855. In some cases blacks did get a redress of grievances in the Courts from overt expressions of discrimination. The Brooklyn City Court for example, in March 1851, found an omnibus driver guilty of assault and battery after forcibly ejecting a black woman from his vehicle. See American and Foreign Anti-Slavery Society, *Eleventh Annual Report*, 154.

There was another form of discrimination, more corrosive than the first in that it involved the proscription of blacks who had the temerity to associate with whites on intimate social terms or be seen publicly in their company in such places as theaters, lyceums, restaurants, etc. The columns of many anti-slavery newspapers, and even the City's popular press, were replete in their reportage of such examples of caste.

On one such occasion, Frederick Douglass, the famous black abolitionist, was assaulted in New York City while walking along the Battery in the company of two white women. Douglass noted that "it is not true that I walked down Broadway with two white females on my arm, in the case alluded to, although I *insist* on the right to do so." Douglass warded off the blows of his assailants with his umbrella, but remained "calm and self-possessed throughout." In recalling the incident he emphasized the fact that he "felt no indignation towards the poor miserable wretches who committed the outrage. They were but executing upon me the behests of the pro-slavery church and clergy of the land; doing the dirty work of the men who despise them, and who have no more respect for them in reality than they have for me."[69]

Sometimes the circumstances surrounding these cases often approached the hilarious. William P. Powell, for example, the keeper of the Colored Sailor's Home, wrote a letter to the editor of the *National Anti-Slavery Standard*, noting that on "Saturday, about noon, I had the impudence to walk arm and arm through Cherry street with a white man. Well I never! Oh, dear, I believe I shall go off with a flash! I am so elated or, at least, feel so elated, that whilst I am writing, it is almost difficult for me to sit still. I do wish some one would hold me. I feel—I feel as if the day of deliverance had come."[70]

Powell also was also happy to say that the people who observed the incident were note offended but gave them the freedom of the sidewalk. It turned out that the man whom he walked with was a "*beastly drunk*." Powell discovered that the man was a worker in sheet-iron and tin ware, and on every Saturday had occasion to go off on an old-fashioned "spree." Powell found that the "poor fellow, no doubt was just turned out of a groggery, . . . when, passing along Cherry street, I recognized my old friend; he begged me to assist him

---

[69] *Liberator*, July 5, 1850. (Italics in original)

[70] *National Anti-Slavery Standard*, August 22, 1850.

home which I did." Powell readily conceded that under the circumstances, he would have been "gallant enough, at any time, to take a poor defenseless white woman by the arm and lead her home. Wonder if they would not mob me as they did Frederick Douglass, last May."[71]

In another case of this irrational manifestation of caste, Miss Sarah P. Remond, sister of Charles Lenox Remond, the eloquent anti-slavery lecturer, was expelled from the Howard Athenaeum. She had purchased a ticket with two friends, and upon presenting it to the doorkeeper, was allowed to proceed to her seat. But on entering, an agent of the company forbade her taking it, and finally pushed her down the stairs. For this outrage, the agent and officer involved in her expulsion were brought before the Police Court. One Justice Russell delivered an opinion sustaining the equal rights of black citizens. The defendants were fined a small sum, the agent adjudged to pay costs. Later an action was brought before the Court of Common Pleas for damages, but was afterward withdrawn by Miss Remond, on her expensed being paid by the other party, and the understanding that in the future she should occupy a seat at Howard she chose to pay for.[72]

When Elizabeth Greenfield, the famous "Black Swan," gave a concert performance at Metropolitan Hall on the evening of March 31, 1853, blacks were not permitted to attend. The placard announcing the event included the following admonition:

PARTICULAR NOTICE—No colored person can be admitted as there is no part of the house appropriated for them.[73]

Miss Greenfield nevertheless disregarded this attack on her people and performed.[74] This prompted a number of Negro leaders to request

---

[71] *Ibid.*, August 22, 1850.

[72] American and Foreign Anti-Slavery Society, *Eleventh Annual Report*, 154.

[73] *Frederick Douglass Paper*, April 8, 1853.

[74] Frederick Douglass in commenting on this treatment marveled that "Miss Greenfield can allow herself to be treated with such palpable *disrespect*; for the insult is *to her*, not less than to her race." Douglass was convinced that "she must have felt *deep humiliation and depression* while attempting to sing in the presence of an audience and

that she give her concert where no distinctions would be made as to color. On this occasion the Reverend J.W.C. Pennington, along with five other black ministers, [75] addressed the following letter to her:

> Miss Elizabeth Greenfield: The undersigned profoundly regret that themselves and their numerous colored friends in the city are denied the privilege of attending your concert at Metropolitan Hall, to-morrow evening.
>
> That they may not be left with the present painful impressions, they hereby respectfully request, if consistent with your engagement, you will be so kind as to repeat your concert on Monday evening, the 4th of April at Broadway Tabernacle. Should you decline further benefit for yourself, we suggest that the proceeds, after paying expenses, be divided between the Home for the Aged Coloured Persons and the Coloured Orphan Asylum.[76]

---

under such arrangements which had thus dishonored the people to which she belonged." *Ibid.*, April 8, 1853 (Italics in the original).

[75]   The other five ministers were as follows: Charles B. Ray, pastor of the Bethesda Congregational Church; J.P. Campbell, pastor of the A.M.E. Church; Henry M. Wilson, pastor of the Emmanuel Presbyterian Church; Dempsey Kennedy, pastor of the Zion Methodist Episcopal Church and Sampson White, pastor, Zion Baptist Church. See *National Anti-Slavery Standard*, April 7, 1853.

[76]   *Ibid.*, April 7, 1853. Miss Greenfield sent the following reply: "I received your kind letter inviting me to sing at a concert previous to my visit to Europe, at which the coloured people of this city might have an opportunity of hearing me sing. I regret that you have been debarred from attending this concert to be given at Metropolitan Hall this evening; but it was expressly stated in the agreement for the use of the hall, that such should be the case. I will with pleasure sing for the benefit of any charity that will elevate the condition of my coloured brethren, as soon as the necessary arrangements shall be completed for the same, which must necessarily be arranged for an early day, as I shall take my departure for Europe on the 6th proximo." Quoted in *ibid.*, April 7, 1853.

Rejected by the larger society, a number of blacks, particularly the affluent and refined, sought solace and contentment by creating their own world of social importance devoid of all invidious distinctions. Here within the attractive but illusive confines of "Colored Society" they could dress ostentatiously, party endlessly, live extravagantly, and generally ape the manners and habits of wealthy white society.

"Ethiop," Brooklyn Correspondent for *Frederick Douglass Paper* once contrasted the social life of Colored Society in Gotham, about Fifth Avenue and vicinity and in Brooklyn, which he dubbed the "Church City." In Brooklyn he found a society that was high-stepping but without that "heedless extravagance" which he noted Gotham was famous for. He reported that in the "Church City" in the vicinity of the "Heights," modest church-going gentlemen were usually found. But in Gotham, another world existed which mirrored the excesses and frivolities of "Colored Society."[77]

Once Ethiop was invited to attend a ball sponsored by George T. Downing of Broadway and Wall Street. Downing was a leading light of Gotham Society. Shortly after eleven o'clock that evening when the ball began the Brooklyn correspondent was on hand to note this gay and motley group. Retiring to an unobtrusive corner, he had a fine opportunity for observation:

> While mid the gathered crowd, some scarce remembered face
> Would call many a long forgotten thought to mind
> They little thought these gentle folks
> 'Twas Ethiop, "mong them taking notes."

He was a keen observer indeed:

> Here were matronly ladies; round, plump dames, that are really good to behold . . . There was another seeming change. The young *Bucks*, though well dressed, and with a goodly share of the tinsel about them, yet were less flashy than formally [sic]; another, step, I hope, in the right direction. But Oh! the music, the sweet music of the Harps, not David's of solemn sound . . . to which, in the dance, the merry dance, the giddy dance,
> "Many a light fantastic toe

---

[77] *Frederick Douglass Paper*, April 14, 1854.

Toppled o'er the carpet soft"

He found his thoughts moving from the splendid pageantry around him until at length his "transit was from fact to reverie to bewilderment." "I remembered," he continued, "the jingle of glasses, the popping of champaign [sic], the delicious taste of creams, jellies, etc." The impressions made upon his mind were not to be forgotten. The portrait he drew of "Colored Society" was indeed revealing, for it showed that even among blacks the social life of the cultured and well-to-do was not homogenous, but had its own distinctive tastes, shades and nuances. For Colored Society in Gotham was comparatively a composite of "gaiety, glitter and rollicking fun," while in the Church City it was "pleasant, rather intellectual, stately; the tongue performing what mostly the *heel's* do in Gotham."[78]

Yet, it must be remembered that Colored Society, with all its affection and charm was an exclusive circle which represented only a small cross-section of black New York life. There was another world, larger than the first, in which each man and woman was faced with the daily task of survival—survival, however, in a society which generally denigrated their characters and sought to undermine their progress. Still, in spite of these obviously drawbacks, some blacks did manage to earn their daily bread and others were fortunate enough to carve out a considerable economic niche in which they achieved wealth and respectability.

To a large extent the degree to which blacks succeeded along economic lines was, as was generally true with whites, an accepted index of their standing in society. The objective conditions which depressed some and gave upward social mobility to others will be considered in detail in the following chapter.

---

[78] *Ibid.*, April 14, 1854.

Economic Conditions

Free blacks in New York City were generally thwarted in their efforts to achieve even a degree of economic mobility. Prejudice and custom largely limited their opportunities and would in time consign them to the position of a permanent underclass. Only menial positions would be available to them.

During the 1830's, for example, blacks were found largely in the field of personal and domestic service. Edward S. Abdy, a French traveler, commented on the "advertisements that appear continually in the papers for colored cooks, colored coachmen, colored footmen, etc."[1] About mid-century an English traveler observed that New York seemed more German in origin than was common for an American city, but she hastened to remark that when one "penetrates a little further, and sees the domestic economy, he will find black cooks as well as waiters."[2] A very few years before this, the Englishman Robert Playfair noted that "the greater part of this population, no doubt, consists of household servants, and others in minor employments; but there are many respectable tradesmen amongst them, some said to be very rich."[3]

Blacks could be seen in many of the public establishments of the city. Most of the smaller hotels employed blacks. The Metropolitan had about 60 or 70; other hostelries like the Stuyvesant House, the Earls, the Clifford, and a number of restaurants employed black waiters.[4]

---

[1] Edward Strutt Abdy, *Journal of a Residence and Tour in the United States of North America, from April, 1833 to October, 1834.* 3 vols. (London, 1835), 1:66. (Hereafter cited as Abdy, *Journal of a Residence and Tour.*)

[2] Duncan, *America As I found It.*, 253.

[3] Robert Playfair esq., *Recollections of a Visit to the United States and British Provinces of North America in the Years, 1847, 1848, and 1849* (Edinburgh, 1856), 136.

[4] Haynes, *The Negro at Work in New York City*, 67,

Throughout this period, the opportunities for blacks in the trades and professions were at best minimal. The columns of the *Colored American* were replete with articles, editorials and appeals which indicated the difficulties in this direction.[5] Charles S. Andrews, for example, the white principal of the Manumission Society School for blacks, found to his chagrin that the graduates found every avenue closed against them and he spoke of the difficulties those who had trades encountered, many being forced to become waiters, barbers, servants and laborers.[6]

The massive influx of German and Irish immigrants in the three decades preceding the Civil War presented a number of problems for free blacks. In some cases, the superior training and skill of these foreigners (especially among the Germans) facilitated their securing of employment. Then too, at a time when the supply of labor exceeded the demand, the free black, unable to compete with these whites, was driven not only from respectable positions but also from menial pursuits.[7]

It would, however, be incorrect to assume that the sharp decrease of blacks within the domestic service trade, for example, started with the influx of the Irish during the forties and fifties. A student of this period has noted that from 1826 to 1830, of the 15,000 applicants for jobs in the Society for the Encouragement of Faithful Domestic Servants in New York, "only 2,500 were colored."[8]

The Irish especially tended to impede the forward advance of the black worker. James Dawson Burn, an Owenite, and a keen observer of working conditions in the United States, discovered that they were the most formidable enemies of blacks:

---

[5] *Ibid.*, 68.

[6] Mary White Ovington, *Half a Man: The Status of the Negro in New York* (New York, 1911), 27-28.

[7] Philmore L. Groisser, "The Free Negro in New York State, 1850-1860" (unpublished M.A. Thesis, Columbia University), 1939, 101. Groisser's thesis, white it does throw interesting light on the overall condition of blacks in New York State in the decade prior to the Civil War, has rather limited value as regards the social, economic, and political status of blacks in New York City during this period.

[8] *Ibid.*, 104.

I have often heard the nature and condition of the colored people discussed by my shopmates in America. I have met with a few well conditioned men who look upon the blacks as rational beings; but the strongly expressed opinion of the majority was, that they were a soulless race, and I am satisfied that some of these people would shoot a black man with as little regard to moral consequences as they would a wild hog.[9]

Small wonder then that with the marked increase of the Irish population the African-American would find it virtually impossible to secure employment in the area of the skilled trades. As early as 1833, a French traveler wrote that in not a single trade in New York City were blacks allowed to work with whites.[10]

Yet even in unskilled occupations this mean spirit presented itself. The African Repository, official organ of the American Colonization Society, noted in an editorial:

In New York, and other eastern cities, the influx of white laborers has expelled the Negro almost en masse from the exercise of the ordinary branches of labor. You no longer see him work upon buildings, and rarely is he allowed to drive a cart or a public conveyance. White men will not work with him.[11]

---

[9] Ernst, *Immigrant Life in New York City*, 104.

[10] Abdy, *Journal of a Residence and Tour*, 1:358. Abdy further added that "there are nearly 20,000 of them [blacks] in the city, and more than twice that number in the State. It will hence be seen at once how closely the self-interest of the mechanics and other journeymen is connected with the continuance of a prejudice, which thus shuts the door against so many competitors." *Ibid.*, 358.

[11] The *African Repository*, quoted in Philmore, "The Free Negro in New York State," 101. In many places foreigners refused to work with blacks. A group of sixty Irishmen, for example, engaged as laborers upon a large building being erected on Duane Street in New York City, quit work when the foreman employed a Negro to wheel dirt from beneath the building. See New York *Tribune*, September 30, 1857. See also *ibid.*, editorial, August 3, 1857.

In addition to being barred from driving a cart in New York, all requests of black citizens for porter's licenses were denied by the governors. The *Colored American*, in an article entitled "Municipal Oppression," excoriated the city of New York, "with all her institutions and bibles," for denying to her black citizens the right to these licenses. In a brilliant philippic the paper went on to say that "it is further pleaded on the part of those in authority that it is IN MERCY to the colored man, that they deny him a license. Were they, it is said to license colored carmen and porters, it would bring them into collision with the white men of the same calling, and they would get their horses and carts 'dumped' into the docks, and themselves abused and beaten." The paper made short shrift of this argument and concluded by saying that this was "mercy on the part of our authorities with *A VENGEANCE TO IT*!!! And it is a compliment indeed to our worthy carmen and porters."[12]

To halt this steady deterioration in their labor situation blacks were frequently urged to diversify their occupations. This was a recurrent theme throughout the 1840's. Frederick Douglass on many occasions emphasized this need. He dismissed the oft-repeated argument that blacks were inherently inferior and fit only to occupy menial positions. In order to eliminate invidious distinctions Douglass urged his people to prove themselves competent in every field. Declared Douglass:

> It must be no longer white lawyer, and black wood-sawyer,—white editor, and black street-cleaner; it must be no

---

[12] *Colored American*, September 16 1837. For similar articles on licensing black carmen and porters see also *Emancipator*, July 6, 1837; July 20, 1837; *National Anti-Slavery Standard*, October 9, 1845. As late as 1846, a promoter of the Colonization scheme commented upon the awful economic state to which blacks had been reduced. Owing to the Irish and Germans, blacks were losing many of the occupations which they had customarily held. Said this man: "Who may find a dray or a cart or a hack driven by a colored man? Where are the vast majority of the colored people in the City? None can deny that they are sunken much lower than they were a few years ago and are compelled to pursue none but the meanest avocations." Quoted in Arnett S. Lindsay, "The Economic Conditions of the Negroes of New York Prior to 1861," *Journal of Negro History*, 6 (April 1921):195.

longer white, intelligent and black, ignorant; but we must take our stand side by side with our white fellow countrymen, in all the trades, arts, professions and callings of the day.[13]

Some blacks were already in the process of reversing this trend, for Douglass was pleased to note that "colored persons are becoming farmers, mechanics, lecturers, doctors, lawyers, merchants, teachers, professors, and editors." "The more we have of them," he concluded, "the better; and the sooner will the distinction of which we complain be removed."[14]

Yet while some blacks did manage to diversify their occupations, as we shall see, the overwhelming majority remained in the same positions. The Federal Census of 1850 seemed to bear this out. For, of those blacks gainfully employed, nearly three-quarters were servants, laborers, and other unskilled or occasional workers. In this computation a total of 3,337 individuals were listed:

---

[13] *The North Star*, January 8, 1848. James Freeman Clarke, a prominent white Unitarian clergyman and abolitionist, underscored this theme again and again. Said Clarke somewhat revealingly: "The colored people ought to diversify their occupations. They should not be satisfied with being only barbers, waiters, and sailors. Each one who has a special talent should cultivate it. Let him not try to be a lawyer, unless he can be a good one. Let him not write books, of which we have to say "They are very good, *considering*." But if he can be *first-rate* in anything, so as to be the best dentist, or engineer, or artist, or engraver, or gunsmith, or oculist, or reporter, in the place, then those who wish to have their work well done *must* go to him, and no prejudice will prevent it." See James Freeman Clark, *Present Condition of the Free Colored People of the United States* (New York, 1859), 264 (Italics in the original).

[14] *Ibid.*, January 8, 1858. William C. Nell, a self-taught black man, who became the first publisher of the *North Star*, seemed to have imbibed in some of the ideas that Douglass and others were emphasizing. On one occasion, while passing through New York City, he remarked: "I had the satisfaction of being introduced to a colored carpenter—not a fractional one, but a master workman and contractor for buildings." The *North Star*, February 11, 1848.

1,144	laborers	8	teachers
808	servants	8	cigar makers
434	mariners	7	clerks
122	barbers	7	gardeners
107	coachmen	5	ink makers
95	cooks	4	bakers
44	stewards	4	printers
39	carmen	3	barkeepers
33	butchers	3	druggists
28	boatmen	3	jewelers
24	farmers	3	merchants
24	musicians	2	apprentices
23	shoemakers	2	confectioners
21	ministers	2	merchants ("generally")
21	boarding house keepers	1	blacksmith
12	carpenters	1	gunsmith
12	sextons	1	student
11	hostlers		Also 207 other occupations
9	doctors		(sweeps, scavengers, etc.)

(Source: J.D.B. De Bow, *Statistical View of the United States . . .Compendium of the Seventh Census* (Washington, D.C.), 80-81.)

    In March 1851, a convention was held by blacks in New York City to deal with this problem of upgrading employment. At this meeting Dr. James McCune Smith read a report on the "Social Conditions of the Colored Race." It was an elaborate, fact-laden document. Smith first addressed himself to the advantages and disadvantages of city life. Though recognizing some merit in the former, the overall portrait he drew was dismal. He found that for the majority of black families "our lives are much shortened. Look at the preponderance of widows and children among us. They far exceed the calamities of mere sickness, that our benevolent societies have been obliged to cut off the widows and orphans, in order to help the sick."[15] Then followed what was perhaps the most incisive factor in his whole analysis:

---

[15] New York *Daily Tribune*, March 20, 1851.

City life shuts us from general mechanical employment, while journeymen in the cities refuse to work with us, and colored bosses have either too little capital, or too little enterprise to bring up and employ apprentices and journeymen.[16]

Although Smith had urged a movement of blacks from the city to the country with the object of bettering their lot by engaging in agricultural pursuits, very few of his people followed his advice. One obvious reason for their reluctance was simple because they lacked sufficient capital to make such a transition.

By 1855 the situation had grown somewhat worse. Robert Ernst found, for example, that "of 3,688 gainfully employed Negroes in 1855, about 200, or only four-tenths of one percent were engaged in the skill trades."[17] Even in such a traditional African-American calling as barbering, blacks were being supplanted by Germans, Irishmen, English and French.[18]

Black workers did make a feeble attempt to organize to protect and promote their interests. In July 1850, the American League of Colored Laborers was formed with the object of uniting black men in the trades, and to give mechanical, agricultural and commercial advice. The League recommended that blacks go into independent ventures if possible and that a fund be set up to aid toward this end.[19]

---

[16] *Ibid.*, March 20, 1851.

[17] Robert Ernst, "The Economic Status of New York City Negroes, 1850-1863," in August Meier and Elliott Rudwick ed., *The Making of Black America*, 2 vols. (New York, 1969), 1:258. (Hereafter cited as Ernst, "The Economic Status of New York City Negroes.")

[18] Ernst, Immigrant Life in New York City, 104. That this was undeniably true can be seen from Frederick Douglass' lament when he said: "White men are becoming house servants, cooks and stewards on vessels—at hotels. They are becoming porters, stevedores, wood-sawyers, hodcarriers, brick-makers, white-washers and barbers, so that blacks can scarcely find the means of subsistence—a few years ago, and a *white* barber would have been a curiosity—now their poles stand on every corner." *Frederick Douglass Paper*, March 4, 1853.

[19] On the Executive Committee of this organization were the following blacks: George T. Downing, Edward Clarke, Stephen

Black waiters had early agitated for higher wages, and in 1853 received $16 a month to the white waiters' $12. In such an unusual situation whites held a meeting to force equalization of their wages. A black man who was present at this meeting simply advised whites to strike for $18 a month. The whites did strike for higher wages but were unsuccessful. Some employers "retrained their best waiters at increased wages and fired the rest replacing them with Negroes and women."[20]

Friction between the races increased when blacks were used as strike-breakers. When, in January 1855, the stevedores of the Morgan Line went on strike for higher wages, blacks were employed in their places. Fighting soon erupted between the unemployed Irish and the blacks. A month later nearly all the blacks had been replaced by white longshoremen.[21]

Despite the fact that many blacks encountered increasing difficulty in their fights to earn a decent livelihood, there were some who managed to accumulate a considerable amount of wealth. They represented largely the business and professional class. While hard data are lacking concerning the socio-economic status and family backgrounds of most of these individuals, it is reasonable to assume that some were the scions of the well-to-do, and had achieved their fortunes by inheritance, but the vast majority started out on the lower economic rungs, and through hard work and thrift managed to obtain a comfortable existence.

Prior to the Civil War Henry Scott of New York City founded and promoted for a number of years one of the most successful pickling establishments in that metropolis. His business was principally confined to supplying vessels.[22] Edward V. Clark, another

---

Myers, William Topp, James McCune Smith, Charles B. Ray, Samuel R. Ward and Frederick Douglass. See New York *Tribune*, July 1850.

[20] Ernst, *Immigrant Life in New York City*, 104-105. See also New York *Tribune*, April 26, 1853; May 3, 1853.

[21] New York *Tribune*, January 18, 1855; February 15, 1855.

[22] J.H. Harmon, Jr., "The Negro as a Local Business Man," *Journal of Negro History*, 14, No. 2 (April 1929):120. Martin R. Delany, a pioneer black emigrationist, who later became the first black major in the United States Army, said of Scott: "There have doubtless been many a purser, who cashed and filed in his office the bill of Henry Scott, without ever dreaming of his being a colored man." See

businessman, conducted a prosperous jewelry establishment requiring much capital. His name had, moreover, a respectable standing even among the dealers of Wall Street.[23] Thomas B. Downing, a well-known caterer, was for thirty years the proprietor of a first-class restaurant, near the corner of Wall and Broadway Streets. Downing was prominent in the black community life of the City, and it was said that he had made "three fortunes."[24] One Mr. Hutson kept for years an intelligence office in New York. He was succeeded by Philip Bell, an excellent business man.[25]

In addition to the above-named business establishments, there were several grocery stores,[26] at least one china ship,[27] and a great number of boarding houses run by blacks.[28] There were also at least two dry goods stores,[29] two coal yards,[30] and several refectories and eating houses.[31]

Martin R. Delany, *The Condition, Elevation, Emigration, and Destiny of the Colored People of the United States. Political Considered* (Philadelphia, 1852), 102. (Hereafter cited as Delany, *Condition of the Colored People.*) See also Eugene Monroe Boykin, "Enterprise and Accumulation of Negroes Prior to 1860," (unpublished M.A. Thesis, Columbia University), 1934, 42.

[23] Delany, *Condition of the Colored People*, 102; Lindsay, "The Economic Condition of Negroes in New York Prior to 1861," 197.

[24] Daniel Alexander Payne, *Recollections of Seventy Years* (New York, 1888), 46; Delany, *Condition of the Colored People*, 103.

[25] Bell later became proprietor of the *Colored American*. His intelligence office was patronized by people from all parts of the city. Delany found him to be "highly sensitive and very eccentric, but withal a warm, good-hearted man." See Delany, *Condition of the Colored People*, 102-103.

[26] *Weekly Advocate*, January 14, 1837; *Colored American*, July 13, 1839.

[27] *Colored American*, May 11, 1839.

[28] *Ibid.*, January 13, 1838; July 7, 1838; September 28, 1839.

[29] *Ibid.*, September 29, 1838; *Weekly Advocate*, January 14, 1837.

[30] Haynes, *The Negro at Work in New York City*, 96-97.

[31] *The Emancipator*, October 19, 1837; *Colored American*, January 12, 1838; June 27, 1840.

Among New York's black professionals was Dr. James McCune
Smith, a prominent physician and civic leader, who carried on a
lucrative practice. He advertised weekly in the Colored American and
Frederick Douglass Paper. One such advertisement read as follows:

> Dr. James McCune Smith may be consulted at his office 93
> Broadway from 7 till 10 A.M., from 2 till 3, and from 8 till
> 10 P.M.   House, 151 Read Street, two doors from
> Greenwich.[32]

Smith, along with Philip A. White, also operated an apothecary
establishment. William C. Nell described both as "practical men,"
who "conduct their business, preparing medicines, etc., etc., with as
much readiness and skill as any other disciple of Galen and
Hippocrates."[33]   Another black man, T. Jennings, was   a surgeon-
dentist who practiced at 185 North Broadway.[34]

Generally speaking, however, few blacks entered the professions.
The difficulties that lay in this direction were obvious and yet Robert
Ernst found on the basis of the manuscript returns of the New York
State Census of 1855 that at least 50 black professional men were
listed. Half this number consisted of teachers and clergymen. There
were also fifteen African-American musicians, five physicians, a
dentists, a lawyer and an artist.[35]

Blacks did make considerable gains in the accumulation of real
and personal property. In 1837, for example, the *Colored American*
reported that blacks had from $50,000 to $80,000 in the savings banks

---

[32] Colored American, March 14, 1840. During the years 1856
and 1857 Smith was taxed on real property worth $13,200. He was
listed as having had, however, no personal property. See W.H. Boyd,
*New York City Tax Book, being a List of Persons, Corporations and
Co-Partnerships, Resident and Non-Resident, who were Taxed,
according to the Assessors Books, 1856 and 1857* (New York, 1857),
184.

[33]   *North Star*, February 11, 1848.   White's Druggist
establishment was located on the corner of Frankfort and Gold Streets.

[34] *Ibid.*, February 11, 1848.

[35] Ernst, "The Economic Status of New York City Negroes," in
Meier and Rudwick eds., *The Making of Black America*, 1:259.

of New York City.[36] A writer for the *African Repository* reported that in September 1846, of the 14,000 blacks in New York City, 4000 approached comfort, while 1000 had substantial wealth.[37]

To further the economic well-being of this community, Dr. James McCune Smith proposed the establishment in March 1851 of a Mutual Savings Bank. In his report on the "Social Conditions of the Colored Race" unveiling this scheme, Smith outlined a plan whereby all the depositors in the bank would have the power to buy and sell real-estate, to discount paper, to lend money on bonds and mortgages, and to deal in merchandise. In concluding his report, Smith noted that blacks already owned $40,000 to $50,000 of investment in the savings banks in Wall Street.[38]

Although nothing seems to have come of Smith's proposal, blacks continued to improve their general economic standing. By 1852 it was estimated that the cities of New York, Brooklyn, and Williamsburg contained more than a third of the state's black population. The amount of money invested by blacks in businesses carried on by themselves was as follows:

In New York City.	$755,000
In the city of Brooklyn.	76,200
In the city of Williamsburg	7,900
Total.	**$836,100**

---

[36] *Colored American*, May 22, 1837.

[37] The *African Repository*, 22 (September 1846):278.

[38] New York *Tribune*, March 20, 1851; Arnett G. Lindsay, "The Negro in Banking," *Journal of Negro History*, 14, No. 2 (April 1929):158. At a national convention of blacks held at Rochester, New York, in 1853, a resolution was passed which seemed to underline the necessity of Smith's proposal. It said: "Resolved, that it is now expedient and necessary for those who have accumulated some means, to employ such means in some one or more of the general avenues of business and profit, and to make for themselves a better business character than we now possess, and thus secure the way for the development of new business, and right business talent." *Proceedings of the Colored National Convention held in Rochester, July 6th, 7th and 8th, 1853* (Rochester, 1853), 39.

Apart from business enterprises, blacks held real-estate, deducting incumbrances, in the following amounts:

In New York City...................	$733,000
In the city of Brooklyn...............	276,200
In the city of Williamsburg...........	151,900
Total........................	**$1,160,000**

(Source: *National Anti-Slavery Standard*, March 20, 1852)

By 1857 there was an even more marked improvement. For in that year 1000 black persons were found to have owed and paid taxes on real-estate, and to have savings deposits, as follows:

Taxed real-estate in the city of New York owned by colored persons.............	$1,400,000
Untaxed by colored persons (churches)...	250,000
Personal estate......................	710,000
Money in savings banks..............	
	1,121,000
Total...........................	**$3,481,000**

(Source: The *Anglo-African Magazine*, 1, No. 7 (July 1859): 222-223.)

Commenting upon this remarkable economic progress, James Freeman wrote in 1859:

> Twenty years ago, when this population was three-fourths of what it is now, the property was less than half what it is now. The only colored beggars seen in New York are those who ask for money to help them buy their wives, their sons, or their daughters.[39]

Yet as Robert Ernst has correctly concluded, only a small portion of the African-American population benefited from the economic advances made during this period. He termed this group a "colored aristocracy," which had definitely appeared by the middle of that century. The great mass of black families experienced no substantial improvement in their lot. Moreover, their condition steadily

---

[39] James Freeman Clarke, "Conditions of the Free Colored People of the United States," *The Christian Examiner*, 66 (March 1859):254.

deteriorated, for "wages failed to keep pace with rising rents and the prices of provisions, while in depression years, as in 1857, unemployment swelled the relief rolls." These factors, among others, contributed to the drastic decreases in Manhattan's black population during the 1850's.[40]

There was one more facet to this economic picture which for a brief period seemed to offer opportunity for improvement to a part of New York's black population. This involved a private project for the free distribution of farm land.

On August 1, 1846, Gerrit Smith of Peterboro, New York, set aside from his huge private holdings, 120,000 acres of land to be distributed among that state's black population. Smith, in addition to being one of the outstanding philanthropists in the United States, was an ardent land reformer who believed that every man who desired a farm should have one.[41]

Even though there were many poverty-stricken whites in the state, Smith would not include them in his bequest, since they were immune from the peculiar disabilities which affected blacks. Whites, for example, enjoyed one distinct advantage: even though penniless they could vote. Blacks were barred from suffrage unless they owned property worth at least $250.[42] To carry out this scheme Smith appointed four committees in different parts of the state and authorized them to select a specified number of beneficiaries from each county. He envisioned that a total of 3000 individuals would settle upon this land. It would be broken up into parcels of from 40 to 60 acres for each family.[43]

---

[40] Ernst, "The Economic Status of New York City Negroes," in Meier and Rudwick eds., *The Making of Black America*, 1:260.

[41] Octavius B. Frothingham, *Gerrit Smith, A Biography* (New York, 1909), 102-103.

[42] Frothingham, *Gerrit Smith*, 103. See also Zita Dyson, "Gerrit Smith's Efforts in Behalf of the Negroes in New York," *Journal of Negro History*, 2 (October 1918), 356-357; Ralph V. Harlow, *Gerrit Smith: Philanthropist and Reformer* (New York, 1939) 243. (Hereafter cited as Harlow, *Gerrit Smith*.) The issue of the suffrage will be dealt with in detail in a subsequent chapter.

[43] Frothingham, *Gerrit Smith*, 105-106.

The committee appointed from New York County consisted of three well-known blacks: Reverends Charles B. Ray, Theodore S. Wright, and Dr. James McCune Smith.[44] Gerrit Smith, however, imposed the following restrictions upon those who were to receive the land:

> 1st. That upon it there be the name of no persons younger than twenty-one and no person older than sixty.

> 2d. That there be upon it the name of no person who is in easy circumstances as to property; and no person, who is the owner of land.

> 3d. That there be upon it the name of no drunkard—and I had almost added of no person who drinks intoxicating liquor—since to drink it, though ever so moderately, is to be in the way of drunkenness.

> 4th. That the total number of names in the list be one thousand nine hudred and eighty-five.[45]

By late November 1846, Smith already had deeds made out for 2000 people. He admitted, however, that the lands he had given away were not entirely paid for and that there were unpaid taxes due on some. Nevertheless, he remained confident that all outstanding debts would be liquidated within two years. He ventured the hope that the grantees would pay taxes regularly once they got the deeds. "I should be grieved," he reflected, "and have abundant reason to be, should any of the grantees suffer their parcels of land to be sold for non-payment of taxes."[46]

---

44   Theodore S. Wright, *An Address to the Three Thousand Colored Citizens of New York Who Are Owners of One Hundred and Twenty Thousand Acres of Land in the State of New York, Given to Them by Gerrit Smith Esq. of Peterboro* (New York, 1846), passim.

45   Subsequently the total number of persons was increased to three thousand. See Frothingham, *Gerrit Smith*, 104. The Committee from New York was requested to submit the names of 861 individuals.

46   Harlow, *Gerrit Smith*, 243. Yet what Smith feared most seemed to have actually happened. For in 1854, the Reverend Charles

Almost immediately Smith encountered difficulties in getting a sufficient number of persons to acually settle upon the land. On September 26, 1846, for example, he asked Mrs. Anna H. Shotwell, directress of the Colored Orphan Asylum, whether any pupils from that institution might be suitable recipients of his offer.[47]   Mrs. Shotwell replied by saying that she approved the motive actuating his generous offer of land to indigent families, but that the Board of Trustees of that institution declined to take up his proposal, because the recipients would probably be unable to mangage and make the land productive.[48]

While blacks in New York City generally applauded Smith's munificence,[49] many feared that unless the lands were settled quickly the gift would be meaningless. This theme was echoed at a national convention of blacks meeting at Troy, New York, in 1847.   The convention as a whole praised Smith and urged a plan of immediate occupancy by suggesting that blacks select their lots and move to them.   The Reverend Charles B. Ray, chairman of the convention's committee on agriculture, underlined this point by introducing a series of resolutions. One said:

> Resolved, That we recommend to our people, also throughout the country, to forsake the cities and their employments of dependency therein, and emigrate to those parts of the

---

B. Ray and Dr. James McCune Smith, two of the original committee members, issued the following notice: "Circular: To *Gerrit Smith Grantees, Redeem Your Lands.* The people who accepted land from Smith and later relinquished it on account of unpaid taxes, due for the year 1849, can now reclaim their property by paying back taxes." U.S.W.P.A., *Calendar of the Gerrit Smith Papers*, 2:186.

[47] U.S.W.P.A., *Calendar of the Gerrit Smith Papers*, 2:5.

[48]   Anna H. Shotwell to Gerrit Smith, May 22, 1854 in *ibid.*, 2:167.

[49]   Samuel E. Cornish, for example, was convinced that land had its redeeming qualities by making one become more self-reliant, virtuous, physically health and economically independent. See Jane H. and William H. Pease, *Bound With Them in Chains: A Biographical History of the Anti-Slavery Movement* (Connecticut, 1972), 145-146.

country where land is cheap, and become cultivators of the soil, as the surest road to respectability and influence.[50]

One other problem that arose which threatened to undermine Smith's whole program centered around the widespread rumor, generally propagated by his detractors, that the lands he had offered for settlement were not productive. They accused him of making a reputation for philanthropy by giving away worthless tracts.

Some of these lands were indeed found unfit for cultivation, as Gerrit Smith himself admitted,[51] but quite a few seemed valuable for their rich timber resources.[52] Yet the controversy which swirled around this issue refused to die. Even though deeds of possession had been made out to blacks in New York City, as elsewhere, they did not settle upon these lands as readily as Smith had hoped. And some who did settle did not succeed. Arnett G. Lindsay, a student of this period, came to the conclusion after extensive investigation that "on account of the intractability of the soil, the harshness of climate, and, in great measure, inefficiency of the settlers, the enterprise was a failure and

---

[50] *Proceedings of the National Convention of Colored People, and Their Friends, held in Troy, N.Y., on the 6th, 7th, 8th, and 9th October, 1847* (Troy, 1847), 30. In a private letter to Gerrit Smith, shortly after the Troy Convention, Ray emphasized his gratitude for the benefaction: ". . . God has not intrusted you with such large possessions for nothing, and He means to show the world why He wanted it, and to which, in due time, He would devote it. O, how exalted the position, to be God's stweard, and to have committed to one, great trusts, and how honored to be God's almoner to the poor!" Ray Family, *Sketch of the Life of Charles B. Ray* (New York, 1887), 21-22.

[51] Frothingham, *Gerrit Smith*, 105.

[52] A black newspaper published in New York City made the following comments: "As these lands are well watered by streams suitable and easy to erect saw mills, forges and factories, we would not only secure breadstuff in abundance, but also be able to furnish the market with other staples, such as timber, leather, iron, furniture and clothing, as cheap as other men." The *Ram's Horn*, November 5, 1847.

offered no relief to the economic condition of blacks in New York City."[53]

Since land did not turn out to be the economic panacea it had been hope for, blacks began to concentrate their attention in other directions. There existed at this time the strongly-held belief that their ultimate elevation within American society could be secured only to the extent to which they improved their mental capacities. Thus, in their search for education would blacks hope to achieve that which had eluded them so often in other endeavors.

---

[53] Lindsay, "The Economic Condition of the Negroes of New York Prior to 1861," 195.

The Search for Education

Free blacks in New York City early evidenced a keen interest in the education of their children. Although the formal movement in this direction was begun under interested white auspices, the blacks themselves would in time play a key role in its support. The first organized attempt to found an institution dedicated specifically to the education of black youth was initiated by the New York Society for Promoting the Manumission of Slaves,[1] which established the African Free School in 1787.[2]

When the school started, it experienced considerable opposition, owing to the widespread prejudice of the surrounding community, which tended at first to check its growth. In the beginning the number of pupils in attendance hovered between forty and sixty.[3] By 1801, however, the school came under increasing favor so that the American Convention on Abolition Societies could say that "Negroes become more generally impressed with the advantages and importance of

---

[1] This group, founded in January 1785, was officially known as "The New York Society for Promoting the Manumission of Slaves, and Protecting Such of Them as have been or may be Liberated." John Jay, first Chief Justice of the United States Supreme Court, was its first president, Alexander Hamilton, its second. See Dwight Lowell Dumond, *Antislavery: The Crusade for Freedom in America* (New York, 1961), 47. Hereafter cited as Dumond, *Antislavery*.)

[2] This school, referred to subsequently as the African Free School No. 1, was located by 1812 on William Street near Duane. See William O. Bourne, *History of the Public Society of the City of New York With Portraits of the Presidents of the Society* (New York, 1873), 671-672.

[3] Enid Vivian Barnett, "Educational Activity By and In Behalf of the Negroes in New York, 1800-1830," *Negro History Bulletin*, 14, No. 5 (February 1951): 99.

education and more disposed to avail themselves privileges offered them."[4]

The majority of the students contributed to the maintenance of the school, a fact which the Society felt would produce more community pride and respect. Still, the resources of the Manumission Society and the contributions of the parents proved insufficient to meet the needs of the school. Accordingly, a state law of March 12, 1813, provided that the African Free School should be one of the institutions to receive a portion of the school funds received by the city and county of New York.[5]

With this Provision for its support the school underwent phenomenal growth. African School No. 2, located in Mulberry Street near Grand, was erected and opened in May 1820.[6] In November 1831, School No. 3 was opened in Nineteenth Street, near Sixth Avenue.[7] In May of the following year, the female department of No. 2 was re-organized as African School No. 4.[8] Then during the summer of 1832, No. 5 was opened at 161 Duane Street, under the care of Jane A. Parker, and No. 6, at 108 Columbia Street, under the

---

[4] *Ibid.*, 99.

[5] *Ibid.*, 99. This law was renewed in 1822. *Ibid.*, 99. In 1824 the New York Common Council appropriated a portion of its funds to support the African Free Schools. See Carter G. Woodson, *Free Negro Heads of Families in the United States in 1830.* (Washington, D.C., 1925), li-lii.

[6] In 1829 for example, the pupils in No. 1 numbered 262, while No. 2 reported a registration of 452. See Bourne, *History of the Public School Society of the City of New York*, 673-674.

[7] Attendance at this school was good, the number of pupils being about 80, but its growth was soon to be checked by an inconvenient location. Objections had been made by the people in that vicinity to the presence of a black school, so the Trustees chose a building in Amity Street, near Sixth Avenue. See *ibid.*, 673.

[8] *Ibid.*, 673.

care of John Peterson—both of whom were black teachers.[9] Finally, in June 1833, School No. 7 was opened at 38 White Street.[10]

Not until the 1820's, however, with the sharp increase of the free black population in the city, did the African Free Schools gain greater visibility, and acceptance within the community. As it was generally hoped that with the development of a strong curriculum of instruction, attendance would improved, a vigorous campaign to this end got under way:

> Notice—Parents and Guardians of Coloured children are hereby informed, that a *male* and Female School has long been established; for coloured children, by the Manumission Society of this city—where the pupils receive such an education as is calculated to fit them for usefulness and respectability. The male school is situated in Mulberry street near Grand street, and the female school in William street, near Duane street; both under the management of experienced teachers. The boys are taught Reading, Writing, Arithmetic, Geography and English Grammar—and the Girls in addition to these branches, are taught Sewing, Marking and Knitting, etc.[11]

Although attendance steadily increased for a time, the African schools did not lack their share of problems. Early in their administration, a monitoring committee was formed, composed chiefly of members of the Board of Trustees, who made weekly visits of inspection. Some of the observations were quite interesting. Isaac Sherwood, for example, visited African School No. 1 on January 5,

---

[9] *Ibid.*, 674. About this time the number of pupils in the schools was as follows: No. 1, 144; No. 2, 272; No. 3, 385; No. 4, 298; No. 5, 179; No. 6, 161—total, 1,439. *Ibid.*, 674.

[10] In September of the same year, No. 3 was divided, and the female department was known as Female School No. 3. *Ibid.*, 674.

[11] *Freedom's Journal*, January 11, 1827. Admission terms were quite reasonable, eligibility being limited to those between the ages of five and fifteen. The cost varied from twenty-five cents to one dollar per quarter, depending on the circumstances of the parents. Those children who could not afford the required fee were admitted free of charge. *Ibid.*, January 11, 1827.

1827 and reported on more than just the educational progress of the pupils:

> This day I visited the school in the morning. The weather being cold to ascertain whether the stove was sufficient to warm the room so as to render the school more comfortable and I am of the opinion it would be sufficient provided the fire was made about one hour previous to the school hour and I would suggest the propriety of allowing the teacher a moderate compensation to procure a competent person to perform that service it being believed this is one cause why the school is so thinly attended.[12]

While the issue of daily attendance would later pose serious difficulties for the Managers of the African schools, those black children who did attend generally made considerable educational progress. On January 16, 1827 another trustee, David S. Brown, called at School No. 1 which he discovered was "very small only 68 [students] present," but found them "well engaged under the good management of the teacher."[13] When the Annual Report for School No. 1 was issued in May 1827, it was found that 174 pupils had been promoted in Reading, 129 in Arithmetic and 35 in Writing, for a total of 358.[14]

The improvement of blacks attending these schools continued apace. The report of the Manumission Society to the American Convention of Abolition Societies in 1828 showed that the African

---

[12] African Free School Papers. *The Regulations, By Laws and Reports, 1817-1832*, 1:43. New York Historical Society. Volume one records the observations of members of the Board of Trustees who visited School No. 1 during the period 1817 to 1832. This was the school located at 245 Williams Street.

[13] *Ibid.*, 43.

[14] *Ibid.*, 45. The Annual Report for School No. 1 covered the period from January 1, 1826 to May 1, 1827. The report was also pleased to note the following: "Scholars on Register 236 of which No. are capable of Reading the Scripture, 94. Writing on paper 78, in Arithmetic 108. Scholars in Sewing department 108 of which No. are acquainted with making garments, marking, knitting, etc., 48. The rest are progressing in the lower branches." *Ibid.*, 45.

Free Schools enrolled over 800 scholars. Of this number, "250 were able to read the Scriptures, write, and do arithmetic, English Grammar, composition, geography [and] astronomy." It was also observed that the "use of globe and map drawings were pursued with interest and advantage by several of the male pupils."[15]

By 1830, 620 pupils attended the schools with the daily attendance not exceeding 400. The library consisted of 400 books at the boys' school on Mulberry Street and 200 at the girls' school on William Street.[16]

During the years 1827 to 1828 attendance at the African Free Schools had dropped off considerably. This was due to indifference or inability on the part of some parents to provide their children with the necessary clothing to attend. The Board of Trustees of the schools appointed the Reverend Samuel E. Cornish, editor of *Freedom's Journal*, to look into the problem, and his initial investigation confirmed his worst fears. He discovered that the dire poverty of many black families operated to limit the opportunities for their children's advancement.[17]

Yet, as has happened so often in the history of Afro-Americans, the women rallied around a program of relief:

> An Association of coloured females has lately been formed, the object of which is to procure by donation, second hand clothing, hats, shoes, etc., for the poor children, who are found or may be found so destitute as to be unable to attend

---

[15]   Barnett, "Educational Activities By and In Behalf of the Negroes in New York," 100. In the late 1820's the school on Mulberry Street introduced an innovation when a room was set aside with a collection of mineral and "natural curiosities" for the older male students. This program, however, was not organized to give the pupils a systematic knowledge of these minerals; their acquaintance with the materials was only superficial. *Ibid.*, 100.

[16]   *Ibid.*, 100. See also Charles C. Andrews, *The History of the New York African Free Schools, from their Establishment in 1787, to the Present Time: Embracing a Period of More than Forty Years; Also a Brief Account of the Successful Labors of the New York Manumission Society* (New York, 1830), 103, 133. (Hereafter cited as Andrews, *The History of the New York African Free Schools*.)

[17]   *Freedom's Journal*, March 7, 1828.

school. (The *Agent* has found a great number in this situation.) The Association is called the AFRICAN DORCAS ASSOCIATION, and is governed by a constitution drawn up for that purpose. [18]

The Association hoped that the "charitably disposed may exert themselves in the cause of a purpose so praiseworthy and let many a poor and destitute child have cause to say—'I was naked and ye clothed me·'"[19] It was largely due to the indefatigable labors of this benevolent group that many black children in succeeding years were enabled to attend school.

Another problem that later arose in the administration of these schools revolved around the treatment of its white and black teachers. The Trustees of the New York Manumission Society had early made a distinction between them, paying the white teachers higher salaries than the black without reference to the qualifications and competence of these individuals. A French traveler, commenting upon this situation, noted that "a man of color, of the name Hughes, receives but 500 dollars a year; while a white man, whose name it would be invidious to mention, as he is acknowledged to be inferior to the other in every respect, has 600, for performing the same duties in a school of the same class."[20]

In 1834, the African Free Schools were taken over by the Public School Society of New York, and later became, a part of the Public System of that City. Before tracing the subsequent history of these events, however, it should be emphasized that by 1850 the African Schools were only *one* among the educational outlets designed for the improvement of blacks.

Mutual Instruction Societies were also established, which were conducted solely by the black member's of the community. According to *Freedom's Journal* there existed:

At least two schools of this description in operation among our brethren of this city, and if we are not mistaken, under

---

[18] *Ibid.*, March 7, 1828.

[19] *Ibid.*, March 7, 1828.

[20] Abdy, *Journal of a Residence and Tour*, 1:8. This problem was not remedied until the African Free Schools were taken over by the New York City Board of Education.

their own superintendence. Here, we have the privilege of communicating to each other the little store of knowledge which we may have industriously acquired, at one and the same time supplying ourselves and importing to others from the same common fountain.

These schools were open to both sexes; the registration fee was one dollar for the year.[21] Blacks also established in March 1828, the B.F. Hughes School for Coloured Children, located in the basement of St. Philip's Protestant Episcopal Church, and open to both sexes. Among the subjects taught were "READING, WRITING, ARITHMETIC, ENGLISH GRAMMAR, GEOGRAPHY with the use of Maps, and Globes and History," The fee was from two to four dollars per quarter.[22]

---

[21] *Freedom's Journal*, April 13, 1827; September 14, 1827. In November 1827, *Freedom's Journal* announced: "It is with much pleasure we learn, that the *African Mutual Instruction School* has a great number of scholars this season than during any former year. There is nothing like perseverance to overcome difficulties frequently considered as insurmountable for a proof of which we need only refer our readers to several individuals in this school, who for years previously, thought *impossible* to read and write. . . .We hope that many of our brethren, who have always thought it impossible for them to read and write will give the subject a trial this season, as delays are always dangerous, and whatever can be accomplished today ought not to be delayed till the morrow." *Freedom's Journal*, November 23, 1827. (Italics in the original.)

[22] *Ibid.*, March 7, 1828. The New York Association of Friends, for the Relief of those held in Slavery, and the Improvement of the Free people of Color, founded about 1841, established a school to educate black adults. Even though day schools for black children were already in operation, it was found that there was "a large body of *adults* in this city, who had grown up without opportunity of literary instruction, which they would gladly obtain, but whose age, and daily avocations, excluded from availing themselves of the benefits of day schools." The Association opened a school four evenings a week and was glad to report an average attendance of about fifty person. See *National Anti-Slavery Standard*, February 10, 1842.

With the avenues to education opening almost overnight, some blacks in this city still felt that not enough was being done. When an "Infant School for Coloured Children" was established in Philadelphia in 1828, the editor of *Freedom's Journal*, John Russwurm, attacked his fellow Negro New Yorkers for not following Philadelphia's example. He observed that while "so much time was being spent by our friends here in *councils* and *palaver*, our neighbors were actively engaged in the cause of humanity."[23]

It should be remembered, however, that while the Mutual Instruction schools and others of a similar nature contributed much to the education of Blacks in New York City, they still operated mainly within the orbit of the African Free Schools. It was in the latter that the great majority of black children gained their education.

The transfer of the African Free Schools to the Public School Society of New York City in 1834 culminated a process which had begun in 1825, when the real-estate of the 24 African schools was leased to the Society.[24] Eight years later the Board of Trustees, acting under the orders of the of New York Manumission Society, approved the change. It was not, however, until the following year that the actual transfer of property occurred.[25] At the time of its transfer the name *African* Free School was changed to the Colored Free Schools in recognition of their pupils' change of status.[26] Thereafter the quality

---

[23] *Ibid.*, May 9, 1828.

[24] Bourne, *History of the Public School Society of the City of New York*, 93. In 1825 there were about 1,000 students attending the African Free Schools. *Ibid.*, 94.

[25] *Ibid.*, 164. At the time of transfer the real-estate consisted of a house and a lot in Mulberry Street, near Grand, a house in William Street, near Duane, on ground held by a perpetual lease from the city for school purposes, and furniture and fixtures of the school. The actual turnover of this property was to be made on condition that the Public School Society purchase it at a fair valuation. The Street property was appraised at $12,130.32 The Mulberry Street property was appraised at $1000. The fixtures of the schools were put at $1,630.32. *Ibid.*, 164, 676.

[26] Eve Thurston, "Ethiopia Unshackled: A Brief History of the Education of Negro Children in New York City," *Bulletin of the New York Public Library*, 69 (April 1965): 219. While the change of the name *African* Free Schools to *Colored* Free Schools was largely

of these schools began to decline. As Carter G. Woodson noted: "The administrative part of the work almost ceased, the schools lost in efficiency, and the former attendance of 1400 startlingly dropped."[27] Then too, it was also revealed that many blacks, frequently intimidated by race riots due to a reactionary climate in the city, either left town or kept their children at home for safety.[28]

---

technical in nature, since the appellation *African* was the distinctive title under which the Manumission Society ran these schools, there was still an underlying "ideological" reason for this substitution. During the latter half of the 18th Century, and the first third of the 19th, many black educational, benevolent, and religious organizations preferred use of the term *African* because this expression connoted their racial and spiritual identification with their long lost motherland, or so it would seem. By the middle of the 1830's, however, use of the word African gained increasing disfavor by certain blacks, who argued that in blood and in nativity they were really Colored Americans. This change of attitude was also closely linked with their implacable opposition to the program of the American Colonization Society, founded in 1816. Since that organization frequently claimed that blacks were basically Africans not Americans, no alternative remained but for these people to quit the United States and return to Africa." In rejecting the term *African*, blacks by implication, reaffirmed their commitment as native Americans.

[27] Carter G. Woodson, *The Education of the Negro Prior to 1861* (New York, 1915), 313. (Hereafter cited as Woodson, *The Education of the Negro.*) But as early as 1827, complaints were voiced concerning the quality of these schools. A subscriber writing to *Freedom's Journal*, sharply criticized the caliber of some of the teachers. He remarked: "We are so skeptical that we cannot believe that almost *anyone* is qualified to keep schools for our children. Enemies may declaim upon their dullness and stupidity; but we respectfully enquire have they not had dull and stupid instructors, who if placed in any but a coloured school would hardly be considered as earning their salt." *Freedom's Journal*, June 1, 1827 (Italics in the original).

[28] *Ibid.*, 313. Samuel E. Cornish, for example, deeply regretted the fact that only a quarter to a third of the eligible black children in New York City attended school in 1837, and he prodded ministers and parents alike to take more interest in education of their youth, urging

In 1855 the schools of the Public School Society were in turn transferred to the Board of Education. Nine years prior to this event, however, blacks had formed a group designed to address itself to many the problems concerning their children's education. The organization, known as "The New York Society for the Promotion of Education Among Colored Children," was founded in July 1846. It aimed among other things at greater access for blacks to the various educational institutions of the city.[29] In the spring of 1847, this group established a high school for black youth, but financial difficulties forced it to close. Its membership numbered twelve when it began but two years later attendance had jumped to one-hundred and twelve.[30]

At the Annual Meeting for the election of the society's officers held at St. Philip's Church on May 12, 1851, William F. Powell, President, noted with disappointment the refusal of the City's Free Academies to accept black children, thus making it necessary for a "separate" educational organization. "We have proclaimed our fitness," Powell maintained, "to superintend and extend the means of Education to thousands of children unprovided for; we have claimed the right to *act* separately, though reluctantly unwilling to yield the principle or to strengthen this invidious distinction; yet we are *compelled* to take this last resort, and make the sacrifice from motives of necessity, or else suffer our children to grow up in ignorance, vice and dissipation."[31]

In the schools established by the Society, an all-out effort was made to encourage attendance. But the difficulties remained considerable. It reported, for example, that Primary School No. 1, located in Center Street near Leonard, had a total of 143 seats, 119 of which were registered for, but an average attendance of only 68,

---

systematic visits of parents in some cases to check the apathy. See Pease and Pease, *Bound With Them In Chains*, 150.

[29] *North Star*, May 19, 1848.

[30] *Ibid.*, May 19, 1848. The officers of the Society were as follows: President, William P. Powell; Vice President, John Berrian; Secretary, Philip A. White; Treasurer, James McCune Smith; Board of Trustees: Henry Scott, Samuel E. Cornish, George Lawrence, John S. Kenny, Louis H. Armand, Patrick H. Reason and Charles B. Ray. See *National Anti-Slavery Standard*, May 22, 1851.

[31] *National Anti-Slavery Standard*, May 22, 1851 (Italics in the original).

leaving about 80 seats vacant. School No. 2 in Thomas Street, had 83 seats in the male, 85 in the female, and 96 in the Primary department for a total capacity of 264. The average attendance, however, was only 200, making the number of seats vacant 64.[32]

Although the Society for the Promotion of Education Among Colored Children made notable achievements in improving the overall level of black education, its work was eclipsed somewhat when the Colored Free Schools of the Public School Society were taken over by the Board of Education in 1855. This event signaled the beginning of a complete overhaul in the administration of these schools. The new school directors "reclassified the lower grades, opened other grammar schools, and established a normal school according to the recommendation of an investigation committee of 1835."[33]

Efforts were also begun at this time to erect school houses for black children. The teachers too were black. One of the chief difficulties, however, was the problem of pupil attendance, owing in part to the fact that some of the boys and girls had to travel "long distances."[34]

Yet even though supervision of these schools became more centralized they still fell short of the desired objectives. For example, some of them were placed under the care of so-called ward officers. Many of these officers neglected their duties, while others gave the work no attention at all. Another problem involved the location of some of these schools in areas that were distinctly hostile to the progress of blacks. Indeed, as Carter G. Woodson has pointed out, the "attitudes of the people in a few wards were distinctly proslavery."[35]

There was also a considerable disparity in the funds appropriated for white and black schools. For example, The New York Society for the Promotion of Education Among Colored Children found in 1855 that there were 3,000 black children in the city of New York as compared with 159,000 white. The former attended the public schools in proportion of 1 to 2.60; the latter in proportion of 1 to 3.40. Proportionally nearly twenty-five percent more black children than

---

[32] *Ibid.*, April 3, 1851.

[33] Woodson, *The Education of the Negro*, 314.

[34] Thomas Boese, *Public Education in the City of New York: Its History, Condition and Statistics. An Official Report to the Board of Education* (New York, 1869), 146.

[35] Woodson, *The Education of the Negro*, 314.

white attended the public schools.   Yet the Board of Education expended $1,600,000 for white schools and only $1000 for the black ones.[36]

In addition to the differentials in funding, black schools often suffered from being housed in buildings that were found to be in a decrepit condition.   These schools were also sometimes located in areas considered unwholesome to the health and morals of the pupils. Thus Public School No. 2, erected in Laurens Street around 1835 by the old Public School Society, was said to be in "one of the lowest and filthiest neighborhoods, and hence, although it has competent teachers in the male and female departments, and a separate primary department, the attendance has always been slender, and will be until the school is removed neighborhood where children may be sent without danger to their morals."   The story was the same for School-house No. 5 located in an old building at No. 19 Thomas Street, but in "a most degraded neighborhood, full of filth and vice; yet the attendance on this school, and the excellence of its teachers, earn for it the need of a new site and building."[37]

A question immediately comes to mind.   Since blacks paid taxes, why did they tolerate such a gross disparity in the funding and up-keep of their schools?   For it was found that "the colored population of this city, in proportion to their numbers, pay their full share of the general

---

[36]   The *Anglo-African Magazine*, 1, No. 7 (July 1859), 222-223. See also Appendix.

[37]   *Ibid.*, 222-223.   Said Richard Warren, Esquire, on his election as President of the New York City Board of Education in January 1859: "I cannot refrain from calling the attention of this Board to the present condition of the schools for colored children in our midst. This class of persons, deprived as it is, of the social and political privileges which others occupy, is certainly entitled to receive more care in the education of their children than it has had.   Many of the school-rooms in which they assemble, are, in every respect, unsuited for them, and unfit for the purpose for which they are occupied. . . .It is a duty, then, we are called to perform to watch with kindness and care over the places where they meet together, and to aid the young to rise to a more elevated position than has been generally attained by those who have lived in our cities. . . ."   *Douglass' Monthly*, March 1859.

and therefore the school taxes."[38] The answer is simple: since blacks were largely politically unorganized they were thus not in a position to make a significant impact upon the community.

Blacks in New York City also pushed for the higher education of their youth. Unfortunately for them, however, the opportunities in this field were severely limited, for while there were numerous public schools in the metropolis, they specialized in the teaching only of the preparatory branches of an English education and not in the higher ones.

An indignant subscriber wrote to the *Colored American* noting this glaring deficiency, and while he had general praise for the public schools, he found to his chagrin "*there is not in this City nor in its vicinity a private school where the colored youth can even obtain a knowledge of the higher branches, nor be fitted to follow any profession which requires a liberal education*" He observed that there was one institution in the city which attempted to perform this task—the New York Select Academy, established in May 1859, under the auspices of St. Philip's Church. He was convinced that had this institution been well-supported it could have remedied the deficiencies in this area, but was disappointed to find that the patronage given the school was not even adequate to pay the salary of its principal.[39]

Higher education was not encouraged among the friends of the African-Americans with any degree of intensity in the 1820's. Indeed in that decade it was very difficult for blacks to attend white institutions of learning. This no doubt accounts for the founding of separate institutions for blacks during the middle of the Nineteenth Century. *Freedom's Journal* pointed up the influence of the lack of higher education of the black student when it queried:

> What are the incentives held out to a lad of colour? Are there higher schools to stimulate him to greater exertions? Is he placed and considered equal, with other boys of the same rank?[40]

---

[38] *Ibid.*, 222-223.

[39] *Colored American*, October 19, 1839 (Italics in the original).

[40] Barnett, "Educational Activities By and In Behalf of the Negroes in New York," 102.

The New York Manumission Society made short shrift of this problem. The Trustees of that organization were really not interested and discouraged efforts along these lines. Informing the parents of the students of the African Free Schools, it observed:

> There is no disgrace incurred by the pursuit of any honest calling however humble. It is the duty of everyone to do all in his sphere in which Providence has placed him.[41]

By the 1830's the question of establishing collegiate institutions for blacks was to receive increasing attention with the emergence of the Negro Convention Movement. At a national black convention meeting in Philadelphia in 1831 a proposal was introduced asking for the establishment of a black college in New Haven, Connecticut.[42] As originally set forth it called for the raising of about $20,000 to finance the plan.[43] One-half of the original sum was to be raised by the convention. One thousand dollars, it should be noted, had already been subscribed by one of the three men who introduced the plan—probably Arthur Tappan, the New York abolitionist.[44]

When New Haven declined to have the college located in its vicinity, the attempt by Samuel E. Cornish and others to raise funds for the institution was temporarily aborted. It was felt that meaningful action on this issue could only be taken at a subsequent convention. Nothing came of this scheme.

When the second Negro convention was held the following year, the group merely reaffirmed the objects and sentiments on the question

---

[41] *Ibid.*, 102.

[42] William Lloyd Garrison of Massachusetts, Simeon S. Jocelyn of New Haven, Connecticut, and Arthur Tappan introduced the proposal. See Howard Bell, "A Survey of the Negro Convention Movement, 1830-1860," (unpublished Ph.D. Thesis, Northwestern University), 1953, 20.

[43] *Minutes and Proceedings of the First Annual Convention of the People of Colour, Held by Adjournment in the City of Philadelphia, from the Sixth to the Eleventh of June, Inclusive, 1831* (Philadelphia, 1831), 5-6.

[44] Bell, "A Survey of the Negro Convention Movement," 21.

of education set forth by the first.[45] A visible change had taken place by 1835, for in that year it was found that there were at least five colleges which admitted blacks on equal terms with whites. They were: Oneida Institute in New York, Mount Pleasant in Amherst, Massachusetts, Canaan in the state of New Hampshire, the Western Reserve in Ohio, and one in the city of Philadelphia.[46]

Blacks however, continued to press for separate institutions for their people. As late as October 1847, a convention meeting in Troy, New York, voted favorably on such a proposal.[47] The issue was kept alive largely because of the persistent discrimination meted out to those blacks who were already enrolled or sought to attend white colleges. William G. Allen, for example, a black professor at New York Central College at McGrawville, New York, wrote Gerrit Smith on May 25, 1852, asking him to support a number of young black men in New York City who were interested in medical education. Said Allen:

> I have received intelligence from New York City that there are quite a number of colored young men there desirous of obtaining a medical education. Some of these young men

---

[45] *Minutes and Proceedings of the Second Annual Convention of the People of Colour, Held by Adjournment in the City of Philadelphia, from the Fourth to the Thirteenth of June, Inclusive, 1832* (Philadelphia, 1832), 34.

[46] *Minutes and Proceedings of the Fifth Annual Convention of the People of Colour, Held by Adjournment in the City of Philadelphia, from the First to the Fifth of June, Inclusive, 1835* (Philadelphia, 1835), 17. While the Convention did not mention it, Bowdoin College, located in Brunswick, Maine, also admitted blacks on terms of equality.

[47] By this time, however, a deep split had developed on the issue. As reported out of committee the tally stood at 26 for, to 17 against. James McCune Smith, Charles B. Ray, and Alexander Crummell of New York City, all voted in the affirmative, while Thomas Van Rensselaer of the same city and Henry Highland Garnet of Troy, voted in the negative. Garnet favored merely the establishment of "Colored Academies" rather than colleges. See *Proceedings of the National Convention of Colored People and Their Friends held in Troy . . . 1847*, 10.

have already spent some time with distinguished physicians in the City but on application to Medical Colleges for the purpose of attending lectures found admittance there denied them. One who had attended one term in Maine found on going the second. time that the doors were closed against him.[48]

This picture would remain generally unchanged until long after the Civil War. But one should not forget that this discrimination, though potent and seemingly insuperarable, did not completely overwhelm. blacks. Indeed, all too often, it simply offered them the opportunity to launch out boldly in other endeavors. Throughout this period we see clear and substantial evidence of this movement. Education, though vital to the elevation of any people, represented merely one facet in their continuing struggle for social improvement. But blacks were also establishing benevolent and literary societies and using their press as a powerful tool toward advancement. No history of these people in New York City could be considered complete without an objective assessment of the role and influence of their organizations.

---

[48] Benjamin Quarles, "Letters from Negro Leaders to Gerrit Smith," *Journal of Negro History*, 27 (October 1942), 438-439. In New York City, for example, two black men, students at the University of New York, were ejected from the medical hall of that institution when they attempted to hear a lecture, opened, it was said, to the "public generally." American and Foreign Anti-Slavery Society, *Ninth Annual Report* (New York, 1849), 67.

Societies and the Press

One of the most salient characteristics of New York City's free black population was a marked tendency toward organizing societies having either a benevolent or a literary objective. These organizations, along with the influential black press, would figure decisively in welding a stronger, more cohesive, community.

On January 21, 1837, the editor of the *Weekly Advocate,* Samuel E. Cornish, announced that an attempt would be made to catalogue all the various organizations of blacks within the city. Thus began the task of "collecting the names and residences; together with the various occupations of our people . . . to which will be annexed a list of our churches, where situated; and a concise account of our various Benevolent and Literary institutions, to be carefully prepared from the most official sources."[1]

When Philip Bell became editor of the paper two years later, he urged the secretaries of the various organizations to send him information, but apparently the enterprise languished, since no further reference is made to it in subsequent issues of the paper.[2]

Although data are lacking as to the precise number of societies formed in New York City, one student has estimated that at least 50 were launched between the years 1800-1860.[3] Quite a few were weak and short-lived, but others flourished and grew into formidable organizations.

Each of these groups, except for a few that later received municipal support, relied wholly upon a paid membership to weather financial difficulties. Thus, in a general sense, only those blacks who had the wherewithal and leisure time to spare were likely to join.

The benevolent groups were the first to emerge, since blacks had early shown an acute interest in providing for those of their race who

---

[1] *Weekly Advocate*, January 21, 1837.

[2] Daniel Perlman, "Organizations of the Free Negro in New York City, 1800-1860," *Journal of Negro History*, 54, No. 3.

[3] *Ibid.*, 182.

were sick, homeless and destitute. Such an organization was The New York African Society for Mutual Relief formed in 1810, which had as its purpose "to raise a fund to be appropriated exclusively towards the support of such of the members as shall by reason of sickness and infirmity be incapable of attending to their usual vocation of employment and also towards the relief of the widows and orphans of deceased members."[4] This Society grew rapidly, so that by 1852 its yearly income from rents and properties amounted to $2000, while its membership dues for that year totaled $197.25.[5]

Another chartered Mutual Aid Society incorporated in 1829 was "The African Clarkson Association." It was founded as a "charitable society of African descent to afford mutual means of education to the members thereof and relief to their families in case of sickness and death." According to its constitution, members had to be between the ages of 21-40 and pay dues of 25 cents per month in order to provide a fund for sick benefit payments of $2 per week for three months to members of one year's standing. Widows were guaranteed $20 per year in addition to a $15 burial allowance.[6]

Black women were also active in forming philanthropic societies. Though none of them, according to Perlman, "achieved the formal status of incorporation, they were active element in the Negro community." These organizations were largely church sponsored and were similar to the present day "Ladies Auxiliaries" and "Ladies Aid Societies." The Female Mite Society, for example, met regularly during 1837 and 1838 at the Zion Church on the corner of Leonard and Church Streets and helped to raise funds in support of the ministry.[7] The African Dorcas Association was one of the most active. It was formed by women connected with the African Free School for the purpose of "providing and making garments for the destitute."[8] The group was so successful that in 1829 it could report that it had

---

[4] *Ibid.*, 182.

[5] *Ibid.*, 183-184.

[6] *Ibid.*, 186.

[7] *Ibid.*, 187.

[8] The Dorcas Society believed that "in so large a city as this, we must always expect that there will be hundreds of destitute little ones; and though we cannot procure suitable clothing for all, we are in duty bound to do all in our power—as the widow when she cast her mite into the treasury." *Freedom's Journal*, January 9, 1829.

clothed 49 boys and 25 girls during the year and had distributed a total of 232 garments, including shoes and hats.[9]

Another women's group, the Abyssinian Benevolent Daughters of Esther Association, was patterned closely after the men's mutual aid societies. Those between the ages of 16 and 50 were eligible for membership, but it excluded "any person addicted to inebriety or having a plurality of husbands." Dues were 75¢ quarterly. Included in the benefits to the members was a $2 weekly payment for six months, "provided the sickness is not the result of immoral conduct." Benefits were also provided, in case of the incapacity of husbands of members, but it specifically barred any allowance in case of pregnancy.[10]

One of the greatest benevolent enterprises begun during this period for the improvement of blacks was the founding of the Colored Orphans Asylum. About 1855, Miss Anna H. Shotwell and Miss Mary Murray laid plans for establishing a home for colored children. The public was appealed to for support and a fund of $2,000 collected. Then in 1836, a board of twenty-two lady managers was elected with an advisory committee of five men. A constitution was adopted, and the organization fully launched under the title of the "Association for the Benefit of Colored Orphans."[11]

Severe difficulties were encountered in trying to secure a proper building owing to the widespread prejudice against blacks prevalent in the city. Property owners, for example, could be induced on no conditions to lease an empty dwelling for such use.[12] Finally a small building was acquired in Twelfth Street, near Sixth Avenue, for the

---

[9] Perlman, "Organizations of the Free Negro in New York City," 187. See also Andrews, *The History of the New African Free Schools*, 105.

[10] *Ibid.*, 187.

[11] (Rev.) J.F. Richmond, *New York and Its Institutions, 1609-1872* (New York, 1872), 302-303. Article 2 of the Association's Constitution noted: "The object of this Society shall be to provide and maintain a place of Refuge for Colored Orphans, where they shall be boarded, clothed, and suitably educated, until of an age to be found out or apprenticed. In admitting children to the Asylum those means be afforded, half-orphans shall be received." See Association for the Benefit of Colored Orphans, *First Annual Report* (New York, 1837), 13.

[12] *Ibid.*, 302-303.

sum of $9,000. The Trustees of the residuary estate of the late Lindley Murray granted $1,000 towards this purchase, which enabled the Association to complete a payment of $3,000, allowing $6,000 to remain on the mortgage.[13]

In the first year of its operation, the Association was pleased to note that it had 23 destitute children under its care. Several were half-orphans who had been admitted on the same terms required of the Half-Orphan Asylum. Most of these it reported "have been rescued from scenes of misery, which can only be conceived those acquainted with the extreme wretchedness and degradation of the lower classes of our colored population."[14]

At its second anniversary in 1838, the Association reported that it had received 64 children under its care. Of this number 33 were orphans, 29 half-orphans, 1 had been sent to the House of Refuge and 9 died.[15] The degradation and utter lack of care of many of the

---

[13] Association for the Benefit of Colored Orphans, *First Annual Report,* 5. See also *Colored American*, October 28, 1837; December 30, 1837. A mortgage of $6,000 did remain for some years on the property. In 1838 the society was duly incorporated by act of the Legislature. The building purchased soon proved too small, and after repeated applications to the Common Council, a grant of sixteen City lots on Fifth Avenue and Forty-Third Streets was made to which several were subsequently added by purchase, and a suitable edifice erected at an expense of $7,000. See J.F. Richmond, *New York and Its Institutions*, 302-302. See also John Jay, *An Address in Behalf of the Colored Orphan Asylum, Delivered at their Seventh Anniversary, December 11, 1843* (New York, 1844), 5.

[14] Association for the Benefit of Colored Orphans, *First Annual Report*, 6. The first officers of the Association were as follows: Martha Codwise, First Directress; Sarah C. Hawxhurst, Second Directress; Anna H. Shotwell, Secretary; Mary Murray, Treasurer, *Ibid.*, 3.

[15] Association for the Benefit of Colored Orphans, *Second Annual Report* (New York, 1838), 2. According to James MacDonald, physician of the Colored Orphan Asylum, death of the nine children was ascribed to the following five causes: "1st-The peculiar constitution and condition of the colored race; 2nd-The admission of sickly and feeble children; 3d-Most of the children admitted particularly the entire orphans, being the offspring of unhealthy

orphans who came under the charge of the institution, can be seen in the following:

> J___ A___ , a little boy three years old, after having been cruelly beaten by an intemperate mother, was turned into the street on one of the coldest days last winter. He was discovered in this situation by a benevolent colored woman, who carried him to the police, whence he was sent by the presiding magistrate to the Asylum. His whole, body was shockingly lacerated and disfigured, when brought to the institution. No inquiry after him has ever been made by his father or step-mother. [16]

The Association progressed so rapidly that by 1843 it was financially' strong enough to move into new quarters on Fifth Avenue. In a speech at its Seventh Anniversary celebration, John Jay, grandson of the first Chief Justice of the United States, and a vigorous fighter for black rights observed:

> You have already heard that the building of the Colored Orphan Association will accommodate 150 children, and that the present number is only 70. Eighty more friendless and destitute are now pining amid want and sickness, in miserable tenements and damp cellars, exposed to the frosts and snows of winter, whom your charity may enable the managers to remove to their comfortable asylum, and, feed and clothe, mature and educate. Eighty mortal beings may, through your instrumentality, be rescued from vice and crime, and trained in the path of virtue, to become useful during their own lives and transmit worthy examples and pure principles to generations yet unborn.[17]

---

parents; 4th-Neglect during the early periods of life—improper diet—bad air—and want of clothing—by which means constitutions naturally feeble, are greatly impaired; 5th-The prevalence of epidemic disease among the children since their admission in the Asylum." *Ibid.*, 20.

[16] *Ibid.*, 5.

[17] Jay, *An Address in Behalf of Colored Orphans*, 12.

The children who were received into the Colored Orphan Asylum advanced considerably under a healthy and proper regimen. Particularly was this evident in their educational standing.[18] In 1849, the Teachers' Report of that institution issued the following information:

Number of scholars, including 9 day-scholars	152
Read with ease	70
" imperfectly	53
" in spelling only	13
" in the alphabet.	28
Beyond the rules of Arithmetic	25
In Division	6
" Multiplication	6
" Subtraction	7
" Addition	62

(Source: New York City, *First Annual Report of the Governors of the Alms House, New York, for Year 1849* (New York, 1850), 64-65.

So effective was the work of the Colored Orphans Asylum that it soon attracted municipal and state support. As early as 1847, the Commissioner of the City's Alms House Department was directed to pay out of his appropriation fifty cents a week for certain of the inmates; this amounted to $200 per month.[19]

---

[18] At the Annual Meeting of this Association held in December 1844, it was reported that the "appearance of the children was highly creditable to the Managers, and the various exercises in which the scholars exhibited were performed with as much precision, and evidence of improvement, as would be shown by a company of whites of the same age. They spoke up as boldly, read as distinctly, did their sums as readily, and spelt as correctly, as if their skins had been as white as little girls' aprons." Quoted in the *National Anti-Slavery Standard*, December 19, 1844. See also Duncan, *America As I Found It*, 254.

[19] New York City, *Annual Report of the Alms House Commissioner, Comprising Reports from the Several Departments Embraced in the Institution, etc., etc., For the Year Ending December*

In February 1851, a committee of the New York State Legislature formed to inquire into the financial condition of this institution[20] found that its funds were from three sources: contributions, annual subscriptions and legacies. The committee reported that the total amount of moneys from these sources since the formation of the Association was $8,612.65.[21] It also pointed out that since its founding the Asylum had received 524 children.[22]

Another prominent benevolent organization founded during this period was "The Society for the Relief of the Worthy, Aged, Indigent Colored Persons" more popularly known as the Colored Home. The plan to establish such an institution originated with two women, one Miss Jay, daughter of: the distinguished New York jurist, John Jay,

---

31, 1847. Board of Aldermen. Document No. 44. February 14, 1848 (New York, 1848), 36.

[20] In that year the Association had petitioned the Legislature for aid to help relieve a $2,758,000 indebtedness. The committee concluded that the institution was "eminently deserving of aid from the State." It further observed that "at a period when the whole community have been agitated by questions affecting the welfare of the colored population elsewhere, let it not be said that neglect the interests of those at our own doors. Let us make a practical application of the motto, 'Charity begins at home,' and enlarge the means and the usefulness of the only asylum in the State, at least the only one of any extent, yet opened for the benefit of the African race." See "Report of the Committee on Charitable and Religious Societies on the Petition of the Managers of the Association for the Benefit of Colored Orphans, in the City of New York." New York State Assembly. *Documents,* 74 Sess., 1851, 2, No. 43, 3.

[21] *Ibid.,* 2.

[22] *Ibid.,* 2. The committee discovered that most of the children at the time of their admittance were very young—one-half under eight of age. They remained at the institution until the age of twelve, when they were apprenticed in the country. During this time an annual stipend was paid for their services which was placed in the savings bank for them until the age of twenty-one. For boys, the stipend amounted to $100; for girls a payment of five dollars per year was required. Half-orphans whose parents paid a small amount for board, could receive custody of their children at the age of twelve, provided they could prove their capacity to take charge of them. *Ibid.,* 2.

and Miss Anna H. Shotwell, a founder of the Colored Orphans
Society. The former donated $1,000 to a few women who convened at
the residence of her sister, Mrs. Maria Banyer, in the autumn of 1859.
The sum appropriated was designed for the relief of the "*sick and
respectable Colored aged.*"[23]

The Society was incorporated by the State Legislature in 1845
under the title of "The Society for the Support of the Colored Home."[24]
Also at this time a petition was presented to the Legislature for the
repeal of certain acts passed March 11, 1839, and May 26, 1841
(which appropriated $10,000 for a State Hospital in the City of New
York), asking a transfer of the money therein named to the Colored
Home.[25]

These acts were repealed, a new one passed, and the money in
question transferred to the Managers of the Colored Home.[26] This
money was to be applied to the erection of a permanent building on the
real-estate belonging to the said Home in the City of New York, for the
relief and support of disabled black sailors,[27] and other infirm and
destitute colored people.[28]

---

[23] Mary W. Thompson, *Sketches of the History, Character, and
Dying Testimony, of Beneficiaries of the Colored Home, in the City of
New York* (New York, 1851), 75. (Hereafter cited as Thompson,
Sketches of the History . . . of the Colored Home.) See also J.F.
Richmond, *New York and Its Institutions*, 439; *Colored American*,
January 23, 1841. (Italics in the original).

[24] *Ibid.*, 75.

[25] *Ibid.*, 75-76.

[26] The Legislative Committee to which the petition was referred
agreed to the transfer of this money since the Marine Fund from which
it originated was nearly depleted. The Committee found in this
institution a "guarantee that these funds . . . will prove a permanent
good to that class of the community which it is designed to benefit."
See "Report of the Committee on Charitable and Religious Societies
on the Memorial of the Colored Home in the City of New York, and
the Memorials etc., in relation to the state Hospital in Said City," New
York State Senate. *Documents*, 68 sess., 1845, 3, No. 112, 2.

[27] It was found that the Colored Home was the "only institution
in the city of New York where disabled colored sailors can obtain
relief." Black sailors were not admitted into the Alms House or the

The Society later made arrangements with the Commissioner of the Alms House, to receive into its institution, at a very low rate, all black paupers of the city, reserving the right to reject such applicants as the resident physician should medically pronounce unfit for the Colored Home.[29] In 1848 the Society purchased 44 lots of ground lying on Sixty-Fifth Street, Between Avenue A and First Avenue and started constructing its buildings, which were completed the following year.[30]

The progress of this Society was truly phenomenal. By 1852, the Colored Home was accommodating upwards of 200 persons, many of them aged and decrepit and others sick. This was also its twelfth year of operation. Its average annual admission was about 500 persons. The Report of the Treasurer from May 1, 1851, to April 30, 1852 showed a collection and disbursement of about $9,000, leaving $123.11 in the treasury. Of the above receipts, $7,691.41 came from the city authorities. The remainder was raised principally by subscriptions and donations.[31]

The last major benevolent enterprise organized by blacks in this period was the Colored Sailors' Home. The Home, located at 61 Cherry Street, was founded in 1839 by William P. Powell, a prominent

---

Sailors Snug House, even though they had contributed about $4,000 annually to the mariners fund. *Ibid.*, 2.

[28] Thompson, *Sketches of the History of the Colored Home*, 75-76.

[29] *Ibid.*, 76. The Colored Home became by 1847 a branch of the Bellevue Alms House. In that year, the total expenses of this home, which had an inmate population of 297, averaged $9,278.88. Unlike the other branches of the Alms House department, distinct arrangements were made for the support of this institution. A contract was drawn up by the Alms House Commissioner, in January 1845, with the Managers of the Colored Home, to board and clothe the colored paupers at 60 cents per week. See N.Y.C., *Annual Report of the Alms House Commissioner 1842*, 28.

[30] *Ibid.*, 76. See also Richmond, *New York and Institutions*, 439.

[31] *National Anti-Slavery Standard*, June 24, 1852. At this time the officers of the Society were as follows: Mrs. Mary Ann Wells, First Directress; Mrs. Samuel J. Bebee, Second Directress; Mrs. W.W. Chester, Recording Secretary; Mrs. N.E. Russell, Corresponding Secretary; and Mrs. John Harper, Treasurer. *Ibid.*, June 24, 1852.

New York black active in its civic and political life. While Keeper of this establishment, Powell helped many destitute and homeless sailors who found themselves denied admission into the regular city units set up for that purpose.[32]

While a small fee was required of the inmates to help defray the expenses of the institution, a few gained admission free of charge. Still the home remained a financially successful enterprise. The Report of the *Colored Sailors Home in New York* from November 1, 1839 to January 1, 1841, showed the following:

Total amount received from 425 boarders . . .	$2,234.39
Amount due from delinquents.	676.93
Total.	**$2,911.32**
Whole amount of current expenses	
exclusive of rent	$2,097.55
Balance in favor of the house.	813.77
Deduct for debts due as above	676.93
Net Profit of the House.	**$136.84**

(Source: *National Anti-Slavery Standard*, May 6, 1841)

In an article entitled, "Gleanings by the Wayside," William C. Nell described the Colored Sailors Home as "an *Oasis* in the desert, when compared with the many houses where seamen usually congregate." "Here," Nell continued, "The Banner of Reform floats conspicuous." Its literary activity was an added attraction, as "an excellent Library and other reading-room facilities, are at the disposal of inmates."[33]

To accommodate the increasing numbers of seamen, a large and spacious three-story brick building was acquired at 230 Pearl Street in 1849.[34] In that very year, William Powell could report:

---

32 *Ibid.*, May 6, 1841. One year after its founding, the Home reported that it had received and accommodated 283 boarders at an expense of $970.32. The inmates area generally found the place well-conducted, where "after escaping the dangers incident to the life of a sailor," they could enjoy "repose and quiet, and none to molest nor make them afraid." *Ibid.*, February 24, 1842.

33 *North Star,* February 11, 1848.

34 *Ibid.*, April 7, 1849.

The whole number of boarders has been about 4,175 or an annual average of 400. Of the whole number, 560 destitute sailors, true objects of charity, have received relief in board and clothing, on an average of each, amounting to $1, 680.[35]

The literary societies established by blacks during this period proved to be an important element in their efforts toward improvement. Writing to the *Colored American* in March 1837, a subscriber had this to say concerning these groups:

> Mr. Editor—It is certainly gratifying to know that there is in existence, in this city, a number of associations, male and female, devoted to the mental and literary improvement of our people. Their establishment has been procured by the spirited efforts of individuals, who have deeply at heart, whatever concerns the interest of the oppressed; and for years have been diffusing among us their benign influences. I care not how many societies, whose objects are moral and mental improvement are raised up. They will do good among us. They will tend to clear us from the charge of indolence, or indifference, to our own welfare which has been heaped upon us. These societies will be productive of the happiest, and most beneficial results, and will not fail to win the approbation of the wise and good of every community. If academic privileges are withheld, they prove a readiness in us to avail ourselves of every means of improvement which lies within our reach. They show, too, that we are not a people given up to revelry and licentiousness as we have been basely misrepresented, but that the leisure hours of many are devoted to thought and literary advancement.[36]

The literary societies formed by blacks were indeed varied and numerous. Some flourished and became valuable pillars of the community; others experienced abrupt careers. One of the earliest of these was the Hicks Society, an organization which met on Wednesday nights every month for at least two years before it passed out of

---

[35] *Ibid.*, April 7, 1849.
[36] *Colored American*, March 11, 1837.

existence. Other short-lived societies included the Franklin Forum, the Tyro Association, and the Eclectic Fraternity.[37]

One of the most celebrated of these groups was the Phoenix Literary Society, founded in 1833, which included such blacks as Christopher Rush, Thomas L. Jennings, Theodore S. Wright, Peter Vogelsang, and white Arthur Tappan.[38] Tappan, the wealthy New York City philanthropist and abolitionist, remained the chief financial backer of the group.[39] The Reverend Christopher Rush was the President of the Society. He later became a bishop in the African Methodist Episcopal Church. The Reverend Samuel E. Cornish was an agent of the Society, his salary being paid by Mr. Tappan, who was treasurer.[40] The board of directors was composed of both white and black persons.[41]

The object of the Society was to promote the improvement of blacks in morals, literature, and the mechanic arts. In a circular the officers stated that "the society is made up of no particular sect or party. It is designed to be the goal of the entire colored population, and of their friends, in New York City." The circular further stated that "no foundation of society can be strong without more virtue and the arts which are essential to universal industry, are to be promoted as the means of wealth and domestic comfort." It noted that "a spirit of improvement is now moving the colored people in various places to secure for themselves and their children advantages which they have heretofore but partially enjoyed."[42]

Under the program of the group the city was to be divided into ward societies, the aims of which were so ambitious and interesting as to merit full quotation:

> This Society will aim to accomplish the following objects: To visit every family in the ward, and make a register of every colored person in it—their name, sex, age, occupation, if they

---

[37] Perlman, "*Organizations of the Free Negro in New York City*," 191.

[38] Benjamin Quarles, *Black Abolitionists* (New York, 1969), 102.

[39] Lewis Tappan, *The Life of Arthur Tappan* (New York, 1870), 158.

[40] *Ibid.*

[41] *Ibid.*

[42] *Ibid.*, 158-159.

read, write, and cipher—to invite them, old and young, and of both sexes, to become members of this society, and to make quarterly payments according to their ability—to get the children out to infant, Sabbath, and week schools, and induce the adults also to attend school and church on the Sabbath—to encourage the women to form Dorcas societies to help clothe poor children of color if they will attend school, the clothes to be loaned, and to be taken away from them if they neglect their schools; and impress on their parents the importance of having the children punctual and regular in their attendance at school—to establish mental feasts, and also lyceums for speaking and for lectures on the sciences, and to form moral societies—to seek out young men of talent, and good moral character, that they may be assisted to obtain a liberal education—to report to the board all mechanics who are skillful and capable of conducting their trades and with respectable farmers for lads of good moral character—giving a preference to those who have learned to read, write and cipher—and in every way to endeavor to promote the happiness of the people of color, by encouraging them to improve their minds, and abstain from every vicious and demoralizing practice.[43]

The Society normally held its gatherings at New York City's famous Broadway Tabernacle. Here literary presentations were often given by its members. At its Semi-Annual meeting in February 1837, the Society followed a program patterned roughly along the lines of its other meetings. On this occasion Samuel R. Ward, the brilliant black orator and abolitionist, gave the opening address. He was followed by Thomas Sydney, whose lecture on "The Influence of Intellectual Ability" was a discourse which "abounded with beauties showing imagination and a depth of research and evidence. . . ."[44] A prize essay was read by Charles L. Reason on the subject the "Influence of the Press," which was a work, in the words of the judges, "showing profound thought and extensive inquiry." George T. Downing, son of

---

[43] *Ibid.*, 159-160. See also *Address to the People of Color, in the City of New York by Members of the Executive Committee of the American Anti-Slavery Society*, 8.

[44] *Weekly Advocate*, February 18, 1837.

Thomas Downing, read an essay on the "Possibility of Great Changes," which was an address "abounding with facts and some very cogent arguments." The judges concluded by saying of Downing, "this young gentleman has power, but he is not conscious of it; we would advise him to exert himself more." Then a poem entitled "Alonzo," composed by Henry Highland Garnet, was recited. Garnet was a member of the Society and at the time was pursuing his studies at Oneida Institute.[45]

The Phoenix Society did not limit itself to mere literary exercises. It also attempted to work for practical objectives. Thus a committee with Samuel Cornish as chairman tried to raise a subscription of $10,000 for the purpose of "erecting a building that would house a library, reading room and museum where colored youth and others might enjoy some of the advantages provided by the white community."[46]

The Phoenix Society made a major contribution with the establishment of a School for Colored People, which met three times per week under the Broadway Tabernacle, now home base of the Society. Tuition was $3 per quarter; the monies helped defray the cost of rent, heat, supplies and teacher salaries. Instruction was offered in reading, writing and geography.[47]

The opening of the school in 1837 aroused much interest among the community. Within two weeks it had employed 13 teachers and was advertising for 7 more.[48] The school continued to operate for a

---

[45] *Ibid.*, February 18, 1837. Commenting on this evidence of literary excellence, Robert Sears, editor of the *Weekly Advocate*, praised the work of the Phoenix Society for encouraging the intellectual improvement of Afro-Americans. He noted that the *Weekly Advocate* was devoted to the "*mental*, as well as moral and political improvement of our people" as it was only by the "*commanding, ascending* and *transcendent* influence of *intellectual* ability," that blacks could rise in the scale of being. *Ibid.*, February 18, 1837. (Italics in the original).

[46] Perlman, "Organizations of the Free Negro in New York City," 193.

[47] *Ibid.*, 193.

[48] *Ibid.*, 193. The Day School consisted of both a male and female department with about 60 students in attendance. An Evening

period of two years, thereafter undergoing a sharp decline. Arthur Tappan's loss of $40,000 worth of merchandise in a fire which swept New York City in 1835 probably brought about the withdrawal of the school's chief source of support.[49]

By early 1839, the Phoenix Society itself had passed out of existence. In February of that year, a subscriber wrote to the editor of the *Colored American* expressing concern that the books presented to the Society were no longer being used for the mental improvement of blacks. While noting that the library of the Society was second to none he was upset over the fact that it would pass into the hands of some other literary association which he feared would be a great loss to "the colored people of this city."[50]

The literary society that outlived all the others and seemed to have exerted considerable influence over many aspects of black New York, life was the Philomathan Literary Society. This organization, founded in 1829 for the avowed purpose of "devoting itself to the improvement of literature and useful knowledge,"[51] met regularly on Tuesday evenings in its own hall on Duane Street. At its gatherings debates and recitations were presented along with select readings on moral and scientific subjects. Membership was limited to those with a "good moral character and the desire to improve the mind."[52]

It was said of the Philomathan Society that "its members are numbered among our most talented young men. . . .It embodies more talent and moral worth, than any other institution existing among us with which we are acquainted."[53] Its roster of members included such distinguished Negro leaders as Dr. James McCune Smith, the physician, and Philip Bell, owner of the *Colored American*, who was also active in the New York African Society for Mutual Relief.[54] Henry Sipkins, one of the founders of the New York African Society for Mutual Relief, a delegate to the National Negro Convention in

---

School was also conducted which the managers characterized as being "in a very flourishing condition." *Weekly Advocate*, January 14, 1837.

[49] Quarles, "Letters from Negro Leaders to Gerrit Smith," 437.

[50] *Colored American*, February 16, 1839.

[51] *Ibid.*, April 15, 1837; April 29, 1837.

[52] *Ibid.*, May 2, 1840.

[53] *Ibid.*, November 4, 1837.

[54] Perlman, "Organizations of the Free Negro in New York City," 194.

Philadelphia in 1830 and a contributor to the *Colored American*, was also a member of the Philomathan along with Isaiah G. DeGrasse, minister of the Second Colored Episcopal Church. By 1837 the Philomathans owned a library of over 500 books and were still anxious to expand.[55]

Another organization founded during this period was the New York Garrisonian Literary Society. Formed in 1834, it emphasized religion, literature, and the overcoming of prejudice. It was maintained for black youth from 4 to 20. Initiation fees were 12 1/2¢ and dues were 1¢ per week for anyone of good moral character who subscribed to the constitution. Its meetings were devoted to singing, praying, and readings of original essays.[56]

While the benevolent and literary societies founded by blacks played an invaluable role in their uplift, no instrument for their improvement figured more prominently than the black press. It stood in the forefront of the liberation struggle.

In 1827, the first black newspaper ever published in America, *Freedom's Journal*, appeared. Samuel E. Cornish, the eloquent black orator and reformer, served as senior editor,[57] and John Russwurm, the second black college graduate in the United States, as junior editor.[58] In its first issue, which appeared on March 16, 1827, the editor outlined the purpose of the new paper:

---

[55] *Ibid.*, 194.

[56] *Ibid.*, 195.

[57] Samuel Elias Cornish was born in Sussex County, Delaware in 1795. He died in Brooklyn, New York in 1858. Educated in Philadelphia for the ministry, he became a member of the New York Presbytery in 1821. He was founder and first minister of the First Colored Presbyterian Church in New York City and later served on the Executive Committee of the American Anti-Slavery Society. After resigning as editor of *Freedom's Journal*, he became School Agent for the New York Manumission Society but resumed his journalistic activities as editor of the *Colored American*. Cornish was active and deeply involved in the religious as well as community life of New York blacks. See Lawrence D. Reddick, "Samual E. Cornish," *Negro History Bulletin*, 5 (November 1941):38.

[58] The first black college graduate was Edward Jones, who received his degree from Amherst College on August 23, 1826.

In presenting our first number to our patrons, we feel all the diffidence of persons entering upon a new and untried line of business. But a moment's reflection upon the noble objects, which we have in view by the publication of this Journal; the expediency of its appearance at this time, when so many schemes are in action concerning our people—encourage us to come boldly before an enlightened publick."

. . . We wish to plead our own cause. Too long has the publick been deceived by misrepresentations, in things which concern us dearly, though in the estimation of some mere trifles; for though there are many in society who exercise towards us benevolent feelings; still (with sorrow we confess it) there are others who make it their business to enlarge upon the least trifle which tends to the discredit of any person of color; and pronounce anathemas and denounce our whole body for the misconduct of this guilty one. . . .[59]

According to one student of this period the advent of *Freedom's Journal* marked the beginning of a national movement among the black masses "and ushered in the Negro Renaissance. It was the first attempt at national race-solidarity."[60] This paper also played an influential role in the calling of the first national Negro Convention in 1830.[61]

In its format, *Freedoms Journal* was a small newspaper of eight pages, yet its interests and appeal were universal. Each issue was filled with articles on morals, literature, philosophy, history, science and an occasional news story. Sometimes it carried a brief summary

---

Russwurm graduated from Bowdoin College on September 6, 1826. See Philip S. Foner, *The Voice of Black America: Major Speeches by Negroes in the United States, 1797-1971* (New York, 1972), 33. (Hereafter cited as Foner, *The Voice of Black America*.) See also William M. Brewer, "John B. Russwurm," *Journal of Negro History*, 13, No. 4 (October 1928): 413-422.

[59] *Freedom's Journal*, March 16, 1827.

[60] Bella Gross, "Freedoms Journal and the Rights of All," *Journal of Negro History*, 17, No. 3 (June 1932): 245.

[61] *Ibid.*, 245.

of events in the nation along with some personal notices of marriages and deaths. Advertisements were placed by local black businessmen and frequently by those in other major cities. The cost was three dollars per year.

Under the capable guidance of its senior editor, Samuel E. Cornish, the paper enjoyed a ready appeal among certain whites, who in some cases became subscribers, as well as among the free African-American population of the United States. Cornish was a radical thinker and an uncompromising idealist who gravitated toward all kinds of reforms. All of the journals he edited were stamped with his personality and style.[62] As long as he was connected with the paper his favorite motto "Righteousness Exalteth a Nation," appeared on the front page of every issue; when he resigned, it was discontinued.[63]

Under his successor, John Russwurm, the journal witnessed a rapid deterioration. The new editor lacked originality and frequently compromised on key issues. Soon complaints were voiced and readers sent in letters of protest demanding explanations. Russwurm was openly charged with having sold the interests of his people to their worst enemies—in this case, the Colonizationists.

The free Negro population of the United States viewed the American Colonization Society, founded in 1817 by Henry Clay and others as its arch foe.[64] Formed to remove the newly manumitted slaves of the South to Africa, it also encouraged the voluntary expatriation of free blacks in the North. Blacks felt this country was their only true home and were unwilling to leave, hence their violent reaction to Russwurm when he came out in support of this scheme.

While Russwurm at first opposed colonization, his belated about-face on the subject virtually insured his ineffectiveness as editor of *Freedom's Journal*. Not long after his conversion, he was forced to resign.[65] With John Russwurm gone, Samuel Cornish again became

---

[62] *Ibid.*, 248.

[63] *Ibid.*, 248.

[64] This issue will be discussed more fully in a separate chapter.

[65] *Ibid.*, 279. But while Russwurm was repudiated by his own people, his support did not go unnoticed by the American Colonization Society. Shortly after receiving his Masters Degree from Bowdoin in 1829, he was sent to Liberia as Superintendent of Public Schools. He became editor of the Liberia *Herald*, and engaged in politics. He then

the editor, changed the name of the paper,[66] and outlined incisively in the prospectus the source of his disagreement with Russwurm on colonization:

> A word on another subject and I am done. The sudden change of the late Editor of "The Freedom's Journal" in respect to colonisation, has excited much astonishment, and led to many inquiries; to me the subject is equally strange as to others and I can only dispose of it, by classing it with the other novelties of the day. I conclude by saying my views, and the views of the intelligent of my brethren generally, are the same as ever in respect to colonisation; we believe it may benefit the few that emigrate, and survive, and as s missionary station, we consider it as a grand and glorious establishment, and shall do all in our power to promote its interests, looking toward the glorious period, when civilization and religion shall have spread over the vast and important continent of Africa. But as it respects three millions that are now in the United States, and the eight millions that in twenty or twenty-five years will be in this country, we think it in no wise calculated to meet their wants or ameliorate their condition.[67]

Samuel Cornish considered the *Rights of All*, not as a continuation of *Freedom's Journal*, but as an entirely new publication—hence its change of name. The first issue of the paper came out on May 29, 1829, two months after the suspension of the first journal (March 28, 1829).

In format the *Rights of All* was small in size and contained eight pages, three columns to a page in each issue. It was originally planned as a weekly but the second issue appeared in June, two weeks after the first, and thereafter monthly until October 1829. Its original cost was two dollars a year; when it became a monthly its price was reduced to one dollar. Income from the paper was mainly from subscriptions and

---

became governor of the Maryland Colony of Cape Palmas in 1836, a position which he held until his death in 1851. *Ibid.*, 280.

[66] Now known as the *Rights of All*.

[67] *Rights of All*, May 29, 1829.

commercial advertisements.   Its agents were found in the United States, England, Canada and Haiti.

With the demise of the *Rights of All* several years elapsed before another black newspaper appeared.   Philip A. Bell of New York began publishing in the middle 1830's an ephemeral newspaper called the *Struggler*, followed in January 1837 by the *Weekly Advocate*.[68]

In February 1837, the Reverend Samuel Cornish became editor of the *Weekly Advocate*, while Robert Sears directed his energies to improving the circulation of the newspaper. Philip Bell, the Proprietor, thought the time was appropriate to change the name of the newspaper and suggested upon reflection the name the *Colored American*. This term was preferred because he believed it was "short, emphatic and distinctive. We are *Americans*—colored Americans, brethren—and let it be our aim to make the title *Colored American* as honorable and as much respected before the world as *white* Americans or any others."[69]

When some objections were raised, largely by whites, as to the correctness of the title, Cornish wrote that "in complexion, in blood and in nativity, we are decidedly more exclusively 'American' than our white brethren; hence the propriety of the name of our paper *Colored American*." He continued by making this penetrating observation:

> We are written about, preached to, and prayed for, as Negroes, Africans, and blacks, all of which have been stereotyped, as names of reproach, and on that account if no other, are unacceptable.[70]

---

[68] This paper was "Printed and Published every SATURDAY, by *ROBERT SEARS*, at his Book and Job Printing Office, No. 2 Frankfurt Street, (2d story) opposite Tammany Hall . . . where Advertisements, Subscriptions, and Communications will be received." The *Weekly Advocate,* January 7, 1837.

[69] *Weekly Advocate*, February 25, 1837. (Italics in the original.)

[70] *Colored American*, March 4, 1837. See also *ibid.*, January 20, 1838.   James McCune Smith, however, generally favored the use of the term "Black" in describing Afro-Americans; "Negroes," "Colored People" "African Race" came under his attack.   He frequently excoriated Horace Greeley of the New York *Tribune* for applying the term "African Race" in particular.   In reply to his strictures on the issue, Greeley wrote: "Mr. Smith proceeds to cavil at the designation 'African Race' as applied to his people.   We used it because we found

Cornish remained in his editorial post through May 1839. In January 1839, James McCune Smith became associate editor but served only until Cornish left the newspaper. When the paper suspended operations between November 1839 and March 1840, no one was listed as editor. Then in the latter month, Charles B. Ray became editor and proprietor. The *Colored American* continued to appear every week until the issue of March 13, 1841.

Throughout its illustrious career the *Colored American* remained the most effective organ of the free black population of the United States. The columns of this newspaper addressed themselves boldly and uncompromisingly to the many problems and issues facing the African-American community. The items in the paper covered a wide range of events. Foreign news was usually noted in a small section of each issue while national politics was commented upon as it affected black Americans. As early as March 1837, a subscriber who signed himself as a *Friend*, wrote to Samuel Cornish, on the great good the paper was accomplishing in the community:

> I must acknowledge, Sir, when this paper was laid upon my table, I felt an unaccountable lukewarmness and indifference toward it. I was well aware that such a paper was wanted. I also knew, that a paper conducted by colored men, would prove either a curse or a blessing; hence I said but little and have formed my opinions very cautiously. . . .I hope sir you will not accuse me of flattery, when I boldly assert that I have spent hours in scrutinizing the last three numbers, published under your editorial supervision, to ascertain the true character of the "Colored American," seeking as much for

---

none other so expressive and inoffensive; 'Negro' is deemed (however improperly) a term of disparagement; and, besides, those of mixed blood are not properly Negroes. 'Colored American' is indistinctive—all men have more or less color, and our Aborigines a good deal. We use the term 'African Race' to designate those descendants wholly or partially from negroes, who are specially 'the African Race' though other Races are found inhabiting some portions of Africa especially near its coasts. Surely, he who cavils at this term manifests a captious spirit and unamiable temper." New York *Weekly Tribune*, September 6, 1851.

faults as for excellence, and I hesitate not to say, that our white brethren may safely recommend it to their friends, as worthy of taking first rank among the periodicals of the day. . . .[71]

From the beginning, however, the *Colored American* encountered severe financial difficulties. The cost of the paper per year was one dollar and fifty cents, but many of the subscribers proved delinquent in sending in their payments. Samuel E. Cornish, for example, virtually served without salary. On one occasion he said:

 The paper ought to be taken up by every free colored man, and his friends. On the contrary it has but about *nine hundred* subscribers, mostly in this city. Its income, as yet, will not pay for the paper and the printing, The Editor has not received *one cent*, nor asked for any pecuniary compensation as yet; and the Proprietor—worse still—*is in debt.*[72]

It was this lack of sufficient financial support which hampered the efforts of the paper to expand. For as Cornish pointed out, "its present size contains one-half the matter we wish to throw out weekly to our communities, white and colored. . . .We can *barely* crowd in the domestic affairs of the community in which we live. . . ."[73]

This problem was relieved somewhat with an increase in subscribers.[74] But, at the same time, the cost of the periodical shot up from one dollar and fifty cents to two dollars a year, for past experience had taught the editor that "a paper depending almost wholly upon its subscription list for support cannot be supplied for the small sum of *one dollar and fifty cents.*"[75]

---

[71] *Colored American*, March 25, 1837. (Italics in the original.)

[72] *Ibid.*, June 17, 1837. Later the paper called upon its readers and friends to contribute five dollars each in support of a plan to pay the editor's salary. See *ibid.*, December 16, 1837.

[73] *Ibid.*, September 16, 1837.

[74] On June 9, 1838, the *Colored American* reported it had 1800 subscribers. One year earlier there were only 900 subscribers most of whom lived in New York City. *Ibid.*, June 17, 1837.

[75] *Ibid.*, June 2, 1838. One month before the *Colored American* increased in price, a delegation consisting of the Reverends Theodore

It was perhaps indicative of the paper's precarious financial base that it continued to change hands in one form or another. In January 1838, it was announced that the *Colored American* had passed from its original proprietor, Philip Bell, to a Committee on publications, composed of several men. Some felt that this move would restore public confidence and increase subscriptions. The editor (Samuel Cornish), still retained temporary control of the paper but was ultimately responsible to the Committee.[76]

But in June 1838, the Publishing Committee transferred control of the organ to Charles B. Ray, Philip A. Bell, and Stephen H. Gloucester. In addition to this move arrangements were made to publish the paper simultaneously in New York and Philadelphia so that the subscribers could be "furnished with interesting items of intelligence from both cities."[77]

None of these actions, however, seemed to put the paper on a strong financial footing, for it continued to make desperate appeals for support. As late as November 1839, it said:

> Whether the Colored American shall survive the present shock, pay its weekly visits during the present distress, and live though another year, depends altogether upon its PRESENT FRIENDS, SUBSCRIBERS and AGENTS: yes brethren whether we shall enter upon another volume at all, depends almost absolutely upon what you will do for us, between this and the first of January.[78]

S. Wright, Charles B. Ray, and William Yates, the abolitionist, waited upon the Business Committee of the American Anti-Slavery Society to solicit aid. after brief deliberations, the Committee resolved that "this society regards the 'COLORED AMERICAN' as an efficient and useful auxiliary in the cause of human rights and entitled to the patronage and support of the friends of the cause, in all parts of the country." American Anti-Slavery Society, *Fifth Annual Report*, 13; *Emancipator*, May 10, 1838.

[76] *Ibid.*, January 13, 1838.

[77] *Ibid.*, June 9, 1838. Stephen H. Gloucester was to conduct the newspaper in Philadelphia.

[78] *Ibid.*, November 23, 1839. For similar appeals for support see ibid., September 26, 1840; December 5, 1840; January 9, 1841; February 20, 1841; March 13, 1841.

Even before the *Colored American* had ceased publication in 1841, there were a few other short-lived black newspapers in New York City. During 1831 and 1832, John G. Stewart edited a paper in Albany, New York, entitled the *African Sentinel and Journal of Liberty*. In November 1838, he proposed publishing in the City of New York, a weekly paper to be known as *The Champion of Equal Rights*. Unfortunately, no copy of either paper has been found.[79]

David Ruggles, a militant black abolitionist and Secretary of the New York Vigilance Committee, a group which rescued many blacks who were kidnapped or threatened, began publishing in 1837 the *Mirror of Liberty*. This was designed to be a quarterly magazine and was probably the first of its type to be published by a black man. The first issue was scheduled to appear on July 7, 1838,[80] but it was delayed until August[81]. A second issue appeared in January 1839, followed by a third in August 1840. The *Liberator* makes reference to a fourth, dated May 1841,[82] but no copies are known to exist.[83]

Early in 1838 issues of a paper called the *Colored Man's Journal* appeared in the city. It was published by White and Owen of No. 1 Doyer Street. Samuel Cornish found it to be a "neat little sheet, got up with some taste and talent." But he discovered to his chagrin that "not a single article it contains was written by a colored man."[84] Finding it to be a deceptive colonization organ, he would not lend it his support.[85]

The *Ram's Horn*, another short-lived black newspaper published in this period, was edited by Thomas Van Rensselaer and Willis

---

[79] *Ibid.*, November 10, 1838. See also Martin E. Dann, *The Black Press, 1827-1890* (New York, 1972), 48-49.

[80] *Emancipator*, July 5, 1838.

[81] *Colored American*, October 20, 1838; *Emancipator*, December 27, 1838.

[82] *Liberator*, August 13, 1841. See also *ibid.*, November 26, 1841.

[83] Ruggles later published between 1845 and 1847 a paper known as the *Genius of Freedom*.

[84] *Colored American*, March 3, 1838.

[85] Cornish noted that "it is the spirit of Colonization, garbed in sheep's clothing, which has got up that Journal." *Ibid.*, March 3, 1838.

Hodges. It appeared sporadically during 1846-1848. Only one issue (dated November 5, 1847) is known to have survived.

The *Anglo-African Magazine* was perhaps the most interesting periodical to be published by blacks in New York City. It was founded in 1859 by Thomas Hamilton of Brooklyn. As a monthly it appeared regularly from January 1859, through February 1860.[86] Its columns, however, were a virtual forum for some of the leading black intellectuals of the time. For twenty-five cents a copy to one dollar a year, the reader was introduced to the views and talents of James McCune Smith, Frances Ellen Watkins, Martin R. Delany, William C. Nell, J.W.C. Pennington, Edward Blyden, Thomas Holly, Daniel A. Payne, George B. Vashon, John B. Vashon, John Mercer Langston, J. Sella Martin, Amos Gerry Beman, Charles L. Reason, and Frederick Douglass.

The Black Press and the Societies exerted a powerful impact on the African American community that should not be underestimated. The one articulated the felt needs and yearnings of that community, while the other served to channel its energies along more constructive lines.

Overshadowing these, however, stood the Black Church, an institution whose tentacles touched nearly every aspect of black life—social, political and economic. Yet the Black Church must first be seen in the role for which it was essentially designed—a religious institution which developed out of the peculiar circumstances surrounding the free black in New York City.

---

[86] The last issue was delayed until April 21, 1860 and then the magazine ceased publication. A weekly newspaper known simply as the *Anglo-African* succeeded it and appeared intermittently until 1865.

Religious Life

The Black Church has traditionally been a major source of stability and continuity for the Afro-American community. In New York City, in the period after 1850, it developed into a dynamic force in providing leadership and direction for that community.

In the period before General Emancipation most of the major black church denominations were already in existence, reflecting the diversity of black New York life. Nearly every one was founded as a reaction to the prevailing caste within the larger American Church, The earliest to be established represented some variety of African Methodism: the African Methodist Episcopal Church, the African Methodist Episcopal Zion Church, the *Asbury* African Methodist Episcopal Church, and the African Methodist Union.[1]

The African Methodist Episcopal Zion Church subsequently became the largest among blacks in New York City. It was founded in 1796[2] when blacks withdrew from the John Street Methodist Episcopal Church. Leading in this movement were Peter Williams,[3] father of the first black priest in the Protestant Episcopal Church; James Varick, elected first bishop in 1822; George Collins; and Christopher Rush.

These men had earlier received permission from the Reverend Francis Asbury, then Bishop of the Methodist Episcopal Church in the United States, to hold meetings in the intervals of the regular

---

[1]   Jonathan Greenleaf, *A History of the Churches of All Denominations in the City of New York, From the First Settlement to the Year 1846* (New York, 1846), 320-331. (Hereafter cited as Greenleaf, *A History of the Churches of All Denominations.*) Another small sect known as the African Free Meeting Methodist Society was founded in 1812. See New York County, *Religious Incorporations*, 2 vols. (1784-1886). 2:76-77.

[2]   It was incorporated on February 16, 1801. See New York County, *Relgious Incorporations*, 1:28.

[3]   Peter Williams, Sr. was a trustee of this church. See *ibid.*, 28.

preaching hours of the white ministers.[4] However, since no one in either the Episcopal or the Methodist Church would ordain and consecrate their elders, they were obliged to undertake this themselves.[5]

Soon a building was obtained in Cross Street between Mulberry and Orange Streets. At this time (1797) there were only "three colored preachers and one exhorter in New York City."[6] Three years later, the congregation built a new edifice on Church Street, at the corner of Leonard Street, which opened in September 1800. When this building was found to be too small, it was demolished in May 1820, and its replacement measuring 55 feet in width by 70 feet in length, was opened for worship in August of the same year. This building was destroyed by fire in 1839[7] but another building was erected in April of the following year. The Reverend Charles B. Ray characterized the new structure as "undoubtedly the largest and most commodious *Protestant* house of worship, owned and occupied by [the colored] people, in the world."[8] The *National Anti-Slavery Standard* subsequently noted that Zion was "considered to be the largest and wealthiest church of the coloured people in this city—perhaps in this country."[9]

There were branches of the A.M.E.Z. Church throughout the city. One, called "Little Zion," was established in Harlem in 1843. Another branch was organized in Twenty-Second Street near Seventh Avenue. By 1846, the Reverend J.A. King, the preacher in charge, could report

---

[4] Greenleaf, *A History of the Churches of All Denominations*, 321.

[5] John Hope Franklin, *From Slavery to Freedom: A History of Negro Americans* (New York, 1967), 163.

[6] Greenleaf, *A History of the Churches of All Denominations*, 322.

[7] *Ibid.*, 322. In this year Zion Church had 800 or more communicants and a congregation reported to be between 1200 and 2000. See the *Colored American*, September 28, 1839.

[8] It had a seating capacity of 1,500 people. See the *Colored American*, March 28, 1840; April 18, 1840.

[9] *National Anti-Slavery Standard*, April 19, 1849. See also Bishop J.W. Hood, D.D. L.L.D., *One Hundred Years of the African Methodist Episcopal Zion Church* (New York, 1895), *passim.*

that there were 1196 members at the Mother Church, 66 at Harlem, and 14 at Twenty-Second Street.[10]

The African Methodist Episcopal Church was the next largest of the four major black Methodist churches in the city. While on a national basis this denomination considerably outstripped Zion in membership and churches, Zion continued to be the largest of "individual congregations in the Negro community in the city."[11]

The A.M.E. Church traces its origins back to 1787, when officials of the St. George Methodist Episcopal Church in Philadelphia proposed segregating its black and white communicants. Richard Allen, a former slave from Delaware, and now a young minister, opposed this plan and suggested that his people form a separate house of worship. When, on one occasion, officials of the church pulled Allen, Absalom Jones, and William White from their knees during prayer, the die was cast. Allen immediately withdrew and organized the Free African Society, with the help of Absalom Jones.[12]

By 1793 the membership of this seceding group had increased considerably. In the following year, Allen organized the Bethel Church in Philadelphia. It was dedicated by Bishop Asbury and later became known as the Bethel African Methodist Episcopal Church.[13]

Branches of the A.M.E. Church sprang up in the North and South. The church grew so rapidly that by 1816 it was possible to

---

[10] Greenleaf, *A History of the Churches of All Denominations*, 322. A later branch was established in Yorkville on Eightly-Fifth Street between Seventh and Eighth Avenues. In the following year it became the African Methodist Zion Branch Church Militant. See New York *Tribune*, August 4, 1853; August 5, 1853.

[11] Freeman, "The Free Negro in New York City," p. 388. Frederick Douglass noted, for example, that Bethel Church (A.M.E.) in Philadelphia was the "largest church in this Union, and from two to three thousand worship there every Sabbath." But he also observed that Zion Church in New York City "exerts a contreolling influence over the next largest colored denomination of the country." See the *North Star*, July 14, 1848.

[12] Franklin, *From Slavery to Freedom*, 162. See also Carol V. George, *Segregated Sabbaths: Richard Allen and the Emergence of Indipendent Black Churches*, 1760-1840 (New York, 1973), *passim*.

[13] Greenleaf, *A History of the Chruches of All Denominations*, 325.

bind them into a formal organization. At its first General Conference, held on April 11, 1816, the Reverend Allen was unanimously elected Bishop.[14]

The members of this connection were at various times called "Allenites" and their churches are usually called the "Bethel Churches" after the name given the first church in Philadelphia. When Bishop Allen died in 1831 he was succeeded by the Reverend Morris Brown, his assistant.[15]

A branch of this church was founded in New York City by the Reverends William Lambert and George White. Fire destroyed the original structure, but in 1835 a new building was erected on Second Street. A branch of the main church was established in Harlem in 1843. By 1846, 716 members were at the Second Street location and 13 at Harlem.[16]

Little is known of the *Asbury* African Methodist Episcopal Church, it being a relatively small sect. The church was incorporated on February 3, 1814[17] and was located on Mulberry Street, between Hester and Walker.[18]

The Methodist African Union was established in 1826 with a body of seven members. The group met at first in a small room in Seventh Avenue, near Eighteenth Street. One Mr. Campbell and Isaac Barney were the ministers. In 1835 the building in which they were housed was destroyed in the disastrous conflagration of that year. The congregation temporarily took up quarters over a stable in Sixth Avenue near Fourth Street, where it met until 1840, when it succeeded in erecting a brick building on Fifteenth Street, near Sixth Avenue. By this time the membership had increased to 350.[19]

---

[14] *Ibid.*, 326.

[15] *Ibid.*, 326. See also Christopher Rush, *A Short Account of the Rise and Progress of the African Methodist Episcopal Church in America* (New York, 1843), *passim*.

[16] *Ibid.*, 327-328. Later in 1858 another branch of this church was established in Yorkville. It was located on Thrid Avenue near Eighty-Fourth Street. See New York *Tribune*, July 10, 1858.

[17] New York County, *Religious Incorporations*, 1:78-79.

[18] *Colored American*, March 25, 1838.

[19] Greenleaf, *A History of the Churches of All Denominations*, 328. See also *Colored American*, March 25, 1837. According to Greenleaf there was "little real difference between these four bodies of

At least three Protestant Episcopal churches were established by blacks in New York City during this period. They were: St. Philip's, St. Matthew's, and the Church of the Messiah.

St. Philip's was organized by a group of black parishioners of Trinity Church in 1809 as a Sunday School African-American children.[20]   Originally located on the corner of Franfort and Willis Streets, the congregation moved in 1812 to a room on Cliff Street. Seven years later, three lots of ground were obtained on a lease for 60 years, which afterward was to be held as a gift.   At this time the church was located on Collect (now Centre) between Anthony (now Worth) and Leonard Streets.[21]

Through the contributions of many persons, the church was enabled to erect a wooden building at a cost of $5,000, which was consecrated by the Reverend John Henry Hobart, Bishop of the Protestant Episcopal Church, in July 1819, and called "St. Philip's Church."   In the following year, the church was incorporated according to statute[22] and Peter Williams Jr., having been ordained a deacon, was placed in charge. On December 24, 1821, the church building was destroyed by fire and rebuilt of brick in the following year, at a cost of $8,000. Upon his elevation to the priesthood in 1827, Williams became the regular rector of the church. Under his auspices the church flourished. He died suddenly on October 18, 1840, after having ministered to this church for 28 years.[23]

African Methodism, their doctrines, discipline and practices, being substantially alike," *Ibid.*, 320-321.

[20]   U.S.W.P.A., *Inventory of the Chruch Archives of New York City.   The Protestant Episcopal Church in the United States of America.   Dioceses of New York* (New York, 1940), 71. (Hereafter cited as U.S.W.P.A., *Inventory of the Church Archives of New York City. The Protestant Episcopal Church.*)

[21]   Greenleaf, *A History of the Churches of All Denominations*, 80.

[22]   This incorporation was recorded on November 14, 1820. See also New York County, *Religious Incorporations*, 1:96-97.

[23]   Greenleaf, *A History of the Churches of All Denominations*, 80-81. B.F. De Costa, *Three score and Ten: The Story of St. Philip's Church, New York City* (New York, 1889), 23. Williams' funeral was held on an unprecedented scale; its size was extraordinary. Among the officiating clergy were the Episcopal bishops of both Christ and

St. Matthew's was organized in 1836 but never incorporated.[24]
Four years later, the prominent black minister, Isaiah G. DeGrasse,
became its pastor. The members first worshipped in a Hall on the
corner of Elizabeth and Grand Streets, but later removed to Mott
Street. DeGrasse preached here about two years, and attracted a
considerable congregation. Illness, however, cut short his ministry; on
a visit to the West Indies to regain his health, he died and his
congregation ceased to meet.[25]

In April 1845, efforts were made to revive this church. Alexander
Crummell, a young black minister, was obtained and services began in
a Hall at 592 Broadway. The church was later reorganized with about
20 members. Shortly thereafter, it was found that another church had
been formed under the name of "St. Matthews," so the Reverend
Crummell's church styled itself "The Protestant Episcopal Church of
the Messiah"[26] and was incorporated on October 1, 1846.[27] Services
were held at 592 Broadway until the congregation removed to a
building at 472 Houston Street, where it remained until 1849.
Another move brought it to Wooster Street, its home until 1862 when
the congregation dispersed. [28]

Shiloh Church was a prominent black Presbyterian ongregation in
the city. Organized in 1822 by the Presbytery of New York, it

---

Trinity Churches. The event was unique. No other black was given a
public funeral of this type before the Civil War. See also *Colored
American*, October 24, 1840. See also *ibid.*, November 7, 1840.

[24] U.S.W.P.A., *Inventory of the Church Archives of New York
City. The Protestant Episcopal Church*, 86.

[25] Greenleaf, *A History of the Churches of All Denominations*,
97.

[26] *Ibid., 98.* Crummell continued as rector until the early fifties;
his successor was probably white. Some of New York's most
prominent blacks served as wardens and vestrymen in the church.
These includd: John Peterson, Prince Loveridge, John J. Zuille,
George T. Downing, and William Tyson. See Freeman, "The Free
Negro in New York City," 395.

[27] New York County, *Religious Incorporations*, 2:109. See also
U.S.W.P.A., *Inventory of the Church Archives of New York City. The
Protestant Episcopal Church*, 93.

[28] U.S.W.P.A., *Inventory of the Church Archives of New York
City. The Protestant Episcopal Church*, 93.

transferred 18 years later to the Third Presbytery of New York. On March 3, 1823 it was incorporated as "The Trustees of the First Colored Presbyterian Church of the City of New York."[29] Services were held in Rose Street until 1824, when the congregation removed to Elm Street near Canal and later to Duane and Hudson Streets, where it remained until 1831. From 1831 to 1851 it was located at Franfort and William Streets. In the latter year it moved to Prince and Marion Streets and continued there until 1866.[30] The Reverend Samuel E. Cornish served as pastor of this church from 1822 to 1828. He was succeeded by the Reverend Theodore S. Wright, who ministered until his death in 1847. The following year, the Reverend J.W.C. Pennington assumed charge and served until 1855.

Two important Baptist churches founded by blacks in New York City were the Abyssinian and Zion. Abyssinian was organized on July 5, 1809[31] by a group of blacks who had broken away from the First Baptist Church owing to the segregationist practices of that body. The Reverend Thomas Paul, minister of the African Baptist Church in Boston, served the congregation long enough to help it obtain a building and get organized. After three months, he returned to Boston owing to the pressing demands of his own congregation.[32]

The new-born church, with only 18 members, struggled along for several years without any settled pastor. The congregation at first worshipped on Anthony Street, near West Broadway, in a building which had been erected by the Ebenezer or York Street Church. During this time the preaching was performed by the Reverends

---

[29] *Ibid.,* 49.

[30] The Church itself continued in existence until 1888. See *ibid.,* 49. See also Lewis Evans Jackson, *Walks About New York. Facts and Figures Gathered From Variou Sources* (New York, 1865), 23. (Hereafter cited as *Walks about New York*); Payne, *Recollections of Seventy Years,* 49; *Colored American,* March 25, 1837.

[31] It was incorporated on December 30, 1809. See New York County, *Religious Incorporations,* 1:60-61. The church was re-incorporated on December 28, 1815 in pursuance of an act passed by the State Legislature (April 5, 1813) provoding for the incoporation of religious societies. *Ibid.,* 80.

[32] George, *Segregated Sabbaths,* 145; Quarles, *Black Abolitionists,* 72.

Jonathan Van Velsen and Drake Wilson until 1824, when the Reverend Benjamin Paul became its stated minister.[33]

The Reverend Paul remained with this church for about six years and then resigned. In 1832 the Reverend James Hayborn replaced him and served until his own death three years later. Following the ministries of William Loomis and William Moore, the Reverend Sampson White became pastor in 1841.[34]

Throughout these years Abyssinian suffered many financial difficulties and on one occasion even the building in which the congregation worshipped was sold at auction. But the church continued to progress so that by 1850 it could report a membership of more than 450 persons.[35]

Zion Baptist Church was an off-shoot of the Abyssinian Baptist congregation. Formed in 1832, it began with only sixteen members, mostly female.[36] First settled on Spring Street, between Varick and Hudson Streets, the church later removed to Duane Street.[37] The Reverend J.T. Raymond served as its pastor until the Fall of 1859.[38] Thereafter its pulpit was occupied by various preachers, white and black. By 1840, the membership numbered nearly 200.[39]

Toward the close of 1840 the church completed construction of a new building at No. 488 Pearl Street. A permanent pastor was finally obtained in 1843 when the Reverend Stephen Dutton of Buffalo was installed. Three years later, Zion could boast a membership of 446 persons.[40] In 1844, the Reverend Charles B. Ray founded a black Congregational Church in a Hall on Grand Street. Bethesda, as it was called, was sustained principally by the First and Second Congregational churches. The church prospered modestly, so that by

---

[33]   Greenleaf, *A History of the Churches of All Denominations*, (Second Edition, New York, 1850), 240.

[34]   *Ibid.*, 240-241.

[35]   *Ibid.*, 241. See also Evans, *Walks About New York*, 21; *Colored American*, March 25, 1837.

[36]   *Colored American*, December 5, 1840.

[37]   Greenleaf, *A History of the Churches of All Denominations*, 259. 1846 edition.

[38]   *Colored American*, December 5, 1840.

[39]   Greenleaf, *A History of the Churches of All Denominations*, 259. 1846 edition.

[40]   *Ibid.*, 260; Evans, *Walks About New York*, 21.

February 1845, there were about 25 members. Ray continued to carry out his pastoral charge effectively.[41]

Of all the churches founded by blacks in this period the Baptists and Methodists attracted the greatest number of members. Carol V. George found, for example, that the Baptists "offered the kind of service that black people could respond to, one relatively free from the more obvious social elitism of the other groups, but they recognized their opportunity later than the other denominations, and therefore had to meet the competition of already existing programs."[42]

Unlike the Methodists, who had built a national organization under the direction of intelligent men who made a systematic effort to superintend and coordinate the work of their churches, the Baptists relied on local initiative and direction. While there were both advantages and disadvantages to local self-government, this unusual liberty sometimes proved to be a handicap to the Baptists, in that "the standard of the ministry and the moral tone of the churches were not so high as in the case of the Methodist bodies, whose conferences had power to make local churches do the right when they were not so inclined."[43]

It should be emphasized, however, that in the formative years of both the Baptist and Methodist churches organized by blacks, the educational caliber of the clergy was not particularly high, Daniel Alexander Payne, who served the African Methodist Episcopal Church as Bishop from 1852 to 1896, declared that the first four bishops of the A.M.E. Church did not have even a common-school education.[44] And Mary Lundie Duncan, in a visit to New York City around this time, observed that the black ministers while "pious in their deportment," were not very well educated. Surprisingly, she found that a majority of them were of the Methodist persuasion and noted to her disappointment that the pastors were generally in the habit of

---

[41] *Ibid.*, 367.

[42] George, *Segregated Sabbaths*, 39-40.

[43] Carter G. Woodson, *The Histroy of the Negro Church* (Washington, D.C., 1921), 108.

[44] Daniel Alexander Payne, D.D.L.L.D., *History of the African Methodist Episcopal Church*, 2 vols. (Nashville, TN, 1891), 1:419.

"addressing the passions more than the understanding, suiting better the temperament and degree of knowledge of their flocks."[45]

While some black ministers suffered from a want of proper educational training, quite a few found that their congregations were too small to provide them either a salary for their services or support in their old age. Thus a subscriber wrote to the *Colored American* suggesting that some means be found to provide relief for the extremely poor black clergymen of New York City. He noted that "we have numerous institutions of charity in this city, but I am not aware that there exists throughout our land, one single society among the people of color, whose specific object is t*o provide relief for indigent or aged ministers of the Gospel.*" He therefore asked that a society be formed for this purpose and was convinced that the people would support it "if it only properly be brought before them."[46]

It is a tribute to black religious leaders in New York that they early sought to extend their influence to African-American churches and organizations in other parts of the country in order to bring about a greater degree of race consciousness and solidarity on questions affecting their welfare. As early as 1837, the *Emancipator* carried a Circular Letter from "*The Ministers and Pastors of the several Congregations of colored people in the city of New York—To the Free colored citizens of the United States, and to all their Christian brethren and friends.*" The Appeal began by saying: [47]

There is a pressure of responsibility daily accumulating upon us. Every movement in the moral world is full of interest to

---

[45] Duncan, *America As I Found It*, 257. In some cases, however, this lack of educational attainment did not necessarily serve to disadvantage. In an article entitled, "A Colored Female Preacher" the *National Anti-Slavery Standard* reported that "last Sabbath afternoon, we had the pleasure of listening to a very touching discourse from a colored woman, in the Sixth-street Methodsit (colord) church. She was once a slave, and is a fine specimen of natural oratory. In propriety, energy, and grace of action, she beats any teacher of elocution we ever heard." *National Anti-Slavery Standard*, May 11, 1843.

[46] *Colored American*, September 9, 1837. (Italics in the original.)

[47] *Emancipator*, March 2, 1837.

our people. It develops some great future in the public heart, which inspires the hope of speedy deliverance. The world is literally in motion relative to the civil, intellectual, and moral interests of the man of color.

To this end philanthropy and religion on both sides of the Atlantic, are marshalling their hosts. All the elements of natural and revealed truth are combining for his good. The tide is rising higher and higher, and rolling onward and onward with ever-increasing power. In these grand movements, we have an humble, yet vitally important part to act; and that you, in union with ourselves, may adopt your plans and efforts to the necessities of the case, we have desired to write to you, and to spread out before you the following facts. . . .

The ministers then outlined under several broad headings the conditions of blacks in relation to I) Population; 2) Claims of the Colored People; 3) Prejudice against color; 4) Agencies of Negroes; 5) Education; 6) Temperance; and 7) Appeal to whites. They generally found reason for encouragement in each of these areas. [48]

Among their other activities, the black ministers were also intimately involved in education, the societies, the Abolition Movement, and politics. Samuel E. Cornish served as a traveling agent for the African Free Schools to encourage attendance. Other ministers who also served in this capacity were Benjamin Paul, William Miller, and Peter Williams, Jr.[49] The B. F. Hughes School for Coloured Children, established in 1827, and located originally

---

[48] *Ibid.*, March 2, 1837. The signers of the Circular Letter were as follows: Christopher Rush, Superintendent, Zion Church, Methodist Connexion; Isaac Barney, Pastor, African Union Methodist Church; Timothy Etoe, Pastor, Asbury Methodist Church; Zion connexion; James Simmons, Pastor, Zion Methodsit Church; John T. Raymond, Zion Baptist Church; William A. Cornish, Pastor, Methodist Church, Bethel connexion; Theodore S. Wright, Pastor, First Colored Presbyterian Church; and Samuel E. Cornish. *Ibid.*, March 2, 1837.

[49] *Freedom's Journal*, January 11, 1829. See also the *Rights of All,* June 12, 1829.

under St. Philip's Church, received active support from the Reverends Peter Williams, Jr., James Varick, Samuel E. Cornish, Benjamin Paul, and William Miller.[50]

When the African Dorcas Association was organized to provide clothing for children attending the schools of the Manumission Society, the ministers of the African churches comprised the committee.[51]　During the late 1830's and 1840's, the Reverend Theodore S. Wright had attached to his church a Female Education Society, designed to "aid in qualifying poor indigent young men to become teachers and ministers."[52]　Wright was also an active promoter of the Female Wesleyan Society, a black educational group, founded in 1836, which also rendered valuable aid to the New York Vigilance Committee.[53]

In September 1839, the Phoenix High School for Colored Youth was established in New York City with the objective of giving "colored youth of good talent and morals, a more extended education than they can procure for them, in the public school, or otherwise." The school listed the Reverend Theodore S. Wright as a Trustee, and the Reverend Samuel E. Cornish as a member of its Financial Committee.[54]

The growing abolition movement in New York City did not lack for its share of black clerical participation, which early included office-holding in the anti-slavery societies. Samuel E. Cornish, for example, served for over two decades on the Executive Committee of the American Anti-Slavery Society, founded in 1833. He, along with Theodore S. Wright, also served on the executive board from 1834 to 1837; they were members of the Board of Managers for New York State from 1834 to 1836, along with Christopher Rush, Superintendent of the AMEZ denomination, and Peter Williams, director of St. Philip's, who served in 1834 and 1835. [55]

---

[50] *Freedom's Journal*, April 6, 1827.

[51] *Ibid.*, January 25, 1828.

[52] *Colored American*, October 17, 1840.

[53] *National Anti-Slavery Standard*, April 7, 1842.

[54] *Emancipator*, September 19, 1836.

[55] American Anti-Slavery Society, *Annual Report for 1834*, 35, 61; *Report for 1835*, 24, 26; *Report for 1836*, 25; *Report for 1837*, 28. On one occasion the *Colored American* noted: "The [American] Anti-

The Reverends Theodore S. Wright and John T. Raymond served as vice-presidents of the New York City Young Men's Anti-Slavery Society, founded during the middle 1830's. Charles B. Ray, pastor of the Bethesda Congregational Church, was listed as a secretary of this group, and later served on its executive committee.[56]

A number of black city ministers were prominent in the activities of the American and Foreign Anti-Slavery Society, organized in 1840. During the late 1840's and 1850's the Reverends J.W.C. Pennington, Samuel E. Cornish, Charles B. Ray, and Christopher Rush all served as members of its executive committee. Ray, in addition, held the office of recording secretary, from 1850 to 1852, when Dr. James McCune Smith assumed that position.[57]

Since these black ministers constituted only a minority of the membership and workers in anti-slavery organizations, at no time was their influence controlling; yet they were present to articulate their views, to remonstrate when necessary, and to prove by their intelligence and conduct the high potential for their race's advancement.

As for politics, Negro ministers played active roles, which will be examined in subsequent chapters. They spearheaded the campaign by blacks to regain the suffrage and were vigorous and militant spokesmen on a wide spectrum of political issues confronting the black community.

A persistent problem that would surface prominently throughout this period centered around the practice of caste by the American church and clergy. The reader will recall that nearly every independent black church founded in the last third of the eighteenth century and the first quarter of the nineteenth grew directly out of this

---

Slavery society has from the beginning, placed colored men on its executive committee. And at the two last anniversaries, colored men were invited and took a prominent part in the exercises." *Colored American*, repritned in the Emancipator, June 28, 1838.

[56] *Emancipator*, March 14, 1839; February 6, 1840.

[57] American and Foreign Anti-Slavery Society, *Annual Report for 1847*, 32; *Report for 1848*, 4; *Report for 1849*, 5; *Report for 1850*, 153; *Report for 1851*, 113; *Report for 1852*, 25; *Report for 1853*, 191. See also *Colored American*, May 30, 1840.

issue. These independent bodies no longer had to contend with the immediate difficulties which the question raised. But those black churches that remained within the larger white denominations found this prejudice increasingly objectionable and sought in various ways to bring the matter to a head.

Particularly was this true of the Presbyterian and Protestant Episcopal churches, although some white interdenominational bodies were also included.

Lewis Tappan, the famous merchant, philanthropist and abolitionist, was, for example, instrumental in the founding of a Free Church (interdenominational) at No. 165 Chapel Street. He had earlier been responsible for abolishing the "nigger heaven" in the upper galleries, where the black members were seated.[58] Later he used his influence to get Thomas Van Rensselaer, the distinguished African-American appointed as a Trustee of this church. This latter step drew repeated criticism from Charles Grandison Finney, the noted western evangelist and abolitionist. Finney, who was also a member of this church and a good friend of Tappan, thought the move totally unwise. He further insisted that Tappan give up this religious enterprise altogether.[59]

Tappan was saddened by this rebuff from Finney, but he nevertheless remained firm: "As Christians—and Christian abolitionists will not tolerate my associating with my colored brethren in a white man's church it seems my duty to unite with a colored church. But will it not invite insult to my colored brethren."[60]

Tappan seemed to have taken the thought of affiliating with a black church seriously, for in a conversation with the Reverend Simeon S. Jocelyn, the zealous white abolitionist and pastor of a black congregation in New Haven, he told that minister of his intention of joining the Negro church led by the Reverend Theodore S. Wright. Jocelyn advised him against the move, however, because that church (Shiloh, Presbyterian) was endeavoring to pay by subscription the

---

[58] Bertram Wyatt-Brown, *Lewis Tappan and the Evangelical War Against Slavery* (Cleveland, Ohio, 1969), 177. See also *Emancipator*, September 1, 1836.

[59] Lewis Tappan, MSS Diary entry for February 25, 1836. Box 14, Lewis Tappan Papers, Library of Congress.

[60] Lewis Tappan, MSS Diary entry for February 26, 1836. Box 14, Lewis Tappan Papers, Library of Congress.

heavy debt due on its edifice and Jocelyn feared that if Tappan joined some persons not friendly to him might refuse to contribute.[61]

The Reverend Samuel E. Cornish, a Presbyterian and at one time pastor of the Shiloh Church in that city, had some bitter personal experiences with the effect of the spirit of caste on young and tender minds. While editor of the *Colored American* he had occasion to recount a poignant incident which involved two of his own sons:

A few weeks since, it being too cold to send our little son, two miles to church, we said to him go to the Rev. Dr.___ church; he did so, and was handed a pew near the altar and was comfortably seated; he is fair and his hair rather straight.

A sabbath or two afterwards, he concluded to take his brother with him, to hear the same Rev. Dr.____ ; very well my son, but take a back seat, be as modest as you can, he did so, and took his brother, whose color and hair betray his origin with him—and one Christian after another, who through mistake got into the same pew—fled from *them*, as though the leprosy was upon *them*. My little sons discovered the prejudice and were grieved to the heart—and one of them said, "Mother, why do the white people hate us so?"[62]

Even though a member of the Presbytery of New York, Cornish never attended the general assembly of that body, its highest court, although the rule was that every member in turn was to be a delegate. "Like the Declaration of Independence." he cried, "the good brethren did not mean EVERY BROTHER, A COLORED BROTHER. NOT AT ALL—NOT AT ALL!!!"[63]   Later, in an even more stinging indictment of his fellow Presbyterians, he declared:

For ten or fifteen years, with our good brother Wright, [Theodore S.], whose life demonstrates the religion of the

---

[61]   Jocelyn was saying in effect that some blacks, forever suspicious, would not look too friendly on a white man joining their congregation. Lewis Tappan, MSS Diary entry for March 3, 1836. Box 14, Lewis Tappan Papers, Library of Congress

[62] *Colored American*, March 18, 1837. (Italics in the original.)

[63] *Ibid.*, June 17, 1837.

cross to be the light of the world, we have been passed by, and neglected by the brethren. Never exchanged pulpits with, never appointed to any ecclesiastical delegation, nor to fill any vacancy. No, nor never invited to a pulpit neither in the city nor out of the city; so far as the country is connected with our Presbytery.

The brethren, when they take a journey either for health or business, will sooner close their Churches, when they know we are disengaged, than to admit a colored brother to their pulpits. And they have so taught their people, that if a colored minister happens to be present whatever his piety and talents, when their pulpit is unoccupied, they will rather dismiss without preaching and go to their homes, than to invite him to officiate or receive the word of life from his lips.[64]

The practices of the Protestant Episcopal Church also provoked controversy. In June 1839, for example, the Board of Trustees of the General Theological Seminary, composed of the Bishops and clerical lay delegates from the different states and territories, met in New York City. Shortly after the proceedings got under way, the Board was presented a petition by a candidate for Holy Orders in the diocese of New York.   The candidate—the Reverend Alexander Crummell desired to be admitted to the seminary as a student. [65]

The petition was referred to a committee, consisting of the Right Reverend Bishop Benjamin Tredwell Onderdonk, Reverend Doctors James Milnor and Hugh Smith, and Esquires William Johnson, David B, Ogden, and Edward Newton. After considerable deliberation, the committee recommended rejection.[66] Before this decision had been

---

[64] *Emancipator*, November 2, 1837. See also *Colored American*, April 1, 1837.

[65] John Jay, *Caste and Slavery in the American Church* (New York, 1843), 6.

[66] *Ibid.*, 6. See also *National Anti-Slavery Standard*, April 13, and 20, 1843.

reached, however, Bishop Onderdonk sent for Crummell and asked him to withdraw his petition, a request which was refused.[67]

The motion to adopt the resolution of rejection was carried with the Right Reverend Bishop William Croswell Doane entering a protest. Significantly, no reasons were given for the decision to reject, nor was there any intimation in the minutes concerning the disqualifications of the candidate.[68] This was despite the fact that the Protestant Episcopal Church had constitutional provisions clearly guaranteeing to every candidate eligible for Holy Orders the right to enter the Seminary.[69]

In view of this constitutional requirement, Crummell found the decision of the committee inexplicable. Subsequently, in a letter published in the *Colored American*, he declared:

> What gave me still more encouragement to adopt this course (petitioning the Trustees) is the fact, that the great good man, the late worthy and lamented Bishop Hobart, the founder of the Seminary, when spoken with reference to admission of *coloured candidates into the Institution, paused,* and *replied, that they would be admitted , as a matter of course, and without doubt.*

> I had spent three years of perfect equality with upwards of one hundred white students, of a different denomination, at Oneida Institute, and could not, after long consideration,

---

[67] U.S.W.P.A., *Calendar of the Geritt Smith Papers*, 1:117. In a letter to Gerrit Smith, dated July 31, 1839, Dr. James McCune Smith concluded that nothing remained for Crummell now but to go to the British West Indies or Canada to further his training. He called upon the philanthropist to help in providing financial support for this project. *Ibid.*, 1: 117.

[68] Jay, *Caste and Slavery in the American Church*, 7.

[69] Said section I, Chapter VII of the Statutes of the General Theological Seminary: "EVERY PERSON producing to the Faculty satisfactory evidence of his having been admitted a candidate for Holy Orders, with full qualifications, according to the canons of the Protestant Episcopal Chruch in the United States, SHALL BE RECEIVED AS A STUDENT OF THE SEMINARY." Quoted in *ibid.*, 7.

discover any reasons why it should be with those of my own communion— with CHURCHMEN.[70]

Bishop Onderdonk later came out with the surprising revelation that two Presbyters had offered to instruct Crummell if he consented to such an arrangement. It was also revealed that similar arrangements were found to be satisfactory for another black candidate, the Reverend Isaiah G. DeGrasse, a deacon in the Church. Unwilling to disturb the peace of the church, DeGrasse withdrew as a candidate for the Seminary, and was subsequently instructed by two Presbyterian ministers.   Later he was ordained and became a full-fledged clergyman.[71]

Perhaps one of the most heated, divisive and prolonged disputes involving the issue of caste in the church began in 1846. In October of that year, St. Philip's and the Church of the Messiah made application to be formally received into the Protestant Episcopal Convention of the Diocese of New York, the general ruling body of that denomination. Their admission would have had the effect of putting them on an equality with all the other Episcopal churches in the city.   The delegates to the annual convention voted immediately to refer the request to the Committee on the incorporation of the Churches which

---

[70]   *Colored American*, December 27, 1839.   (Italics in the original.)   John Jay, the distinguished jurist, noted that in barring Crummell, the high church officials, "establish a principle which would justify us in regarding the colored man as an inferior being, intended to occupy a lower sphere in the scale of creation; which designate him as one whose constitutional privileges we may innocently annul, whom we may, without a pang of guilt or a blush of shame, insult, injure, and oppress, even though he be one arrayed by episcopal hands in the robes of the priesthood, who walks forth a messenger of the Most High." Quoted in Jay, *Caste and Slavery in the American Church*, 8-9.

[71] Jay, *Caste and Slavery in the American Church*, 14. DeGrasse later condemned Bishop Onderonk for sanctioning caste in the church. He exploded the Bishop's arguement that Providence would open the way for the proscribed blacks, pointing out that men, being the instruments of Providence, were the only ones capable of carrying out its designs. *Ibid.*, 16.

was directed to rule on the issue at the present sitting of the Convention. [72]

By a majority of three, this committee rejected the request of the two churches. In unequivocal language its report began by saying:

We deeply sympathize with the colored race in our country [and] we feel acutely their wrongs,—and not the least among them, their social degradation. But this cannot prevent our seeing the fact, that they are socially degraded, and are not regarded as proper associates for the class of persons who attend our convention. We object not to the color of their skin, but we question their possession of those qualities which would render their intercourse with the members of a Church Convention useful, or agreeable, even to themselves. We should make the same objections to persons of the same social class, however pure may be their blood, or however transparent their skin. [73]

The minority report, issued by Evan M. Johnson and John A. King, differed sharply from that of the majority. It rebuked the majority for basing its decision on the fact that the members of St. Philip's at the time of the ministry of the Reverend Peter Williams, Jr. disavowed any intention of joining the Convention of the Diocese. It correctly pointed out that this self-denying pledge by the congregation of that day was no longer binding on the present members who did not "think as their fathers did on the subject." In a penetrating rebuttal, it summed up these views by observing:

Suppose churches, now to be composed of colored people exclusively, are organized in our principal cities—suppose

----

[72] *Journal of the Proceedings of the Sixty-Second Convention of the Protestant Episcopal Church in the Diocese of New York, Held in St. John's Chapel, in the City of New York, Wednesday, Sept. 30 to Saturday, Oct. 3, inclusive, A.D. 1846* (New York, 1846), 25-56.

[73] *Ibid.*, 73. As if to justify the foregoing statement, the Report added parenthetically that "the colored people have themselves shown their convictions of this truth, by separateing themselves from the whites, and forming distinct congregations where they are not continually humbled by being treated as inferiors." *Ibid.*, 73.

they are refused equal Christian privileges with other
Episcopal Churches—that the Convention of our Diocese
refuse to take them under their charge, and into their
fellowship—will not these churches unite and form a
Convention of their own? And *under such circumstances,*
would they find difficulty in obtaining apostolic succession?
We fear the refusal of our Convention to admit into their
fellowship this portion of their Christian brethren, will
inevitably lead to a schism in the Church, by the
establishment of another Episcopal Church in the United
States.[74]

Four years later the issue came up again at the regular meeting of
the Convention of the Diocese. On this occasion John Jay was
spokesman for the two black congregations, and he made vigorous
representations to have them admitted but was repeatedly overruled by
the chairman, who indicated that new application would have to be
made. The chairman insisted that the Convention was unable to
determine whether the churches in question desired admission, since
four years had elapsed and there had been no renewal of their
applications.[75] The story was the same for 1851.[76]

Jay nevertheless persisted. At the 1852 Convention, he was again
present, seeking admission of the excluded black churches. At this
meeting, he introduced an amendment to Canon IV of the Church
Laws entitled: "Of the Admission of a Church into Union with the
Church of this Diocese." It read as follows:

Sect. III—No church, applying for admission which shall
have been found duly incorporated as above provided, shall be
refused admission into Union with the Convention of this
Diocese, on account of race, lineage, colour or complexion, of
the congregation so applying, or any part thereof, or of the
minister presiding over the same, nor on account of any social
or political disqualifications of any kind whatsoever, that may
attach or may be supposed to attach to them without the
church; and all churches admitted into union with the said

---

74 *Ibid.*, 78-79. (Italics in the original.)
75 *National Anti-Slavery Standard*, October 3, 1850.
76 *Ibid.*, Ocotober 2, 1851.

Convention, shall be admitted-without any condition or disqualification establishing or recognizing caste in the church—upon a footing of catholic Equality and Christian Brotherhood.[77]

Jay's work finally paid off. In 1853, after a battle that lasted seven years he succeeded in gaining the admission into the Convention of St. Philip's and the Church of the Messiah.[78]

The struggle against caste in the church, particularly by those black congregations which found themselves in fellowship or union with the larger white denominations, did bespeak a concern by these churchmen for the unity and harmony of the Christian community, and racial distinctions were totally anathema to this ideal.

Yet it should be remembered that since most of the black churches had their own separate, independent denominations, this issue was no longer one of overriding importance. It was in these separate groups that blacks found greater chance for freedom and expression without the unfriendly and stifling restrictions of the white bodies. Moreover as a student of this period has pointed out, "if colored men did not supply these pulpits and manage their religious affairs, the Negro population would not be attracted to, or retained within a religious community." She further observed that "without these separate churches it is most unlikely that Negro ministers would have had a pulpit at all."[79]

Unfortunately, the success and independence which some blacks achieved in the religious sphere did not follow them as readily in their political endeavors. In this arena they found themselves thwarted and frustrated time and again. Particularly was this true in the long, arduous and heroic struggle of these people to obtain the suffrage. But, as we shall see, blacks did not succumb to these difficulties. Rather, they redoubled their efforts and mounted a campaign unprecedented in

---

[77] *Ibid.*, Ocotober 14, 1852.

[78] *Ibid.*, Ocotober 8, 1853.

[79] Freeman, "The Free Negro in New York City," 380.

New York's history to achieve that instrument without which no free people could ever feel secure.

Agitation for the Suffrage

Of all the ironies and contradictions of the American democratic experience, one of the most glaring has comprised the open, systematic, and successful attempts at legal disfranchisement, based solely on the fact of race. In New York City. For example, access by free blacks to the suffrage had been severely circumscribed by the period of General Emancipation. In order to understand how blacks were virtually eliminated as a political force in the city and, by extension, in the state itself, one must first consider their suffrage status prior to 1821, the year in which constitutional restrictions were placed upon their exercise of the franchise.

During the colonial period many free blacks in New England, the Mid-Atlantic states, and even in the South exercised the suffrage. The practice continued to some extent even after the American Revolution.[1] Gradually, however, as the African-American population increased, some of the states revised their constitutions to include provisions specifically barring blacks from the suffrage. This movement grew largely out of the involved argument, extending back to the federal Constitutional Convention, as to whether free blacks, so called, were in that sense citizens of the states in which they resided. Even though the Constitution of 1787 explicitly provided that citizens of one state should enjoy "all the privileges and immunities of citizens of the several states," and, while some individuals, particularly in the Northern states, believed that definition to include free blacks as well, this view was not generally accepted.[2] It was this failure to define more fully the constitutional and legal status of free blacks that provided the opportunity far many states to apply their own criteria. As

---

[1]   Charles L. Wesley, "Negro Suffrage in the Period of Constitution-Making, 1787-1865," *Journal of Negro History*, 32, No. 2 (April, 1947): 143.

[2] *Ibid.*, 146.

Charles Wesley correctly observed, the "free Negro was known as 'free,' but in none of these states was he as free as the white man.[3]

The New York State Constitution of 1777 included no racial exclusionary provision. As soon as any slave was freed he became a voter, on the same terms as a white man, namely: if he paid taxes to the state, owned a freehold of the value of 20 pounds, or rented a tenement of the annual fee of 40 shillings."[4]

One student of this period has maintained that even this mild qualification operated to exclude many free blacks although he conceded that it did not keep some whites and even blacks from voting illegally under it.[5] When, however, in 1799, New York State decreed gradual Emancipation for its slaves, freeing males at the age of 28 and females at 25, "the free Negro voters increased in number and activity."[6]

As more blacks obtained the suffrage, they soon aligned themselves with the Federalist Party, led, in good part, by wealthy landowners and merchants. This party, as opposed to the Democratic-Republicans, was more liberal in its attitudes toward the African-American population both in New York City and upstate. It was the same party, moreover, which had been in control of the legislature at the time Gradual Emancipation was enacted.[7] This alliance did not bode well for the future prospects of blacks.

By 1813, for example, it was said that the votes of 300 free blacks in New York City decided the election in favor of the Federalists and determined the character of the state legislature.[8] When the Federalist majority was overturned at the next election, immediate steps were taken to check the political influence of the African-American in New

---

[3] *Ibid.*, 148.

[4] Dixon Ryan Fox, "The Negro Vote in Old New York," *Political Science Quarterly*, 32, No. 2 (June 1917): 255. The New York pound was the equivalent of $2.50. *Ibid.*, 255.

[5] Emil Olbrich, "The Development of Sentiment on Negro Suffrage to 1860," *Bulletin of the University of Wisconsin*, 3, No. 477 (1912): 30.

[6] Wesley, Negro Suffrage in the Period of Constiutution-Making," 155.

[7] *Ibid.*, 155.

[8] Olbrich, "The Development of Sentiment on Negro Suffrage," 30.

York City.[9] Thus, in 1814, a law was enacted providing for the recording of certificates of freedom. This law, applicable only to New York City, required that these certificates be recorded in the office of the Registrar. A copy of the same had to be produced by every free black man at elections before he could vote. The obvious intent was to put difficulties in the way of the African-American elector.[10]

The effort to limit the black vote reached its culmination in 1821 with the convoking of a state constitutional convention. One of the avowed aims of the convention was to extend the suffrage to new classes by completely sweeping away those undemocratic property qualifications which were a carryover from the English practice of colonial days.[11] Ironically, many of the delegates who sought to broaden the suffrage to benefit poor whites, at the same time were seeking to eliminate it altogether for blacks.[12]

One of the oft-repeated arguments advanced at the convention was based on the belief in. black inferiority. Since blacks supposedly lacked sufficient intelligence, they could not be relied upon to vote wisely on important issues.[13] Another fear expressed arose from the conviction that since some blacks had been born in slavery and had imbibed the spirit of dependence, they would consequently vote according to the wishes of their employers. This would enable rich men to control their votes and would therefore foster an aristocracy.[14]

---

[9] Fox, "The Negro Vote in Old New York," 257.

[10] Olbrich, "The Development of Sentiment on Negro Suffrage," 30. In the spring election of 1821, for example, only 163 blacks actually voted, although many more tried to vote. It was estamated that if all property qualifications were abolished, at least 2500 blacks would have qualified for the suffrage. *Ibid.*, 30.

[11] Fox, "The Negro Vote in Old New York," 258. For a first-rate study on the democratization of the ballot, with particular respect to New York, see Chilton Willliamson, *American Suffrage from Property to Democracy, 1760-1860* (Princeton, 1960), 201-206.

[12] Fox, "The Negro Vote in Old New York," 258.

[13] Olbrich, "The Development of Sentiment on Negro Suffrage," 31.

[14] *Ibid.*, 31.

General Erastus Root, a delegate from Delaware County and, later, lieutenant-governor of New York[15] cautioned the convention about the potential impact of the black vote on the political Power balance in the state:

> At present the number of blacks who are voters is so small, that if they were scattered all over the state, there would not be much danger to be apprehended, but if we may judge of the future by the past, I should suppose that there was some cause for alarm, when a few hundred Negroes of the city of New York, following the train of those who ride in their coaches, and whose shoes and boots they had so often blacked shall go to the polls of the election and change the political condition of the whole state. A change in the representation of that city may cause a change in your assembly, by giving a majority to a particular party, which would vary your council of appointment, who make the highest officers of your government. Thus would the whole state be controlled by a few hundred of this species of population in the city of New York.[16]

This argument was ably dismissed by Peter Augustus Jay, Federalist, and son of John Jay. In a masterly rebuttal he noted that blacks in New York State constituted less than one-fortieth of the total population. He further maintained that in New York City alone, not more than one-tenth of the inhabitants were black, and of this tenth only a few were entitled to vote.[17]

He asked. "Why are they, who were born as free as ourselves, natives of the same country and deriving from nature the same rights

---

[15]   Allen Johnson and Dumas Malone eds., *Dictionary of American Biography*, 20 vols. (New York, 1937), 16:145.

[16]   Quoted in Fox, "The Negro Vote in Old New York," 260.

[17]   Charles Z. Lincoln, *The Constitutional History of New York from the Beginnings of the Colonial Period the 1905, Showing the Origin, Development, and Judicial Construction of the Constiution*, 5 vols. (Rochester, NY, 1906), 1:661. (Hereafter cited as Lincoln, *Constitutional Hitory of New York*.)

and privileges which we have, now to be deprived of all these rights and doomed to remain forever aliens among us?"[18]

The attempt to restrict the vote to whites was defeated.[19] But October 8 1821 as finally adopted on Article ii, Section I of the new constitution required blacks to possess a freehold estate of $250 "over and above all debts and incumbrances charged thereon" in order to exercise the suffrage. They were also required to have lived in the state for three years and to have paid taxes. Whites could qualify for the suffrage after one year's residence and the payment of taxes or the rendering of highway or military services.[20]

It should be emphasized that under the provisions of the new constitution blacks were not required to serve in the militia. In addition to this, if a black man did not possess a $250 freehold estate, he was automatically exempted except to the from the payment of taxes.[21]

The effect of this $250 requirement was to summarily exclude most blacks from voting. Concomitantly, blacks generally were excluded from the basis of representation; only those who paid taxes were included. Free blacks, however, were included in the basis of national representation.[22]

---

[18] Quoted in Wesley, "Negro Suffrage in the Period of Constitution Making," 159.

[19] Olbrich, "The Development fo Sentiment on Negro Suffrage," 35.

[20] Lincoln, *The Constitutional History of New York*, 1:198-199. In 1826, the property qualification, except as to black voters, was abolished by an amendment to the constitution. Ibid., 1:199.

[21] *Constitution of the State of New York, Adopted in Convention, November 10th, 1821* (Hudson, NY, 1822), 8. See also William Yates, *Rights of Colored Men to Suffrage , Citizinship and Trial by Jury: Being a Book of Facts, Arguments and Authorities, Historical Notices and Sketches of Debates—With Notes* (Philadelphia, 1838), vii. (Hereafter cited as Yates, *Rights of Colored Men to Suffrage*.)

[22] Yates, Rights of Colored Men to Suffrage, vii. In a speech at the New York Convention, Dr. robert Clarke, a delegate from the County of Deleware remarked: "Free people of colore are included in the number that regulates your representation in Congress, and I wish to know how freemen can be represented *when they are deprived of*

A French traveler found these distinctions somewhat disturbing. He began by observing:

> It is singular that, where no political privileges are connected with property, an exception should be made in favor of those with whom vice, not virtue, is supposed to be hereditary; and that the parchment on which the pedigree is written is the skin of the claimant. Equality of civil rights is granted where equality of social rights is denied; and the same man who is admitted to the ballot box, is thrust out of the dining hall.

He concluded:

> Let the "African" carry off the palladium of the constitution; but he must not disturb the digestion of its friends. Plutus must be highly esteemed, where his rod can change even a negro into a man. If 250 dollars will perform this miracle what would it require to elevate a monkey to this enviable distinction?[23]

In the thirty-year period from 1825 to 1855, the number of free blacks in New York City who were eligible to vote remained small. In 1825 for example, of the 12,559 blacks in the city, only 68 were qualified to vote. In 1835, with an estimated Negro population of 15,061, a mere 84 could exercise this right. Ten years later, with a black population of 12,913, some 255 met the requirements. In 1855, of the 11,840 blacks in New York, only 100 could cast their ballots.[24]

In the face of these appalling figures, blacks in the city undertook a program of organized agitation to regain their full and complete suffrage rights. Through meetings conventions, and petitions, they sought to rouse the conscience of the state to action. The 1830's and 1840's would witness their most intense activity in this matter.

One of the first major drives to obtain the suffrage began in 1837. In March of that year blacks met at Phoenix Hall, under Broadway

---

the privilege of voting for representation." *Ibid.*, 13. (Italics in the original.)

[23] Abdy, *Journal of a Residence and Tour*, 2:8.

[24] Franklin B. Hough, *Statistics of Population of the City and County of Nw York* . . . (New York, 1866), 240.

Tabernacle.   A series of resolutions was drawn up praying the Legislature at Albany to receive the petitions of African-Americans from New York and Brooklyn relating to three important issues.   One of these requested an alteration in the constitution of the state to extend "the right of voting to all male citizens of the State, on the same terms, *without distinctions of color.*"[25]

Several months later, on August 19, 1837, the *Colored American* announced that its proprietor, Philip Bell, planned an extensive tour through the River Counties of the state to arouse blacks living there to the necessity of acquiring their political rights.[26]   Furthermore, the "colored young men'" of New York City were urged to use this opportunity to open through Bell a correspondence with the "colored young men" throughout the Northern and Western parts of the state by "deluging the Legislature with PETITIONS," praying that body "to grant to the colored citizens, in common with other citizens of the State, that RIGHT which by the revised constitution of 1821, was taken away from a large portion of the colored inhabitants of the state: a right which they had enjoyed uninterrupted for forty years."   The paper also indicated that a meeting would be held by blacks on August to rally support behind the plan.[27]

This meeting was convened as scheduled at Philomathean Hall with Timothy Seaman, a well-known New York Negro, serving as president, Edward V. Clarke, Henry Highland Garnet, and Charles L. Reason were appointed vice-presidents, and John J. Zuille and George T. Downing, secretaries.   Thomas S. Sydney, a militant black suffrage advocate, then proposed the following motion:

---

[25] *Colored American*, March 11, 1837.   The petitions in question contained the names of 620 men.   The document was 20 feet long. *Ibid.*, March 11, 1837.   See also *Weekly Advocate*, February 25, 1837.

[26] Bell was actualy authorized to make this canvass by a group of blacks consisting of Thomas Downing, Reverend Samuel E. Cornish and Henry Sipkins.   See *Colored American*, August 12, 1837.

[27]   Among the sponsors of the proposed meeting were the following blacks: Edward V. Clarke, John J. Zuille, Henbry Highland Garnet, Thomas S. Sydney, Charles L. Reason and George T. Downing.   *Colored American*, August 19, 1837; *Emancipator,* September 7, 1837.

Resolved, That whereas, the annals of the past and the
developments of the present clearly demonstrate that to
achieve any reform in governmental policy, or effect any
desirable change in public opinion—systematic, organized
effort is absolutely necessary for success; and as history is
replete with evidence which facts and events, continually
transpiring, abundantly corroborate, that in organized efforts
for effecting great moral reformations, or achieving important
political revolutions, young men are important and efficient
agents.

Charles L. Reason then offered a resolution requesting Standing
Corresponding Committee of Ten be appointed "with power to
increase to 15, who shall draw up and circulate the petitions among
the colored young men, for signatures."[28]   To facilitate this plan, a
smaller Committee of Three was authorized for each ward to circulate
petitions. Before the meeting adjourned it was also urged that the
young men of New York City cooperate with their counterparts in
Brooklyn, Jamaica and on Long Island to carry out this scheme.[29]
The suffrage petitions were scheduled for presentation to the
Legislature at its opening session in January 1838. By December 1837
most of the work involved in securing signatures was nearly
completed. Each ward was reported to have organized a committee,
except for Wards 10 and 17.[30]   The lack of a committee in the Tenth
Ward was later remedied when four blacks, Edmund Crosby, Samuel
Hardenburg, Jacob Frances, and William P. Johnson were appointed to
fill this deficiency.[31]

---

[28] *Ibid.*, September 2, 1837. See also *Emancipator,* September 7,
1837.   The following blacks were appointed to the Corresponding
Committee of Ten: Henry Highland Garnet, William J. Wilson, P.P.
Simmons, Thomas S. Sydney, George Kisson, Timothy Seaman,
Thomas Harris, John J. Zuille, Charles L. Reason and Peter Guignon.
Colored American, September 2, 1837.

[29] *Ibid.*, September 2, 1837. See also *ibid.*, September 16, and
18, 1837; November 18, and 25, 1837.

[30] *Ibid.*, December 30, 1837.

[31] *Ibid.*, January 13, 1838. This action was taken on December
26. 1837.

The first petition in the series was printed in full in the *Colored American*. It began by calling attention to the fact that:

> By the former constitution of the state, all citizens, whatever might be their complexion, and from whatever ancestors descended, were placed upon the same footing. Its patriotic framers did not think it consistent with the principles they professed, to divide freemen into castes, and to confer privileges on one caste, which were refused to the other.

It therefore asked for:

> The abolition of an odious distinction, which, while it acknowledges them as citizens, denies them the right which all others possess as attached to that honorable appellation.[32]

Since the Legislature proved unresponsive, blacks decided that if one petition failed, another would be presented. This drafting of petition after petition was the avowed object of the New York Association for the Political improvement of the People of Color.[33] At organizing meeting held in Philomathean Hall on June 1838, Charles L. Reason introduced a resolution urging that similar associations be formed throughout the state and requesting his brethren to "send delegates to a General Political Convention of the Colored People, to be held at Albany, at such time as shall be appointed by the Executive Committee."[34]

The many-sided activities of blacks to secure the suffrage elicited varying degrees of support from influential whites who in some cases

---

[32] *Ibid.*, December 16, 1837, See also *ibid.*, December 9, 1837.

[33] Article II of its Constitution stated: "The Association will aim to acquire for the colored citizens of the state, equal political rights and privileges, as enjoyed and exercised by other citizens.—By Laboring through the means of memorial and petition to effect the repeal of so much of the State Constitution as disfranchises them, and by striving through the agency and influence of the press, in the presentation of truth, argument and appeal, to enlighten the 'public sentiment' which sanctions and tolerates such disfranchisement." *Ibid.*, June 16, 1838.

[34] *Ibid.*, June 16, 1838. See also *ibid.*, December 8, 1838.

claimed to be the "friends" of the African-American, William H. Seward, for example, who later became Governor of New York, was asked by William Jay,[35] and Gerrit Smith in October 1838 whether he was in favor of abolishing all distinctions based solely on race, in the constitutional rights of the citizens of that state. In his reply, Seward noted; that the property qualification was passed mainly as a yardstick to measure those *competent* to exercise the responsibilities of self-government. He believed that "nations and races may become debased by ignorance so as to became destitute of those responsibilities." He qualified this statement by emphasizing that he was opposed to any suffrage restriction "rounded solely on complexion," but favorable to attempts to discriminate between those blacks who possessed the requisite intelligence and capacity to discharge the responsibilities of free men, and those who did not.[36] The obvious weakness in this argument was the failure of Seward to apply equally the same test of *intelligence* to whites, as he did to blacks. This in itself mirrored the racial distinction which he professed to condemn.

The equivocal attitudes on the part of some key whites goaded many in the black community to step up their suffrage efforts. In July 1839, the *Colored American* exhorted: "We must revolutionize the State. The subject must be brought before the people: they must be made to understand it; they must be shown the justice of it, and the necessity ere New York can be called in fact that she professes to be—a Free State."[37]

On April 27, 1840, a convention of blacks assembled in Jamaica, Queens County. A declaration outlining sentiments opened with the statement: "We, the colored citizens of the State of New York being disfranchised, conceive it to be our solemn duty to exert ourselves by the use of all legitimate means, to obtain redress." The group pledged to meet in convention from year to year to agitate the question of their

---

[35] William Jay (1789-1858), the noted judge, author and moral reformer, was the son of John Jay, Chief Justice of the United States, and brother of Peter Augustus Jay. John Jay (1817-1894), mentioned earlier in this study, was his only surviving son.

[36] George F. Baker ed., *The Works of William H. Seward* 3 vols. (New York, 1853), 3:427-428.

[37] *Colored American*, July 27, 1839. See also *ibid.*, August 17, 1839; October 12, and 19, 1839.

political disability. The first state convention was scheduled to convene at Troy in September of that year.[38]

The proposed Troy convention actually assembled that same year in; Albany, New York, on the 18th, 19th and 20th of August.[39] It represented by far the most concert effort on the part of blacks up to that time to regain the suffrage. The convention was reported to have attracted a large audience, with sessions ranging from 40 to 140 delegates and supporters.[40] Austin Steward of Rochester, was elected chairman, while Charles L. Reason of New York, Henry Highland Garnet of Troy, and William Topp of Albany; served as secretaries.

On the third day the delegates passed a series of resolutions outlining the strategy the convention urged blacks to take with reference to the franchise. Continued reliance upon petitioning was a major element in this program. One resolution urged that a committee of seven be set up, consisting of four members from Albany and three from Troy, whose duty "it shall be to correspond with other committees throughout the State, appointed for the same purpose." Another, issued by the Business Committee, requested the establishment of a committee of five from each county in the state "except New York," which would be allowed ten members. These committees were to be known officially as "County Committees." The last resolution provided that the County Committees forward their petitions to the Central Committee, which body was to then forward them to the appropriate legislative committee at the Capitol in Albany.[41]

After adopting these resolutions, an "Address of the New York State Convention of Colored Citizens, to the People of the State," was drawn up and adopted. Its language was eloquent:

---

[38] *Ibid.*, May 9, 1840.

[39] The Call, signed by about 100 people, was drafted by a committee consisting of Charles B. Ray, John J. Zuille, Theodore S. Wright, Charles L. Reason and Timothy Seaman, appointed at a New York meeting on May 29, 1840. *Ibid.*, June 6, 1840. See also *ibid.*, July 25, and August 15, 1840; *National Anti-Slavery Standard*, June 18, 1840.

[40] *Colored American*, August 22, and 29, 1840.

[41] *Ibid.*, January 9, 1841.

. . . We base our claim upon the possession of those common. on and yet exalted faculties of manhood. . . .WE ARE MEN. 1. Those sympathies which find their natural channel, and legitimate and healthy exercise in civil and political relations, have the same being and nature in us that they have in the rest of the human family. 2. Those yearnings and longings for the exercise of political prerogatives, that are the product of the adaptedness of man's social nature to political arrangements, strive with irrepressible potency within us, from the fact of our disfranchised condition, a prevalent and unreasonable state of caste, and the operation of laws and statutes not proceeding from, yet operating upon us. 3. Those indignities and wrongs which naturally become the portion of a disfranchised class, and gather accumulated potency from an increase and intenseness of proscription, naturally and legitimately revert to us. . . .[42]

Immediately after the adjournment of the Albany Convention plans were set in motion to implement its recommendations, particularly with respect to the petition effort. The New York City County Committee was pressed, for example, "to make early and energetic efforts in behalf of the great cause" for which it was appointed.[43] Since the Legislature was scheduled to convene on January 2, 1841, it was imperative that blacks move swiftly. The *Colored American* urged a broad campaign and insisted that "the time has now fully come, brethren, when we should all sign and be actively engaged in circulating petitions, and we have not a week to lose."[44] Later in more emphatic language the editor implored: "*Brethren, one and all, sign the petition.* And you who cannot write your name, get

---

[42] *Ibid.,* December 19, 1840. See also *ibid.,* November 21, and 28, 1840; *Minutes of the State Convention of Colored Citizens: Held at Albany, on the 18th, 19th, and 20th fo August, 1840, for the Purpose of Considering Their Political Condition* (New York, 1840), *passim.*

[43] *Ibid.,* September 5, 1840.

[44] *Ibid.,* November 28, 1840.

some one to do it for you. Secure also the names of your friends, your white friends. SIGN THE PETITION."[45]

The form of each petition was as follows:

To the Honorable the Legislature of the State of New York:
We, the undersigned, colored citizens of the town of_____
County of_____ and state of New York do most respectfully
pray your honorable body to take measures for so amending
the Constitution of the State, that the Elective Franchise may
be extended to us on the same terms as enjoyed by other
citizens. [46]

When the petitions were formally presented to the Legislature it was said that 1700 names came from New York City alone.[47] The signatures impressed at least some of the legislators and, although they failed to take immediate action on the petitions, they did promise Henry Highland Garnet, who later became pastor of the Shiloh Presbyterian Church, an early hearing on the issue.[48]

In March 1841, Garnet appeared before the Judiciary Committee of the State Assembly to testify. Shortly afterwards, the committee reported a resolution introduced by William Duer of Oswego County, providing for an amendment to the state constitution. This amendment would have given the suffrage to all male persons, regardless of color, who could read and write the English language and who were resident in the state for at least six months prior to an election. Garnet, who supported the resolution enthusiastically, found reason to be encouraged:

I think therefore, gentlemen, we may not hesitate in saying to
our brethren throughout the Empire State, that the God of
Israel has written with his omnipotent finger upon our future
prospects, those all glorious words: "*Hold up your heads, ye*

---

[45] *Ibid.,* December 12, 1840. See also *ibid.,* January 2, 1841 (Italics in the original).

[46] *Ibid.,* December 5, 1840.

[47] *Ibid.,* February 13, 1841.

[48] *Ibid.,* February 13, 1841.

wronged and injured people, for victory is declared unto you."[49]

Unfortunately, the resolution was read in the Assembly, and laid on the table.[50] No subsequent action was taken on it.

The inaction of the Legislature was a bitter setback for blacks. Some felt that the time had come to hold another convention to discuss strategy. Garnet issued the call. As head of the Central Committee, he, along with the other six members of that body, believed that the petitions should be resubmitted to the Legislature at its next yearly session.[51]

At the Troy Convention on the 25th, 26th and 27th of August 1841, nothing extraordinarily new emerged from its proceedings. Emphasis upon the use of the petition to gain the franchise was a recurring theme. Its most distinguished achievement was its Address "To the Electors of New York." Denying the widely held notion that granting blacks the suffrage would lend itself to social equality, the Address maintained that "men may be *politically* equal, and yet socially distinct" It pointed out that "the Jews, for example, downtrodden, in every European nation, in our state enjoy *political* equality, and yet maintain their separate identity." To the specious argument that blacks were too ignorant and degraded to exercise the vote, it answered:

> . . . Unfit to vote? Is there anything in our institutions which has a greater power to unfit men to vote, than there is in the tyrannical despotisms of Europe? Have the colored population who have lived under the glorious institutions of

---

[49] *National Anti-Slavery Standard*, March 18, 1841; April 15, 1841. See also "Report of the Committee on the Judiciary, on a Resolution Introduced by Mr. Duer, Relative to the Right of Suffrage," New York State Assembly, *Documents,* 64th Sess., 1841, 5, No. 181, 1-2.

[50] *Journal of the New York State Assembly,* 64th Sess., 540-542 (March 10, 1841).

[51] *Colored American*, August 6, 1841; *National Anti-Slavery Standard*, August 12, 1841. See also Earl Ofari, "*Let Your Motto Be Resistance*" The Life and Thought of Henry Highland Garnet (Boston, 1972), 20-21.

the State of New York less opportunity rightly to appreciate value, and exercise the privilege of voting, than the ten thousand per annum who swarm our genial shores from the besotted and deadening sway of European Kings?[52]

Less than one month after the conclusion of the Troy Convention, the American Reform Board of Disfranchised Commissioners met in New York City. Formed around 1840, it sought to secure the suffrage "immediately" for the African-American.[53] The organization was dominated by David Ruggles, who served as its Corresponding Secretary. At its first annual meeting, on September 8th in the Wesleyan Methodist Episcopal Zion Church. Samuel Hardenburg of New York City was appointed president and William C. Nell of Boston, secretary. The delegates from the city were T.L. Jennings, Prince Loveridge, George T. Downing, Thomas Downing, William P. Powell, and Thomas Van Rensselaer.[54]

While blacks continued to stress the necessity of gaining the ballot, the issue did not receive a serious and extended discussion until 1846. In that year, a constitutional convention was called by the State of New York. It remained in session from June 1st to October 9th. Blacks and their white sympathizers hoped that, with the expected revisions in the Constitution of 1821, the property qualification would be entirely abolished. Unfortunately, sentiment in favor of retaining the restrictive clause was surprisingly strong. Some delegates, however, spoke out vigorously and insistently against what they considered to be an anti-republican provision.

On September 30th, debate on the suffrage began when the first draft of Article ii, Section I of the revised constitution was reported out of committee. it read as follows:

---

[52] *National Anti-Slavery Standard,* September 23, 1841.

[53] Article II of its Consitution stated: "The object of this Society is to promote intelligence, that its members and others may know our true condition; to vindicate equal human rights; to take special cognizance of the oppressive legal or illegal customs, under which we groan; to unite and energize in securing our IMMEDIATE relief and enfranchisement." *Ibid.,* September 23, 1841.

[54] *Ibid.,* September 23, 1841. See also *Liberator,* August 13, 1841; September 24, 1841; October 22, 1841; November 12, 1841.

Every *white* male citizen of the age of twenty-one years who shall have been a citizen for sixty days, and an inhabitant of this state one year next preceding any election, and for the last six months a resident of the county where he may offer his vote, shall be entitled to vote at such election, in the election district of which he shall have been an actual resident during the last preceding sixty days, and not elsewhere, for all officers that now are, or hereafter may be, elective by the people.[55]

Immediately after the introduction of this section, Benjamin F. Bruce, a delegate from Madison County, moved to strike out the word "white" as a requirement for the franchise.[56] This led to a serious and prolonged debate. It is interesting to note some of the arguments advanced as a rationale to keep blacks from voting. John L. Russell, for example, who represented the County of St. Lawrence, opposed striking out the word "white" and even contended that the abolitionists in his constituency were opposed to extending the suffrage to blacks. He felt that if the African-American were given the ballot "our republic would soon be degraded to a level with those of Mexico and South America." He further added in a blunt summation that "we cannot admit you to be voters. If so, we must admit you to an equal seat with us in the jury box, and to hold office."[57]

Another delegate, John H. Hunt of New York County, supported this proposition by adding that blacks were an alien part of the American body politic. The doctrine of his constituents, and of himself, Hunt argued, was this:

We want no masters, and, least of all, no negro masters, to reign over us. We contend for self-government. We hold that no man who is not a part of the Republic's self—who is not a bona fide citizen-shall have any voice in the state. Negroes are aliens, but no longer idolaters,—no longer naked savages.

---

[55] *Debates and Proceedings in the new York State Convention for the Revision of the Consiution* (Albany, 1846), 775. Albany Argus edition.

[56] *Ibid.*, 775.

[57] *Ibid.*, 177.

They have made much progress in the arts of learning of a superior race.[58]

But Andrew W, Young, another delegate, challenged Hunt's position by stressing the fact that the word "colored" did not appear in the Declaration of independence. He added further that blacks were as independent as immigrants and entitled to the franchise.[59]   Elijah Rhoades, representing Onondaga County, regretted Hunt's remarks and could not see how he could advocate the "deprivation of rights, simply on the ground of a difference of complexion or the curl of the hair."[60]   David S. Waterbury, a delegate from the County of Delaware, noted that if equal suffrage was adopted it would place the state on the same footing as Vermont, Massachusetts and Rhode island.   He too believed that any argument based on the fact of color was "unworthy of men of sense."[61]

After considerable debate, the Convention declined to recommend equal suffrage to black persons, but continued, without change, the provision on this subject contained in the Constitution of 1821.[62]   The Convention did, however, submit a separate amendment providing for equal suffrage with the provision that, if adopted by the people, it would become a part of the suffrage article in the new Constitution.[63] In line with this amendment ballots were to be printed with the following words:

Equal suffrage to colored, persons? Yes
Equal suffrage to colored persons? No[64]

---

[58] *Ibid.,* 785-786.

[59] *Ibid.,* 786.

[60] *Ibid.,* 786.

[61] *Ibid.,* 786-787.

[62] *Ibid.,* 842.

[63] *Ibid.,* 852. This amendment read as follows: "Colored male citizens, prossessing the qualifications required by the first section of the second article of the Constitution, shall have the right to vote for all officers that now are, or hereafter may be elected by the people after the first day of January, 1847." *Ibid.,* 852.

[64] *Ibid.,* 852.

When the Convention adjourned on the 9th of October, the state election was a little more than three weeks off. The new constitution was approved by the people November 3, 1846 by a vote of 221,528 to 96,436; and the proposed amendment granting equal suffrage to blacks was rejected by nearly the same vote ,—85,306 to 223,834.[65]

The deficit of the amendment guaranteeing equal suffrage represented perhaps the severest blow to the political prospects of the African-American up to that time. Some blacks found it hard to understand that after years of agitation and protest their just grievance could be so callously brushed aside. One person, however, using the pen-name "Anglo-Saxon, attempted to come to grips with this problem. Writing in the *National Anti-Slavery Standard*, he noted that the question had been '"repeatedly presented to the State Legislature, and also to the people of the, state, for an amendment of the Constitution, by striking out the word '*white*' and all the application of political intrigue—all the inventive genius and arguments of political aspiration—have been brought to bear upon the subject without success. . . ." He was thus forced to the reluctant conclusion that:

> . . .Either the hearts of the people are hard and desperately wicked or there is a substantial, overruling, paramount objection to the admission of this class of people to the rights of free manship. I place that objection on this basis—*The Ignorance of the Negro Race.*[66]

But the charge of the Negro's alleged ignorance was not new. It had been trumpeted by his enemies throughout this period. Even in the face of such gross misrepresentations, blacks did not surrender on this issue. Some saw it as all the more reason to increase their activity.

In September 1855, for example, a convention of blacks meeting at Troy resolved "to give the ear of our Legislature and our fellow citizens generally no peace until they shall wipe from the statute book the anti-republican qualification." This convention also announced

---

[65] Lincoln, *The Constitutional History of New York*, 2:212-213.

[66] *National Anti-Slavery Standard*, October 4, 1849. (Italics in the original.)

through Dr. James McCune Smith the formation of a State Suffrage Association with Frederick Douglass at its head.[67]

As a follow-up to the Troy Convention, blacks in New York City met at Merritt Hall in December 1855 and declared:

> *Whereas*: the State Convention of Colored citizens that assembled at Troy on the 4th September, 1855, recommended a league to secure and promote the political rights of the Colored People of this State, we therefore recommend the formation of an Association for this county. . . .

The New York County League for Political Advancement, as it was called, was to be governed by a president, treasurer, secretary, and a central committee of 18 persons. In addition to this, an annual fee of fifty cents was required of each member as a condition for membership.[68]

The repeated use of the convention by blacks as a mechanism to focus attention upon their suffrage disability soon invited the criticism of some of their declared well-wishers who began to view the whole exercise as useless. The New York *Tribune*, for example, a strong anti-slavery newspaper published by Horace Greeley, attacked one such a gathering, which assembled in New York City in September 1857. In a mordant editorial the paper noted:

> A Convention of Colored Persons has been sitting in this City during a good part of this week. It speaks well for the sagacity and practical good sense of Negroes, that very few of them paid any sort of attention to this movement, That the present disfranchisement of all but a few of the richest of their number is most unjust, they doubtless feel; that they desire to be enfranchised is obvious and rational; but that they can hasten or promote their enfranchisement by holding

---

[67] *New York Tribune*, September 6, 1855.

[68] *Ibid.*, December 25, 1855. The organization was later referred to as "The New York City and State League Asssociation." The following person served as its officers: James Scott, president; Henry M. Williams and Edward Clark, vice-presidents; George W. Levere and Jael F. Still, secretaries; John B. Roberts, general agent and Joseph W.B. Smith, treasurer. *Ibid.*, October 6, 1856.

Conventions, none but the most stupid of their number can believe, though some who are more crafty, and fond of pocketing the hard earnings of others, may affect to believe it.

. . . We have always been in favor of conceding to Black or Yellow men all the political rights which are conceded or exercised by White men. We believe in Equal Rights for All Men, and prove our faith by our vote whenever we have an opportunity. We do not, as The *Express* mistakenly asserts, affirm "the *intellectual* equality of the "Colored with the White man;" but we claim for ourselves, and of course concede to all other adult human beings, political equality irrespective of any claim to intellectual superiority which may be set for or against us. . . .[69]

While conceding a growing lack of interest by the African-American in organized efforts to regain the suffrage, the *Tribune*, unfortunately, was conspicuously silent on what steps blacks could take to hasten the day of their full enfranchisement. It was true that the campaign for the suffrage gradually began to lose momentum, Many blacks had simply grown weary of the struggle, Thus at a meeting of these people held in Williamsburg on October 10, 1859, a number of resolutions were passed touching upon this theme. One said:

Resolved, That the indifference and apathy manifested by so many of the colored people on the subjects of equal suffrage, calls loudly upon us to adopt some more effectual measure for the raising of funds to carry forward the movement, and secure a general cooperation of the whole people in relation to this question.[70]

---

[69] *Ibid.,* September 26, 1857. See also *ibid.,* September 28, 1857. (Italics in the original.)

[70] *Weekly Anglo-African*, October 15, 1859. Nearly one year later the same paper commented: "If during the last few years, this matter [suffrage] has been left to the labors of a few zealous colored men, it was rather because the masses labored under the depression of hope deferred, that they ceased to act with the vigor of former days." *Ibid.,* March 31, 1860.

On the eve of the state and national elections of the issue of the franchise remained high on the agenda of blacks. In September of that year, for example, there were 48 local suffrage clubs in New York City and 18 in Brooklyn. But again, when the equal suffrage proposal was presented to the voters, they emphatically turned it down.[71]

Blacks in New York City did not gain the total suffrage until after the Civil War, when the property qualification was abrogated by the Fifteenth Amendment to the Federal Constitution which took effect in 1870. Yet one should not forget that in the three decades prior to the Civil War the political status of the African-American was by no means one of complete impotence. In certain elections, he sometimes was viewed as holding the balance of power. This in itself had a sobering effect on some officials who might otherwise have run rough-shod over his interests.

On the state and national level blacks expressed their political preferences clearly. As the following chapter will show, support was never given to a party out of blind loyalty; it was always inextricably tied to the position that party took with respect to the suffrage and other vital issues affecting blacks' welfare.

---

[71] The vote stood at 337,900 to 197,00. See Quarles, *Black Abolitionists*, 173; Olbrich, "The Development of Sentiment on Negro Suffrage," 126-127.

Political Alignments

In the period before 1850, free blacks in New York City had voted either for the Federalists, and subsequently the Whigs, or for some third party, but never for the Democratic Party. Earlier reference has been made to the fact that the Federalist Party, composed of wealthy merchants and landowners, had been largely responsible for the passage in 1799 of New York's Gradual Emancipation Act. In the early 1800's, this group continued to remain in the front ranks of those seeking to better the condition of blacks. Yet the support blacks gave to this party, it will be recalled, unfortunately resulted in the movement which led to their being generally disfranchised.

With the demise of the Federalist Party during the 1820's, blacks gradually shifted over to the anti-Jacksonian Whig Party. They could not in good conscience support the Democratic Party because of its strong pro-slavery tendencies. In 1826, for example, when the few remaining suffrage restrictions on whites had been eliminated, it was the Democratic-dominated legislature which voted to retain the property qualifications for blacks.[1]

While the Whig Party, like the Democrats, never *officially* endorsed a program of equal suffrage, owing to the prevailing prejudices, it did include a number of influential leaders like William H. Seward and Horace Greeley, who did favor some extension of the elective franchise to the African-American.[2] This fact was not to be lost upon the black voter. For in the decade after 1830, in the three contests for governor, the Fifth Ward of New York City, where most blacks resided, was carried against Tammany, "apparently" according to Fox, "by Negro influence."[3] The same result was brought about in

---

[1] Fox, "The Negro Vote in Old New York," 263.

[2] *Ibid.,* 265. See also Eric Foner, "Racial Attitudes of the New York Free Soilers," New York History, 46, No. 4 (October 1965): 313.

[3] Fox, *ibid.,* 264. In the gubernatorial contest of 1835, for example, the Whig, William H. Seward ran against William L. Marcy,

New York City in at least three municipal elections, and likewise, according to Fox, "in the eighth ward, next to the fifth, in African-American population," in 1834, 1837, and 1838. [4]

In the gubernatorial contest of 1838, the black vote statewide could have added to the outcome of the election.[5] In that year, William H. Seward and Luther Bradish were the candidates of the Whig Party for governor and lieutenant-governor respectively. Since the Democrats openly opposed granting African-Americans the suffrage, some blacks came out in support of Seward. That gentleman, it will be remembered, had indicated in October 1838, his qualified endorsement of black suffrage. But when queried whether he would support a law granting trial by jury to all fugitive slaves and, additionally, whether he favored the repeal of existing legislation that permitted the importation and detention of slaves in the State of New York for a period of nine months, he responded in the negative, declaring that these subjects did not enter "into the political creed" of his party.[6]

The *Colored American* was disappointed with Seward's response and urged blacks to withhold their vote from either gubernatorial candidate, since neither one was favorable to the rights of black men.[7] This advice went unheeded, for at a meeting of blacks held on the eve of the elections in Wilberforce Hall, blacks were urged to vote the whole Whig Ticket, The meeting also passed three resolutions:

---

a Democrat. Even though Seward lost this election, his vote in the Fifth Ward totalled 1284 to Marcy's 1211, for a majority of 73. See Edwin Williams ed., *The New York Register For the Year of Our Lrod 1835, Containing An Almanac, Civil and Judicial List: With Political, Statistical and other Information, Respecting the State of New York and the United States* (New York, 1835), 52. (Hereafter cited as Williams, *New York Register*.)

   [4] *Ibid.,* 264. In the municipal election of 1834 for example, one Verplanck, a Whig, ran against Lawrence, a Democrat. Verplanck polled 1841 votes in the Eights Ward to Lawrence's 1769, for a vote majority of 72. Williams ed., *New York Register* (New York, 1834), 279.

   [5] *Ibid.,* 264.

   [6] Baker, *The Works of William H. Seward*, 3:426-432. See also *Emancipator*, October 30, 1838.

   [7] *Colored American*, November 3, 1838.

1st.   That since Wm. H. Seward, in his letter to the
Committee of Abolitionists, has shown himself more friendly
to the abolishment of all distinctions as far as regards color,
than the candidates of the Democratic party, we agree to give
him our unanimous support.

2d.   That Luther BRADISH has shown himself the
unqualified friend of Human Rights, and in consequence shall
receive the votes of every colored citizen in this city.

3rd.   That the Congress and Legislative tickets of the Whig
party shall also receive our support.[8]

Seward won the election over his Democratic opponent, William
L. Marcy.[9] He later went on to win the confidence and support of the
African-American community in general.[10]

---

[8] *Emancipator*, November 8, 1838.

[9] *Ibid.*, November 15, 1838.   In the Eighth Ward, for example,
Seward polled 1977 votes, against Marcy's 1938, for a majority of 38.
Williams ed., *New York Register* (New York, 1840), 224.

[10] On December 19, 1842, for example, the Negro people of New
York City met at Union Hall and drew up an address along with
resolutions for the purpose of "expressing the high consideration
which they entertain for his excellencey since he has filled the office of
governor—especially towards the colored citizens."   In that year,
Seward had declined renomination by his party for a third term, and
blacks felt it incumbent upon themselves to show their appreciateion of
his wise and just administration.   The Address, drawn up by the
meeting, noted in part: ". . . .The undersigned would add, that they
are not moved to it by a preference for any political creed; but on the
contrary, isolated from the ferment of political strife, they have calmly
viewed the course of your excellencey in relation to certain great
principles, laid down, but which until the occurrence of your exective
career, had long remained as a dead letter; principles, towards the
carrying out of which, your excellencey has done so much; principles,
the full practice of which, by making New York a free state,
indeed—no portion of her inhabitants being proscribed for physical
peculiarity, or for cherished views—would enable her to advance with

The Whig Party continued to attract the wide support of blacks until the formation of the Liberty Party in April 1840. This new political body reflected the belief that neither the Whigs nor the Democrats could ever strike a blow at slavery because their memberships included hundreds and thousands of slaveowners. In its platform of principles, the Liberty Party pledged itself not only to the "overthrow of slavery" within the limits of national jurisdiction, but also to the "restoration of equality of rights among men, in every state where the party exists or may exist."[11]

In order to understand why some blacks came to support this party, one must view it within the broader perspective of American history. The Liberty Party was a direct outgrowth of the controversy within the anti-slavery movement as to whether political action or moral suasion on the part of the abolitionists could best overcome the constitutional and legal obstructions to emancipation. William Lloyd Garrison, the founder of the .American Anti-Slavery Society, was an exponent of the philosophy of moral suasion, based on the belief that the only effective way to end slavery was by an appeal to the hearts and consciences of slaveholders. Hence Garrison renounced the use of all physical instruments to end the institution. He further urged non-political action and advised his followers not to resort to the ballot. He viewed the Constitution of the United States as a pro-slavery document and insisted that no right-thinking abolitionist could vote or hold office under it.

Garrison's position created a split in his movement which led to the formation of the American and Foreign Anti-Slavery Society in 1840. The Liberty Party, founded in the same year, was the political expression of abolitionism.

Even though the Liberty Party was committed to "the principles of Equal Rights" and had urged its supporters to combat "any inequality of rights and privileges . . . on account of color,"[12] some blacks were at first ambivalent toward it. Especially was this the case as the presidential campaign of 1840 got under way.

---

unfettered strides in her glorious career." New York *Tribune*, reprinted in the *National Anti-Slavery Standard*, January 26, 1843.

[11] Kirk H. Porter and Donald Bruce Johnson eds., *National Party Platforms, 1840-1956* (Urbana, IL, 1956), 4-5.

[12] Foner, "Racial Attitudes of the New York Free Soilers," 312.

Charles B. Ray, the editor of the *Colored American*, for example, who threw his support to the Liberty Party before the campaign had ended, on one occasion said: "We go for thorough-going political action but whether an independent general ticket will best meet the circumstances of the case now, we have many reasons, for and many against."[13]

These reservations were expressed at least six months before the elections. He made it clear, however, that neither Martin Van Buren, the Democratic nominee nor the Whig William Henry Harrison, was acceptable to blacks in 1840. Ray was particularly opposed to Van Buren because, as a delegate to the New York Constitutional Convention of 1821, he had hedged on the question of equal suffrage for blacks.[14]

Unlike Ray, who in the early months of 1840 had only mild misgivings about the possible effectiveness of a third party, Thomas Van Rensselaer expressed his vehement opposition to the Liberty Party throughout the campaign. For one thing, he resented the fact that, even though this party was formed to secure the rights of the African-American, it had refused to give him a place on its ticket where he could plead his own cause. Of course, Van Rensselaer was not oblivious to the fact that blacks simply did not run for political office at this time. He conceded that it would be regarded by many as "contrary to the usages of civilized society to place a colored man on a ticket with a white man. Nevertheless, he felt that this argument was basically weak because blacks numbered about 40,000 in New York State and there were about "5,000 professed abolitionists." In spite of this "constituency," "not a single colored man's voice is to be heard in this new anti-slavery legislature." He therefore urged his brethren in both the city and state is not to lend their support to the Liberty Party.[15]

In reply to Van Rensselaer's position, a white subscriber wrote to the *Colored American* stating that he thought it foolish that a man had to be of a "*certain color*" before he would qualify to legislate for the rights of all citizens. "Is this true abolition doctrine?" he queried. "Have we not agreed to treat that people irrespective of color?" He concluded by saying:

---

13 *Colored American*, April 18, 1840.
14 Freeman, "The Free Negro in New York City," 159.
15 *Colored American*, October 10, 1840.

Why no name of a colored citizen is on any of the electoral tickets, I am not advised, having kept myself aloof from the meetings where electors were nominated; but I suppose that, having, as they supposed worthy objects to carry, the persons concerned selected such names as they thought would be most likely to obtain the greatest number of votes without respect to the color of the skin, the eyes or the hair—either of which should alike be indifferent.[16]

Van Rensselaer's argument made little headway among blacks in New York City. For one thing, Charles B. Ray had already announced his intention of supporting the Liberty Party in August 1840, and his opinions were influential. To blacks who asked, "For Whom Shall We Vote ," Ray urged them to vote for the Liberty ticket, headed by James Birney.[17] He based his stand on the conviction that the candidates of that party were "men of unimpeachable integrity, of sound mind and morals, devoted to *all the interests* of their country, and especially to the paramount interest of Liberty and equal rights to all."[18]

Even though the Liberty Party went down to defeat in the elections of 1840, Ray continued his active association with it. At its convention at Buffalo in September 1843, Ray served as one of its secretaries; Henry Highland Garnet was on the committee to nominate officers. This, Charles Wesley noted, "was the first time in American history that Negro citizens were actively in the leadership of a political convention.[19]

---

[16] The writer signed his remarks, "Principles Not Men." *Ibid.*, October 31, 1840. Van Rensselaer replied by condemning the writer's veiled suggestion that only by putting "whites" on the ticked would the Liberty Party be assured of obtaining the greatest number of votes. He believed that if this indeed was true, "the gentleman ought to have signed his name, MEN not Principles." *Ibid.,* October 31, 1840.

[17] *Ibid.,* October 3, 1840. Birney was the founder of the Liberty Party.

[18] *Ibid.,* October 10, 1840 (Italics in the original).

[19] Charles H. Wesley, "The Participation of Negroes in Anti-Slavery Political Parties," *Journal of Negro History,* 29 (June 1944):44-45. At this convention Garnet presented a resolution to the delegates which was adopted. It read: "Resolved, That the Liberty

In the period after 1840 the Liberty Party provoked wide discussion within the African-American community among those who insisted that blacks remain aloof from all parties, those who continued to support the Liberty Party, and those who thought it dangerous for blacks to identify themselves too closely with *any* party. For example, at a convention of blacks which met at Buffalo in August 1843, the subject of the Liberty Party came up for debate. When a resolution was introduced which attempted to put the convention on record in its support, Frederick Douglass immediately arose to oppose it.[20] He was joined by Charles L. Remond and William Brown of Massachusetts. Henry Highland Garnet, however, spoken defense of the resolution. He was supported by Charles B. Ray, Theodore S. Wright, and James M. Gloucester, all delegates from New York City.

The opposition maintained that the Freeman's Party, to which the resolution referred, was merely the Liberty Party by another name and that they neither believed in it nor would they "enroll themselves under its broad banner." Garnet admitted that by the Freeman's Party the Liberty Party was meant and made clear his intention to support its principles, After considerable discussion on both sides the resolution was adopted.[21]

---

party has not been organized for any temporary purpose by interested politicians, but has arisen from among the people, in consequence of a conviction hourly gaining ground, that no other party in the country represents the true principles of American Liberty or the true spirit of the Constitution of the United States." *Ibid.*, 45.

[20] Douglass at this time was a moral suasionist Garrisonian abolitionist who viewed all political parties as basically corrupt. See *Minutes of the National Convention of Colored Citizens held at Buffalo, on the 15th, 16th, 17th, 18th and 19th of August 1843, for the Purpose of Considering their Moral and Political Condition as American Citizens* (New York, 1843), 15.

[21] [21] It read as follows: "*Resolved*, That we hail with pleasure the organization of the Freman's Party, based upon the great principles contained in the Declaration of Independence, that all men are created equal, and that we cheerefully enroll ourselves under its broad banner, and hereby pledge to each other and to the world, our sacred honor, never to disband until liberty shall be proclaimed throughout all the land, unto all the inhabitants thereof."   15-22.

When the Annual Convention of the Colored Citizens of the State of New York met at Schenectady, September 18-20, 1844, a "Protest" was presented by James McCune Smith and Ulysses S. Vidal, delegates from New York City, against the endorsement of the Liberty Party by the Rochester Convention of 1843, Smith contended that the Rochester Convention, which had been called strictly for the purpose of obtaining the elective franchise, lacked the right to adopt "resolutions extraneous or detrimental to that object."[22]

Although the Schenectady Convention refused to approve the "Protest," the New Yorkers held a meeting after their return home and adopted a resolution stating that, in seeking the franchise, the "colored people by allying themselves with one party had incurred the opposition of the other parties."[23] Furthermore, Sydney Howard Gay, editor of the *National Anti-Slavery Standard* advised blacks against making their claim to the franchise a party issue at all. He noted:

> . . . No surer course could be taken to defeat the purpose of obtaining the extension of suffrage than make the question one of partisan politics. If this right is ever to be obtained by the colored people of this State, it should not be accepted even as the spoils of party triumph, or as a bribe for party support; but should be received only as it should be demanded, as a right pertaining to man, and not a privilege to be granted, or taken away by any party. . . .It should be demanded not of one party but of all parties,—not of a portion, but of the whole people.[24]

Support for the Liberty Party among blacks began to wane after 1844. This was attributable in part to internal dissensions which led to a split in the party by the time of the next presidential campaign.

---

[22] The "Protest" also insisted that the Rochester Convention had linked the attempt to gain the franchise with "the success of a *party* which must never comprise but a portion of the people instead of relying on the will and magnanimity of the whole people." *National Anti-Slavery Standard*, October 17, 1844. See also *ibid.*, October 24, 1844.

[23] Wesley, "The Participation of Negroes in Anti-Slavery Political Parties," 46.

[24] *National Anti-Slavery Standard*, October 24, 1844.

But the greatest reason for its declining fortunes was the emergence in 1848 of a new grouping, the Free Soil Party. Democrats and Whigs who opposed the extension of slavery in the territories met in Buffalo in the summer of 1848 and organized a new party with the proclaimed goals of free soil, free speech, free labor, and free men.[25]

Blacks at first had mixed attitudes toward the Free Soil Party. In Ohio, for example, the party had supported black suffrage, while in Massachusetts Free Soil men waged a successful battle to remove discrimination in marriage laws, transportation, and public schools.[26] Yet its standard-bearer during the presidential campaign of 1848 was Martin Van Buren, a man whose record on black rights "was anything but praiseworthy."[27] But the majority of enfranchised blacks took a half-a-loaf attitude, believing "it wiser," as Gerald Sorin pointed out, "to support the Free Soil Party because it had a chance to win."[28]

While some African-Americans in New York continued to support the Free Soil Party, many remained guarded in their political affiliations. For example, during the municipal election campaign of 1849, blacks held a meeting on October 2 and declared that it would be "inexpedient . . . to identify ourselves with either of the great political parties," but vowed to "favor such of them as will do most for

---

[25] Quarles, *Black Abolitionists*, 185. See also William H. and Jane H. Pease, eds., *The Antislavery Argument* (New York, 1965), lxiv-lxv.

[26] Gerald Sorin, *Abolitionism: A New Perspective* (New York, 1972), 114.

[27] *Ibid.*, 114. This attitude of political pragmatism did not always win them the support of their friends. When, for example, Thomas Van Rensselaer, editor of the *Ram's Horn*, endorsed Van Buren, his actions brought a sharp rebuke from Gerrit Smith, candidate of the Liberty Party. From Smith's viewpoint, the Free Soil candidate shared the prevailing prejudices of the vast majority of Americans in his "views and treatment of the colored race." Thus, Smith contended, blacks could not expect any better treatment from a Free Soil Government than from a Democratic or Whig Administration. In conclusion, he urged blacks not to vote for Free Soilers who "acquiese, and even take part in the proscription and crushing of your race." See Foner, "Racial Attitudes of the New York Free Soilers," 320.

[28] *Ibid.*, 114.

our cause—the cause of freedom, of justice and of rights."[29]   In the
following year, when Washington Hunt, a Whig, ran for the
governership of New York, the Franchise Committee of Colored
Voters endorsed him because he had shown his concern in matters
affecting their interests. Blacks were called upon to support the Whig
Party in the state because it was considered the "most liberal."[30]

In 1854, anti-slavery Whigs, dissident Democrats, Free Soilers,
and Liberty men, joined together to form the Republican Party, a
group committed to the containment of slavery. Despite the fact that
its appeal in part was basically racist, it soon gained a ready adherence
among blacks.[31]   For example, when that party put up a slate of
candidates for state, city. and county officials in 1855, blacks were
unusually strong in their support. The Reverend J.W.C. Pennington
termed the ticket "worthy [of] the support of every man of our race
who has the vote." And Charles B. Ray, echoing the principles which
he had espoused in 1840, urged black voters to show that they
understood "the science of liberty and [were] up to the practical
doctrine of sustaining freedom when brought to the issue of
tyranny."[32]

During the presidential campaign of 1856, the Negro people of
Brooklyn held a meeting in July and endorsed John C. Fremont, the
candidate of the Republican Party. A committee consisting of J.M.

---

[29] *National Anti Slavery Standard*, November 8, 1849. See also
American and Foreign Anti-Slavery Society, *Tenth Annual Report*
(New York, 1850), 125.

[30] Freeman, "The Free Negro in New York City," 163. See also
New York *Tribune*, November 5, 1850.

[31]   A leading student of this period has remarked: "Most
Republicans, of course, shared the prevalent prejudice of their times,
and were by no means ready to afford complete equality to black
citizens. But by their actions in state legislatures and in Congress in
the ante bellum decades, the Republicans demonstrated that they were
willing to guarantee Negroes certain basic rights, and they consistently
fought Democratic attempts to make the legal and social position of
black citizens even worse than it was." Eric Foner, *Free Soil, Free
Labor, Free Men: The Ideology of the Republican Party Before the
Civil War* (New York, 1970), 284-285.

[32] Freeman, "The Free Negro in New York City," 163.

Gloaster, George W. Levere, and Junius C. Morrell drafted the following resolution: [33]

> That in the nomination of Col. John C. Fremont by the Republicans to the office of Chief Executive of the nation, we behold the embodiment of Northern sentiment against Southern impudence and oppression and tender it our hearty good will, pledging as far as we are permitted (by yet the behest of slavery in our own state) to exercise the right of American citizens in the use of the ballot box, to remember him and his contest in the coming election.

In September 1856, a state convention of blacks assembled in Williamsburg. Here, Henry Highland Garnet observed that there were in the state some 5,000 or 6,000 black voters, about half of whom lived in New York City and Brooklyn. He believed the coming election would be closely contested, and urged every black man who possessed the franchise to vote and vote right. "Our people," Garnet continued, "have of late been seized with the spirit of do-nothing. Many do not see the necessity of voting at all. There are not many inducements for colored men to take part in politics, unless upon the broad ground of principle." But he insisted that blacks should act with those who came nearest to supporting their positions and believed that the Republican Party met this requirement. [34]

Garnet was not to be disappointed. Blacks generally rallied around the Republican ticket during that year. "Colored Republican Clubs" and the New York City and State League Association played an active role in this endeavor.[35]

---

[33] New York *Tribune*, July 30, 1856.

[34] *Ibid.*, September 24, 1856. One of the resolutions drawn up at this meeting stated: "*Resolved*, That inasmuch as the Republican Party of this country presents a platform more consistent with the principles of liberty and justice than that of any other party, we therefore pledge ourselves to use our best endeavors to secure the success of the candidate nominated by that party, namely, Fremont and Dayton for President and Vice-President, and King and Seldon for Governor and Lieutenant-Governor." Quoted in the *National Anti-Slavery Standard*, September 27, 1856.

[35] *Ibid.*, October 6, 1856; November 1, 1856.

The story was the same in the municipal and state elections of
1857. Here the ticket was supported despite some misgivings about
the platform. Blacks were pleased, however, to throw their support to
Fernando Wood because that functionary had granted licenses to
colored cartmen and porters, a concession seldom given by other
mayors.[36]

During the gubernatorial campaign of 1858 blacks in the city were
confronted with a dilemma. In that year, Gerrit Smith, candidate of
the Radical Abolitionist Party,[37] was running against the Republican
Edwin D. Morgan and a Democrat. Blacks had to decide whether to
vote for Smith, their longtime friend and benefactor, or the Republican
Morgan. Since the Democratic Party was divided and it was conceded
by nearly all blacks that Smith had no chance to win, the Republicans
under Morgan seemed the more likely choice. But, if too many votes
were given to Smith, the Republicans would very possibly go down to
defeat. Hence it seemed imperative that the black vote not be divided.

The *Radical Abolitionist*, a monthly political paper published in
New York City, editorially dismissed this argument, however:

What part do you propose to take at the approaching State
election? Hitherto, the greater part of you have voted with the
Whig, Free Soil, Free Democratic, and Republican Parties.
You have done so, because you have expected to obtain from
them equal suffrage, and protection against the *Fugitive Slave
Bill*. Your expectations have been disappointed. The leaders
of the Republican party have now ceased to repeat their
former professions of regard for you, as they did when they
were Free Soilers or Whigs. They declare their party to be
distinctively "*The white man's party*."

---

[36] *Ibid.,* November 3, 1857. See also Freeman, "The Free Negro
in New York City," 164.

[37] The Radical Abolitionist Party was organized at Syracuse, New
York in June 1855. It was, as one historian has aptly expressed it,
"simply the Liberty party by another name." Philip S. Foner, *The Life
and Writings of Fredreick Douglass,* 4 vols. (New York, 1950), 2:81.
See also Quarles, *Black Abolitionists,* 188.

. . . Can you refuse to neglect voting for GERRIT SMITH? Can you fail to rally, en masse, and to see to it that every voter among you votes for him?

Remember, it cannot be said, *now* that to vote for him, would be "throwing away your votes"! Nobody believes that the Republican's candidate can be elected, and if he could, you would gain nothing by it. The real struggle will be between GERRIT SMITH and the Democratic candidate. Unless SMITH be elected, a pro-slavery Democrat will be. And the vote of the colored people may, perhaps, decide the election.[38]

Yet this argument apparently had little impact, for at a state-wide convention of blacks at Troy, the delegates were urged to rally around the Republican Party. Stephen Myers, editor of *The Voice of Freedom*, a black newspaper published in Albany, summed up the feeling of the convention when he said:

MORGAN WILL BE THE NEXT GOVERNOR. The Democracy is divided. A house divided against itself must fall. And we, the 11,000 colored voters of the State, must stand just where we can be of some service in the struggle. If we ever gain any political rights we must look to the Republican party, for that is to be the dominant party.[39]

---

[38] *Radical Abolitionist,* October 1858, 4, No. 3 (Italics in the original).

[39] *National Anti-Slavery Standard,* October 9, 1858. William J. Watkins, another delegate, who had been appointed by the convention as a traveling solicitor to drum up Republican votes, praised Smith for his integrity and magnanimity but considered that his "nomination, under the present circumstances, must operate disastrously upon the hope of the disfranchsed colored citizens of the Empire State, and of the country at large; for the precedent now sought to be established, and the result of the present election will tell materially upon the next Presidential contest." He viewed the Democratic Party "of the State and nation as the black man's most determined and efficient enemy, a consolidated despotism which must be utterly overthrown before we can obtain the rights of franchise upon the same basis with our whte

As expected, Gerrit Smith was defeated.[40] The triumph of the Republican ticket did not sit too well, however, with some blacks. Within three months after Morgan's election, Frederick Douglass, echoing the views of many of his brethren in New York City, declared:

> Governor Morgan, whose anti-slavery was so loudly proclaimed to the people before his election finds no occasion in his [Annual] Message, to utter an anti-slavery sentence. How frequently we were told, during the campaign, that we were doing a very wicked thing to advocate the election of GERRIT SMITH, in opposition to the anti-slavery candidate of the Republican party. We feared *then*, what seems to us to be proved *now*, that the anti-slavery of Mr. Morgan was not the kind that would bear the test of office. We have looked in vain, through the entire Message, to find one word of advice to the assembled Legislature of New York in favor of granting the Elective Franchise to all her sons, irrespective of color. . . . [41]

Yet, despite some disappointments, blacks in the city continued to support the Republican Party down to the Civil War. Even the Morgan administration subsequently made a number of moves which won their praise.[42]

Throughout this period blacks demonstrated a shrewd capacity for political pragmatism. They were willing to support the man or party that had a chance of translating at least some of their objectives into reality. Thus the Whig, William H. Seward, won their enthusiastic backing because he had shown himself sympathetic to their cause.

While the Liberty Party, from the beginning, remained weak in its general appeal, blacks rallied under its banner, because it had come out unequivocally for the overthrow of slavery and a program of "equal

---

fellow citizens." New York *Tribune,* October 5, 1858. See also *ibid.,* October 26, 1858.

[40] He received only 5,033 votes. See *ibid.,* November 20, 1858.

[41] *Douglass' Monthly,* February 1859 (Italics in the original).

[42] *Weekly Ango-African,* October 15, 1859. See also *ibid.,* March 31, 1860.

rights for all." Even though the Free Soil Party was never strong in its professions for black rights, the African-American supported it because he saw in its growing influence against the spread of slavery the harbinger of a new and better day.

The story was the same for the Republican Party. Although this new political group "made no special effort to attract black voters," and while part of its appeal rested on the racist notion of "saving the West for the Caucasion,"[43] many blacks came out in its support. This was due primarily to the fact that some Republicans, like William H, Seward and Horace Greeley, did look favorably upon programs for extending to blacks their basic political rights.

In spite of all this, there were some in New York who saw the black man's salvation, political and otherwise, outside of the limits of the United States. In the opinion of these individuals, race prejudice and discrimination were so potent and so imbedded within American society that the African-American would never gain the chance to exercise his full potentialities. Only by emigrating to Africa or some other foreign land, they felt, could the black man achieve the freedom and dignity which he so earnestly desired.

The colonizationists, as they were called, as they were called, numbered among their ranks both whites and blacks. In New York City, some blacks were active promoters of the scheme and established organizations to carry it into operation. While the majority of the African-Americans steadfastly rejected the appeals of the colonizationists, their "solution" to the race problem, as the following chapter will show, was viewed by some as a viable alternative to life in the United States.

---

[43] Sorin, *Abolitionism*, 114.

Colonization

On December 28, 1816, the American Society for Colonizing the Free People of Colour, commonly called the American Colonization Society, was organized. Its declared purpose was "to promote and execute a plan for colonizing (with their consent) the free people of color, residing in our country, in Africa, or such other place as Congress shall deem most expedient."[1]

While the Society failed to win the financial backing of the Federal Government to carry out its program,"[2] it did gain the support of many influential groups which sympathized with its objectives. From its inception, however, the Society engendered the active opposition of most free blacks in the United States. They were convinced that the colonization scheme was but a means of ridding the nation of the free people of color in order to make slavery more secure. Then, too, since the Society viewed the African-American as an innately inferior and degraded class incapable of progress within American society, blacks rightly charged its sponsors with aiding in the spread of racial prejudice and deprivation of rights they already enjoyed.

In New York City, the colonization program came under heavy attack. Beginning in 1827, Samuel E. Cornish, as mentioned above, registered his unequivocal opposition to it. John Russwurm, his associate on *Freedom's Journal*, also opposed it at first, lamenting the vast sums being spent in that enterprise and suggesting that they could better be used in educating the black race. Russwurm's about-face was owing to the fact that his views on the issue had "materially altered." When attacked for inconsistency, he replied that it was "a mere waste of words to talk of ever enjoying citizenship in this

---

[1] *The First Annual Report of the American Society for Colonizing the Free People of Color, of the United States; and the Proceedings of the Society at Their Annual Metting in the City of Washington, on the First Day of January, 1818.* (Washington, D.C., 1818), 3.

[2] Dumond, *Antislavery*, 128.

country; it is utterly impossible in the nature of things; all therefore who pant for these, must cast their eyes elsewhere."[3]

Peter Williams Jr., Rector of St. Philip's Protestant Episcopal Church, was a staunch foe of colonization. On July 4, 1830, he delivered a sharp indictment of the American Colonization Society, stating the case of the African-American as forcefully as he saw it:

> How inconsistent are those who say that Africa will be benefited by the removal of the free people of color of the United States there, while they say they are the *most vile and degraded* people in the world. If we are as vile and degraded as they represent us, and they wish the Africans to be rendered virtuous, enlightened and happy people, they should not *think* of sending *us* among them, lest we should make them worse instead of better.

> . . . We are natives of this country, we ask only to be treated as well as *foreigners*. Not a few of our fathers, suffered and bled to purchase its independence, we ask only to be treated as well as those who fought against it. We have toiled to cultivate it and raise it to its present prosperous condition; we ask only to share equal privileges with those who come from distant lands, to enjoy the fruits of our labor.[4]

---

[3] *Freedom's Journal*, February 14, 1829. Later, on resigning the editorship of that paper, he said: "In many things, it is our duty to experiment until we arrive at the truth; but unless we have reasonable hopes for a favorable issue, they are all uselss; hence then, we conclude that all efforts here, to improve the mass of coloured persons must prove abortive; and this conclusion we adopt from the evidence of our own eyes." *Ibid.,* March 16, 1829.

[4] Foner, *Voice of Black America*, 45-46. (Italics in the original.) Although Williams' opposition to colonization never extended further than the expression of his views, so much antagonism to him developed that he was forced by his bishop (Onderdonk) to resign from the New York Anti-Slavery Society, because of a disturbance in his church. See Lewis H. Mehlinger, "The Attitude of the Free Negro Toward African Colonization," *Journal of Negro History*, 1, No. 3 (June 1916):288.

During the 1830's opposition to colonization within the black community increased in intensity David Ruggles became perhaps the foremost spokesman against the scheme. In a pamphlet entitled, *The "Extinguisher" Extinguished. . .*, written in 1834, he gave his answer to Dr. David Reese's support of the idea. Ruggles was incisive and direct in replying to the doctor's points. He viewed colonization as the offspring of prejudice and summarized his opposition by declaring that the Colonization Society was in reality the daughter of slavery.[5]

Samuel Ennals and Philip Bell referred to the colonizationists as men of "mistaken view" with respect to the welfare and wishes of the Negro people. They protested against the bold effort to colonize the oppressed free people of color on the ground that it was "unjust, illiberal and unfounded, tending to excite the prejudice of the community."[6]

Attacks by blacks, however, did not weaken the determination of the American Colonization Society, so thoroughly convinced it was of the correctness of its course. Throughout the 1830's it stepped up its propaganda campaign to encourage emigration to Africa and to counteract the unfavorable opinions being spread in the African-American community on the subject. On one occasion, the Reverend John T. Matthias, the governor of Bassa-Cove on the West coast of Africa, offered a glowing account of his region in his report to the New York City Colonization Society, an auxiliary of the national body:

> The colored man in this country is incomparably happier than in America, whether he is there a slave or freeman. The climate here is better for him; the soil is better; and the road to wealth and respectability, is open before him. This is the spot for the colored man. . . .We have no fogs, and there is very little variation in the temperature. It is now Christmas, and when you in New York are suffering from the cold, the country around us is dressed in the richest garb, and this will be the case during the year.

---

[5] David Ruggles, *"The Extinguisher" Extinguished or David M. Reese, M.D., "Used Up,"* (New York, 1834), 18-19.

[6] Mehlinger, "Attitude of the Free Negro Toward African Colonization," 285.

Samuel E. Cornish dismissed these appeals in an article entitled, "'Why not let us Alone."[7]

> The American Colonization Society profess to colonize colored people on the coast of Africa, with their OWN CONSENT; yet they, in the character of agents, supernumeraries, ecclesiastics and busybodies, are reconnoitering all the cities, towns and villages of our country, *scheming, begging, threatening* and *beguiling* our people into THAT CONSENT.

> When these officious men, who come to us, outwardly exhibiting sheep's clothing, are *plainly and positively told* and in the best of facts, that we do not wish nor intend to go to Africa WHY NOT LET US ALONE. Why make themselves *morally* and *literally* pests to our communities? We have no longer any faith in such men, *we cannot and will not trust them all.*[8]

In 1840, Cornish, along with the Reverend Theodore S. Wright, published a work entitled, *The Colonization Scheme Considered in Its Rejection by the Colored People . . .* The Authors began by presenting the views of free blacks regarding the entire concept of colonization. They denied that the outset that Afro-Americans "yearned in their hearts for Africa." On the contrary, they wrote, they regarded it as "but little more merciful *than death*." The authors argued that the colonization scheme was organized and maintained to perpetuate slavery. The plan to use blacks as missionaries was attacked as hypocritical in view of the fact that blacks were criticized for their moral laxness here in America.

They concluded by inquiring whether the scheme should be persisted in since it had been patently rejected by blacks from the first and since it only created prejudice against them, it "afflicts us with the feeling that our condition is unstable, and prevents us from making

---

[7] *Sixth Annual Report of the Colonization Society of the City of New York, etc.* (New York, 1838), 7-8.

[8] *Colored American*, October 20, 1838. For similar expressions of Cornish's views see also *ibid.*, January 27, 1838; April 12, 1838; December 8, and 15, 1838. (Italics in the original.)

systematic effort for our own usefulness and happiness and that of our families."[9]

The American Colonization Society was primarily interested in blacks emigrating to Liberia in Africa.[10]   Yet one of the most active colonization ventures, not directly associated with that Society, began in 1838.   In November of that year, the Legislative Council of Trinidad passed an ordinance to facilitate emigration to the island. There was a great demand for laborers in Trinidad at this time, and those who came were guaranteed immediate employment.   The allowance for passage and maintenance for laborers of African descent from the United States was $25, and from Canada, $30.[11]

Attracted by the prospects of immediate employment some blacks in New York City actually left for the island. The government agent from Trinidad, hoping for a mass exodus, sought to encourage more. But Charles B. Ray, editor of the *Colored American*, hastened to warn his people against the scheme. He noted

> Our brethren must not headlong blunder into an operation of such *vital importance* to the present and future generations, without the necessary precaution and preliminary steps.   If they do, ship-wreck and incalculable injury will inevitably, be the result. We are opposed to emigration in toto, in any other light than as in *individual enterprise*, and we forewarn our brethren against moving one step in an enterprise of so much magnitude to themselves and children, until well qualified *scientific agents* have been sent out to examine the whole matter and report.

He concluded by saying:

---

[9] Samuel E. Cornish and Theodore S. Wright, *The Colonization Scheme Considered in Its Rejection by the Colored People. . . .* (Newark, NJ, 1840), 4, 5, 6, 16, 12-16, 20-21, 26. See also *Colored American*, May 9, 1840.

[10] Liberia was founded by the American Colonization Society in 1822.

[11] *Emancipator,* July 25, 1839. See also ibid., September 5, 12, and 26, 1839.

If an emigration to Trinidad is not worth the expense of such agents, to the government of the island, it is not worth entering or encouraging on our part, and if not worth the expenses of an agency to us, it is not worth sustaining even in our thought, and much less in our practice. Brethren beware.[12]

A few blacks who returned to the city from Trinidad brought back unfavorable reports. They were branded by S.R. Buchanan, government agent of the island, as "worthless characters . . . who have by palpable and exaggerated misstatements traduced the inhabitants and institutions of Trinidad." He found that most of those who returned to the United States had failed for lack of industry and frugality and indicated that in the future "none but men of character with families, recommended for honesty, industry and sobriety will be entitled to a free passage . . ."[13]

Yet interest on the part of African-Americans about emigrating to Trinidad had waned considerably. On October 29,1840, blacks met in Asbury Church to discuss the issue. Several persons recently from the island made statements disapproving of the scheme, although the meeting passed no resolution to that effect. Still, as the *Colored American* pointed out:

Public sentiment among our people in this city, had settled down, long since, in opposition to that scheme, and the matter rendered about dead among us; and we trust our humble efforts have added some, to put a stop to it.[14]

Yet despite vigorous efforts on the part of some black leaders to discredit colonization, they were unable to check its influence completely. In October 1851, for example, the Board of Managers of the New York City Colonization Society announced that 36 emigrants had set sail for Liberia. Altogether some $893.70 was expended in supplies for their accommodation and support for six months after their arrival in the new republic.[15]

---

12 *Colored American,* October 5, 1839. (Italics in the original.)

13 *Ibid.,* March 7, 1840. See also *ibid.,* March 14, 1840.

14 *Ibid.,* October 31, 1840.

15 New York *Tribune,* October 23, 1851.

It was also in 1851 that Lewis H. Putnam, a New York City African-American, together with certain colleagues formed an organization known as the Liberian Agricultural and Emigration Society.   This organization was simply a black version of the American Colonization Society.

At a public meeting held by blacks on October 6, 1851, Putnam and his organization came under attack.   A report, submitted by a committee favoring emigration to Liberia, was upon motion, refused even the respect of a reception. The Reverend Samuel E. Cornish, Robert Hamilton, George T. Downing and others supported this move. Putnam and one Jones defended the right of a hearing.

Putnam had campaigned actively for the emigrationist scheme and had collected money from blacks in the city to help finance his program. Cornish advised his people that Liberia was the last place to go, citing the general poverty, spirit of caste, and other demoralizing influences and he emphasized that the greatest obstacle to the advance of blacks in the United States was the American Colonization Society. In addition to this, Cornish accused Putnam of appropriating the funds he had collected for his own private use.

Before the meeting adjourned a series of resolutions was passed. One made clear the fixed determination of blacks to oppose all colonization schemes and declared their "abhorrence" for its designs, whether "Promulgated by the American Colonization Society or by renegade colored men, made under the guise of an emigration society." Another asked Putnam to "disconnect himself from the negroes of New York. · .seeing that he has found it to his interests to connect himself with the American Colonization Society, our enemy and vilifier." A final resolution called upon blacks in the city to refrain from contributing funds towards the "so-called Liberia Emigration Society, as the colored citizens of New York have no connection or sympathy with it."[16]

But Putnam was not to be outdone. Within a few months his critics accused him of having gained Governor Washington Hunt's ear with a plea that state funds be diverted to his colonizationist scheme. It seems that Hunt was favorable to the idea, for in his Annual Message to the New York State Legislature in January 1852, he called

---

[16] *Frederick Douglass Paper*, November 13, 1851.

upon that body to make a "liberal appropriation" to help in colonizing those blacks in New York who were desirous of emigrating.[17]

On the day that the Governor's message was made public, the Committee of Thirteen, a watchdog organization, representing the interests of blacks in New York City and Brooklyn, promptly called upon the Governor to disavow this scheme. They pointed out that the plan would be "pernicious to us and the state," and were apprehensive that "if suffered to go unrebuked" would lead to further deterioration in the status of blacks in New York. The group then announced plans for a state convention to be held at Albany on January 20, 1852 to deal with this problem.[18]

In the meantime a metropolitan area meeting was called for January 13 to fight Hunt's proposal. It was scheduled to convene at the Abyssinian Baptist Church in Anthony Street, near West Broadway. Shortly before the meeting assembled, the Committee of Thirteen issued circulars entitled, "IMPORTANT NOTICE. Coloured MEN AROUSE! AROUSE! AROUSE!" In the circular the Committee declared:

> There are traitors among us—coloured men allied with our oppressors—men who, to satisfy their selfish ends, to put money in their purses, are uniting their influence with those who would drive us from our country. Is this to be! You will not remain indifferent with this fact before your eyes! No! No!

---

[17] The full text of Governor Hunt's Message on the "Expatriation of the Free Coloured People," can be found in the *National Anti-Slavery Standard*, January 22, 1852.

[18] *Frederick Douglass Paper*, January 15, 1852. The Commitee of Thirteen was composed of the following men: John J. Zuille, Chairman; George T. Downing, Philip A. Bell, William J. Wilson, T. Joiner White, Robert Hamilton, Ezekiel Dias, Jeremiah Powers, James McCune Smith, Junius C. Morrell, Thomas Downing, John T. Raymond and William Burnett. See New York *Tribune,* January 7, 1852.

. . . Come one, come all—maidens and mothers, brothers and sisters, fathers and all—come, come, and proclaim to the world your unanimous resolve not to leave the country.[19]

After the meeting got under way a number of resolutions were passed, one of which branded Governor Hunt's colonization program as being "both unchristian and unconstitutional." The resolution continued by saying that it was

unchristian because it does not recommend to the wrongdoer instantaneous cessation from his evil course, and unconstitutional because there is no power given to the Legislature, by the constitution, to make appropriation of public funds for the purpose of removing citizens beyond the bounds of the state.[20]

This meeting was followed by another held at Abyssinian on January 26, 1852. It was called for the purpose of receiving the report from the delegates to the Albany Convention held earlier (January 20th) that month. At this gathering, Philip A. Bell was appointed chairman and George T. Downing, secretary.

Downing gave an extended account of the black delegates who called on Governor Hunt at the Executive Mansion. He reported that the group was kindly received by the Governor who tried to impress upon it the fact that he harbored no hostile attitudes toward the black citizens of the state and only viewed colonization as an attractive alternative to some blacks who wanted to leave. To buttress his argument that he was not an enemy of the African-American, the Governor mentioned the fact that several colonization documents sent

---

[19] *National Anti-Slavery Standard*, January 22, 1852. See also *ibid.*, January 29, 1852.

[20] *Frederick Douglass Paper*, February 5, 1852. At this meeting, Jeremiah Powers, a member of the Committee of Thirteen, vowed that in view of Governor Hunt's policies, blacks would refuse their support to the Whig Party. He promised that "in the future we will vote for no man that will not vote for us and the cause of humanity. We will vote Gov. Hunt out next time. He was elected by only two hundred and fifty of a majority and these were the votes of the Colored population." *Ibid.*, February 5, 1852. See also *ibid.*, February 12, 1852.

to him had remained on his desk without being read. To further indicate his goodwill, he insisted that he would not sign any bill for an appropriation of money for colonization, should one be passed.[21]

Thus the Hunt plan was dead. The massive and overwhelming pressure exerted by blacks in opposition to it proved conclusively that no state-sanctioned program of colonization, however benevolent and well-meaning, could ever succeed.

While colonizationists schemes continued to be touted, it was not until the formation of the African Civilization Society in 1858 that a serious challenge was again presented to blacks in New York.

This Society was founded by the Reverend Henry Highland Garnet, who also served as its first president. It was organized with the avowed purpose of bringing about "the civilization and Christianization" of the Dark Continent.[22] More specifically, it hoped to inaugurate a program to pay the passage of black men who wished to go to Africa to assist in the development of the cultivation of cotton. Since cotton would be made cheaper in the United States by its cultivation in Africa, the "strongest support of slavery would be taken away."[23]

While Garnet, pastor of the Shiloh Presbyterian Church, remained a strong supporter of this plan, the Reverend J. W.C. Pennington came out vigorously against it. He maintained that leaders of the Republican Party, with Horace Greeley at their head, were joining in a crusade with the "*African Civilization Society to secure the expulsion of the free colored people of this country.*" At one time Pennington was in favor of the Society because he believed it was formed for the purpose of "educating young men, and assisting to pay off the indebtedness of our churches," but, having discovered its real objects, he came out vehemently against it.[24]

Like Pennington, most of the prominent black leaders in New York City were opposed to the approach of the African Civilization Society. A call for a meeting of blacks to assemble in Zion Church on April 12, 1860, issued the following appeal:

---

[21] New York *Tribune*, January 27, 1852. See also *National Anti-Slavery Standard*, January 29, 1852; March 4, 1852.

[22] Quarles, *Black Abolitionists*, 217.

[23] *Weekly Anglo-African*, May 5, 1860.

[24] *Ibid.*, March 31, 1860. (Italics in the original.)

> The colored people of New York and vicinity are called upon
> to pass judgement on the African Civilization Society . . . and
> to declare openly whether they approve or condemn that
> society. The undersigned believe that in its operations and
> influence it is of kin to the old colonization scheme—a
> supporter of prejudices—and hence a co-worker in the ranks
> of our enemies.[25]

Preparatory to the actual meeting, circulars were widely
distributed with the following message:

> COLORED MEN READ: It is said we should be slaves! It is
> said we should go to Africa! A new society has been formed
> to send us there. It is collecting money for the purpose.
> Come out. Will you be shipped off? Let nothing prevent you,
> come out, crowd old Zion! Admittance free.[26]

Shortly before eight o'clock that evening the meeting got under
way with nearly 1200 persons in attendance. George T. Downing was
elected chairman and began the proceedings by reading a letter he had
received from Harriet Martineau, the English author. Miss Martineau
revealed that agents of the Society were in Europe asking for financial
support, maintaining that the objects of the group had received the
approval of the free black population of the United States. Most of the
black speakers at this gathering, with the exception of Garnet and J.
Sella Martin, the Boston Negro leader, denounced this claim as a gross
misrepresentation.

As the discussion progressed, the debate between the opponents
and proponents of the Society became heated, and at times led to
serious confusion on the floor. Later, when order had been restored,
Downing read another letter which he had received from Elizabeth
Smith Miller, the daughter of Gerrit Smith, setting forth the views of
her father on the subject. Smith had recently returned from Utica
Asylum and was unable to pen a personal communication. Mrs. Smith
began by saying that her father believed that some merit existed in the

---

[25]   Among the signers of this Appeal were the following:
Jeremiah Powers, Reverend J.W.C. Pennington, George T. Downing.
Ibid., April 21, 1860.

[26] *Ibid.,* April 21, 1860.

program to induce blacks who desired to emigrate to Africa, Haiti, and Central America, but feared that such a plan might work "great evil by the exaggerated views of their importance and effects." She continued by pointing out that "nothing is more indispensable, in his judgement, to the well-being of these Americans than the abiding sense that their native land is their own land; and that they have as much right and as much reason as the whites to look upon it as their home." She concluded by remarking, "let the black man account no white man as his friend, or indeed, as other than his enemy, who does not accord as fully to the black race as to the white, political, civil, ecclesiastical and social rights, as well as on this soil as on any other."

Before the meeting adjourned a resolution was passed which stated:

> *Resolved*, That we wish it to be most firmly fixed in the minds of our fellow-countrymen, the American people, that we as a body, in any number do not intend to leave this, our home—that we intend to stay here; to have our children enjoy victory over hate and wrong, the promise of which is everyday indicating itself.[27]

The African Civilization Society failed in its efforts to organize an effective program of emigration. For, however noble and elevated its objects, as the supporters of this organization believed them to be, it could not overcome the deep-seated feelings shared by many blacks in New York that endorsement of colonization, in whatever form, would only worsen their status in the United States by increasing prejudice against them. They regarded the American Colonization Society as a living confirmation of this belief.

Yet, throughout the 1850's, while blacks in the city generally rejected going to Africa, some did view with growing favor the possibility of increased emigration to Canada and, to a limited extent, even Haiti. In these countries they remained well within the orbit of the United States and could render aid and succor to their oppressed brethren who steadfastly refused to leave their native land.

---

[27] *Ibid.*, April 21, 1860. See also *ibid.*, May 5, 1860.

While some free blacks were truly disillusioned with life in the United States and sought an immediate escape, others gained hope in the growing crusade against slavery. They saw in the powerful abolition movement the dawn of a new day.

Abolition Movement

During the period of General Emancipation blacks played an active role in the Abolition Movement of New York City, particularly as it developed more and more of the militant spirit after 1830.[1] One recent student of this period, for example, has included Theodore S. Wright, Henry Highland Garnet, Samuel E. Cornish, and Charles B. Ray among New York's ten highest-ranking abolitionist leaders.[2]

While white abolitionists in the city, as we shall see, spearheaded the main antislavery drive, it is generally conceded that *Freedom's Journal* and the *Rights of All* were precursors of the Abolition movement among blacks. In the words of Charles Wesley, they were the "first public evidence that there were Negroes who were dissatisfied with slavery, colonization and color prejudice."[3] It should be remembered, moreover, that these two newspapers had taken a strong stance against slavery before the appearance in 1831 of Garrison's *Liberator*, a paper which would later command wide support among blacks.

---

[1] In the 1830's, abolitionists led by William Lloyd Garrison and others adopted the doctrine of Immediatism. As defined by Gerald Sorin, Immediatism described a state of mind which recognized the "sinfulness of slavery, admission of personal responsibility for its existence, and personal committment to make no compromise with it." It also involved a program of direct action designed to achieve total emancipation in the future. Gradualism, which was the dominant theme of abolitionists prior to this period, viewed slavery's demise as inevitable but lacked the moral urgency to agitate for its immediate overthrow. Sorin, *Abolitionism*, 38-39. See also Pease and Pease, *The Antislavery Argument*, xxviii-xxxii.

[2] Gerald Sorin, *The New York Abolitionists* (Westport, CT, 1971), 81-93.

[3] Charles Wesley, "The Negros of New York in the Emancipation Movement," *Journal of Negro History*, 24 (Janary 1839):72.

It was not until the formation of the New York City Anti-Slavery Society that an opportunity was presented for closer cooperation between white and black abolitionists. The circumstances surrounding the establishment of this group are worth noting.

On October 2, 1833, the first meeting of this organization was scheduled to be held in Clinton Hall On the afternoon of that day, however, placards were posted in the streets and persons of pro-slavery sympathies were rounded up to disrupt the proceedings.

The trustees of Clinton Hall, anticipating violence, retracted their contract and refused the building to the group. At the suggestion of Lewis Tappan, a trustee of Chatham Street Chapel, it was agreed to hold the meeting in the lecture room of that building. Oral notices were sent out, and about 5O "stout-hearted abolitionists" gathered at the hour of the meeting. The mob gathered near Tammany Hall, eager to attack the Chapel. Lewis Tappan and his brother Arthur, passed through the crowd unnoticed. The sexton of the Chapel locked the iron gates, and gave the keys to Lewis Tappan, who at once entered the building and told the gentlemen present to transact their business with dispatch before the mob assaulted them. A constitution was quickly adopted, and Arthur Tappan was chosen president and Lewis Tappan named to be one of the board of managers.[4]

As the meeting adjourned the keys were turned over to the sexton, and the members made their exit through the main body of the Chapel to the rear of the street. Soon after the abolitionists had gone, the disappointed mob rushed in, seized a black man, called him Arthur Tappan, placed him in the chair and forced him to make a speech, whereupon he said:

> Gentlemen, I am not used to making speeches, and don't pretend to be qualified to do so. But one or two things I do know: one is, God hath made of one blood all nations; and another is, all men are created equal, and are endowed by their Creator with certain unalienable rights, among them life, liberty, and the pursuit of happiness.[5]

---

[4] Henry Wilson, *History of the Rise and Fall of the Slave Power in America*, 3 vols., (New York, 1872), 1:231-232.

[5] *Ibid.,* 232; Clarence Winthrop Brown, *Arthur and Lewis Tappan* (New York, 1883), 5-7. William Goodell, *Slavery and Anti-Slavery; A History of the Great struggle in Both Hempishperes; with a*

From the outset blacks supported the aims of the New York City Anti-Slavery Society even though they served in no official capacity within the organization.[6] They did, however, assume prominent roles in the American Anti-Slavery Society, founded in December 1833.[7] The First Annual Report of this Society in 1834 lists four blacks from the city as members of the board of managers. They were Samuel E. Cornish, Theodore S. Wright, Christopher Rush, and Peter Williams.[8] All of these except Rush, also served on the executive committee of 12 of which Arthur Tappan was chairman.[9]

Of those blacks who served on the executive committee, Peter Williams Jr., was the only one who was forced to sever his connections with the group. In the summer of 1834 Bishop Onderdonk of the Protestant Episcopal Church in New York advised Williams, as rector of St. Philip's Church, to cease his active work with the American Anti-Slavery Society, and direct his full energies to the ministry. The Bishop, realizing how painful this would be to Williams, nevertheless emphasized that "on whichsoever side right may be, St. Philip's Church will be found on the side of meekness, order, and self-sacrifice to the common good, and the peace of the community." Accordingly,

---

View of the Slavery Question in the United States (New York, 1855), 395. See also New York *Evangelist*, October 5, 1833.

[6] New York *Evangelist*, October 5, 1833.

[7] The object of this Society, as stated in its constitution, was the "entire abolition of slavery in the United States." It was also formed to "elevate the character and condition of the people of color, by encourageing their intellectual, moral and religious improvement, and by removing public prejudice, that thus they may, according to their intellectual and moral worth, share an equality with the whites of civil and religious privileges; but this Society will never, in any way, contenance the oppressed in vindicating thier rights by resorting to physical force." Quoted in Dumond, *Antislavery*, 178.

[8] American Anti-Slavery Society, *First Annual Report* (New York, 1834) 35-36.

[9] Westley, "The Negroes of New York in the Emancipation Movement," 77.

Williams resigned his position as a manager of the American Anti-Slavery Society, and as a member of its Executive Committee.[10]

The American Anti-Slavery Society, particularly in its early years, was constantly seeking "colored agents" to propagate its views. An opportunity presented itself in March 1835, when the agency committee of this society employed the Reverend Israel Monroe to promote the improvement of blacks in New York City. In June of the same year the committee asked Simeon S. Jocelyn, a prominent white home missionary to blacks in New Haven, to persuade one of New York City's leading black ministers, Theodore S. Wright, to accept a temporary assignment in behalf of the educational and general improvement of members of his race. Since, however, no record exists of agency activity by either man, presumably neither was employed.[11]

On December 5, 1855, blacks rounded the "United Anti-Slavery Society of the City of New York." This organization held its first meeting at the hall of the Phoenix Society in Chapel Street. Thomas Van Rensselaer was elected a vice-president of this group. The executive committee of this society consisted of Samuel E. Cornish, William P. Johnson, Thomas Downing, and Theodore S. Wright.[12]

The problem of slavery in New York City was to remain a most difficult one throughout the period General Emancipation, presenting a strong challenge to the abolitionists. Even though slavery was abolished in the state in 1827, the right of slaveholders to reclaim their runaway property was recognized under the Federal Fugitive Slave Law of 1793.

This law empowered the master of an interstate fugitive slave to seize him wherever found, carry him before a federal or state magistrate in the vicinity, and obtain a certificate warranting his removal to the state from which he had fled. The statute allowed no trial by jury and required conviction merely on the oral testimony of

---

[10]   Woodson, *The Mind of the Negro*, 634. The full text of Williams' reply can be found in *ibid.,* 630-634.

[11]   John L. Myers, "American Anti-Slavery Agents and the Free Negro, 1833-1838," *Journal of Negro History*, 52, No. 3 (July 967):203.

[12]   *Emancipator*, December 15, 1836.

the claimant or an affidavit certified by a magistrate of the state from which the Negro was alleged to have fled.[13]

Under the Fugitive Slave Law of 1793 some blacks were claimed on false charges; others were kidnapped and taken South. So widespread had these practices become that New York was forced in 1830 to enact a series of legal provisions to deal with the problem. According to the Revised Statutes of that year, any person who was not an inhabitant of the state, and who possessed property in the form of a slave, could not retain that person within the state beyond a period of nine months from the day of his first entry.[14] Section 8 of this law strictly forbade the selling of any person within the state as a slave under any circumstances. It read as follows:

> No person shall under any colour, or pretext whatever, sell any other person as a slave; and whoever shall offend against this provision, shall be deemed guilty of a misdemeanor, and, on conviction, shall be subject to a fine not exceeding *two* thousand dollars, or to imprisonment in the county jail not exceeding three years, or to imprisonment in the state prison, not exceeding four years.[15]

---

[13] *United States Statutes at Large,* I, Sec. 3, 302-305; Wilson, *Rise and Fall of the Slave Power* 1:69-78. See also C.W.A. David, "The Fugitive Slave Law of 1793 and Its Antecedents," *Journal of Negro History,* 9 (January 1924):18-25.

[14] This provision stated: "Any person, not being an inhabitant of this state, who shall be travelling to or from, or passing through this state may bring with him any person lawfully held by him in slavery, and may take such person with him from this state, but the person so held in slavery, shall not reside, or continue in this state more than *nine* months, and if such residence be continued beyond that time, such person shall be free." *Selections from the Revised Statutes of the State of New York: Containing all the Laws of the State Relative to Slaves, and the Laws Relative to the Offence of Kidnapping, which Several Laws Commenced and Took Efect Janyary 1, 1830. Together With Extracts from the Laws of the United States, Respecting Slaves* (New York, 1830), 5.

[15] *Ibid.,* 5.

The penalties for kidnapping were severe. Any person found guilty of such an offense could be punished by incarceration in the state prison for not exceeding ten years And any person found guilty of being an "accessory" was to be confined to the state prison for not exceeding six years, or in the county jail for not exceeding one year, or by a fine not exceeding $500, or by both such fine and imprisonment.[16] Finally, it was emphatically declared that:

> Every person born within this state, whether white or colored, is FREE; every person who shall hereafter be born within this state, shall be FREE; and every person brought into this state, as a slave except as authorized by this TITLE, shall be FREE.[17]

Yet despite the stringent provisions against slavery and kidnapping, many free blacks in the city lived with the ever-present danger of being enslaved on the questionable evidence of Southern slaveholders or their agents. For example, on July 23, 1836, George Jones, a "free colored man," was arrested at 21 Broadway, by certain police officers, upon the pretext of his having "committed assault and battery." Jones, confident that no such charge could be sustained against him, refused to go with the officers. His employers, however, advised him to go and answer to the charges, promising him assistance if he should need it. Being thus assured, Jones went with the officers and was locked up in Bridewell prison. Between one and two o'clock that afternoon he was brought before the Honorable Richard Riker, Recorder of the City of New York. In the absence of his friends, and in the presence of several notorious kidnappers, who asserted under oath that he was a runaway slave, the Recorder declared him to be a slave. In less than three hours after his arrest, he was bound in chains and dragged through the streets "like a beast to the shambles" and carried South. Said David Ruggles in reference to this case:

> My depressed countrymen, we are all liable; your wives and children are at the mercy of merciless kidnappers. We have no protection in law, because of the legislators withhold justice. We must no longer depend on the interposition of the

---

[16] *Ibid.*, 16-17.
[17] *Ibid.*, 5.

Manumission or Anti-Slavery Societies, in the hope of peaceable and just protection; where such outrages are committed, peace and justice cannot dwell. While we are subject to be thus inhumanely practiced upon, no man is safe; we must look to our own safety and protection from kidnappers, remembering that "self defence is the first law of nature."[18]

Eight months prior to the Jones incident, the New York Committee of Vigilance had been formed to render assistance to blacks who were in danger of being enslaved. The Committee sought to prevent, if possible, the return of fugitives to slavery and to ascertain the extent of kidnapping. It also attempted to aid the fugitive in providing him with legal counsel and securing to him the right of trial by jury. David Ruggles was the well-known secretary of this organization.[19]

At the end of its first year in operation the Vigilance Committee called on blacks in New York City to remain firm in their determination to protect fugitive slaves and it was happy to report that "we have found them efficient coadjutors. To them we have been principally indebted for funds, in them we find steady and uniform agents, and by their exertions, we trust this work will not only spread extensively in this city, but throughout the states."[20]

In the report of its proceedings the Committee directed its attention to the following subjects:

1st. The arrival of persons (needing their aid and counsel) from the South and other parts.

2d. The arrival and departure of vessels, [sic] suspected as slaves, or having persons on board claimed as slaves, or who were in danger of being kidnapped and sold.

---

[18] *Emancipator*, July 28, 1836. See also *ibid.*, August 4, 1836; September 1, 1836; October 6, 1836.

[19] *The First Annual Report of the New York Committee of Vigilance for the Year 1837, Together With Important Facts Relative to their Proceedings* (New York, 1837), 3.

[20] *Ibid.*, 11-12.

3d. The arrival and proceedings of slave agents and kidnappers.

4th. The arrest of persons claimed as fugitive slaves.

5th. The abduction of persons by kidnappers.

6th. The recovery of persons detained in the South.

7th. The recovery of property due to colored people by wills, etc.[21]

Much of the success of the New York Committee of Vigilance can be credited to David Ruggles. He was the most vocal and active of all its workers. One contemporary noted that he was "a General Marion sort of man for sleepless activity, sagacity and talent."[22]

Ruggles personally aided hundreds of runaways. The case of Frederick Douglass was a typical one. Ruggles sheltered the young Douglass for nearly two weeks, made his marriage arrangements, and sent the newlyweds to New Bedford, Massachusetts, with a five-dollar bill and a letter of introduction to a locally prominent black man, Nathan Johnson.[23]

---

[21] *Ibid.,* 13-14. Of the seven outlined objectives, the act of kindapping received the strong attention of the Vigiliance Committee. The whole free black community was constantly being told to be on the alert. On one occasion even the *Emancipator* warned its black readers: "Look out for kidnappers! We are informed that the notorious NASH has returned from the South, and is prowling about the city for more victims. Colored people should be on their guard. Let no man into your house unless you know who he is, and what his business is. If he says he is an officer and has a warrant to arrest a fugitive slave, *don't let him in unless he shows a search warrant.* He has no right to go or stay without [one]." *Emancipator,* March 2, 1837. (Italics in the original.)

[22] Quarles, *Black Abolitionists,* 151. See also Helen Boardman, "David Ruggles," *The Negro History Bulletin,* 5 (November 1941):39-40.

[23] Foner, *Life and Writings of Frederick Douglass,* 1:23.

Ruggles also boarded incoming ships to see whether slaves were being smuggled in. On one occasion he was successful in having an indictment brought against a Frenchman from Guadeloupe, who had clandestinely brought in a slave. His efforts in this particular case in winning freedom for the slave produced a volley of criticism. The New York *Express*, for example, a violent *Whig* organ, in commenting upon this case, denounced Ruggles because his actions tended to "embarass trade." Said the *Express*:

If these embarassments to commerce, of trading and freighting vessels between the Free States and the West Indies, or Southern ports, are to be thus designedly created by colored Abolitionists, and made a matter of persecution for innocent men, every man of business will soon see that such Abolitionism is nothing but a pick-the-pocket business, by which traps ["set"] to extort costs, or bribes from captains and owners of such vessels. A business community will not put up with it. Indeed, it would be a pretty lucrative business, this, of extorting a one hundred dollars, or more, from the captain of the vessel, when in a hurry to sail, after any negro should swear that he was a slave, brought out in such a vessal, provided some great captain of emancipation would drive the bargain hard.[24]

Despite numerous attacks and misrepresentations, Ruggles continued his work on behalf of the Vigilance Committee. He resigned, however, as secretary and agent in February 1839, because of failing eyesight and a clash with the committee over funds. Receiving a salary of four hundred dollars per year, he had expended on several occasions more money than he was entitled to. An audit committee appointed to examine his accounts found him indebted to the committee for $326.17. Ruggles, secure in his own sense of honesty, vigorously denied this accusation.[25]

---

[24] The New York *Express*, repritned in the *Emancipator*, August 30, 1838.

[25] *Emancipator,* October 24, 1839. The *National Anti-Slavery Standard* in its issue of the August 20, 1840, devoted six columns to an airing of the quarrel between Ruggles and the Committee.

With the resignation of Ruggles the New York Committee of Vigilance lost its driving spirit and much of its influence But the committee's record since its founding had been commendable. It is reported that during the first seven years of its activities no less than 1,373 persons came under its cognizance.[26] The committee also won public acceptance of its contention that persons claimed as fugitives should have a trial by jury, a measure they had advocated at their opening meeting A bill requiring such a guarantee was passed by the New York Legislature in 1840 and signed by Governor Seward in May 1841. A month later the Vigilance Committee held a victory celebration at Asbury Church, The presiding officer, Charles B. Ray, hailed the measure for sweeping clean from the statute books the last vestige of slavery in the state. [27]

On September 18, 1850 another major challenge was presented to the black community in New York City with the passage by Congress of a Fugitive Slave Bill. Under the provisions of this act the African American claimed as fugitive—by a master's affidavit presented before a United States judge or Commissioner—was given no jury trial. Furthermore, the official's fee was ten dollars if he found the black person to be a fugitive, five dollars if he did not. Only the testimony of a white man was acceptable in determining the status of the Negro. In

---

[26] *Fifth Annual Report of the New York Committee of Vigilance, for the Year 1842, with Interesting Facts Relative to Their Proceedings* (New York, 1842), 38.

[27] *Emancipator*, June 17, 1841. Unfortunately, the new law was not vigorously enforced, and before it could even prove its effectiveness was nullified by a Supreme Court decision (*Prigg v. Pennsylvania*, 1842) giving Congress the *exclusive* right to enforce the Fugitive Slave Law. Then in April 1843, the New York State Assembly voted 60-45 to repeal the law requiring trial by jury. The Assembly bill sough to repeal not only the jury law of 1840, but the provision of the Revised Statutes requiring proof that persons claimed as fugitive slaves were really such, and even nullified so far as it related to slavery, the time honored *writ of homine replegiando*, by which a man held in bondage might challenge his master to show cause why he should be so constrained. Fortunately, the bill did not come before the State Senate; so the law of 1840 remained on the statute books. See *National Anti-Slavery Standard*, April 27, 1843.

addition, all citizens were subject to call to assist in the prosecution of the statute.[28]

Unlike the Fugitive Slave Law of 1793, which proved ineffectual because it was not rigorously enforced, the law of 1850 struck terror into the hearts of the African-Americans because an intense arid vigorous effort was made to carry out its provisions. A free black, for instance, who had worked honestly and industriously earning a respectable livelihood was subject—often upon false charge—to be thrown into slavery. Then, too, since kidnapping was rampant during this period, no black could be guaranteed immunity from the operation of the law. Thus through a vicious combination of force and fraud, many blacks in the North found themselves in a precarious position.

Yet from the beginning, blacks in New York as elsewhere in the North made clear their strong determination to resist the law's enforcement. Meetings and conventions were called to outline a program of action.

One of the most effective of these meetings held by the Negro people of the city took place on the evening of October 1, 1850, when more than 1300 blacks jammed into Zion Church. Preparatory to this gathering circulars were issued exhorting the blacks to "resist oppression! Shall we defend our liberties? Shall we be freemen or slaves?"

Shortly after the meeting convened, William P. Powell took the podium as chairman and launched into a stinging attack on the Fugitive Slave Law, He asked blacks whether they would tamely submit to the "sweet music of passive obedience," and they responded with a resounding, No, No![29] Then he went on to put the question that had been on the minds of everyone present, including not only the blacks, but also a large group of white abolitionists. He phrased it this way:

Shall the iniquitous Fugitive Slave Bill [continue], which subjects every free colored man, woman and child to be seized upon, handcuffed, and plunged into perpetual slavery? Shall the blood-thirsty slaveholder be permitted by this unrighteous law to come into our domiciles or workshops, or the place

---

[28] *United States Statutes at Large*, 9, Sec. 1, 462-465.

[29] *National Anti-Slavery Standard*, October 10, 1850.

where we labor, and carry off our wives and children, our
fathers and mothers and ourselves without a struggle . . .

The response was instant and unanimous; loud cries of No! No!
No! reverberated throughout the auditorium. Powell concluded his
speech with a Garrisonian flourish. He declared that the Fugitive Slave
Law was a "covenant with Death and an agreement with hell and must
be trampled underfoot, resisted and disobeyed at all hazards."[30]
After his speech, Powell read to the gathering a letter he had
communicated to Charles S. Woodhull, the Mayor of New York City,
asking that functionary what "protection we, the free colored people,
may expect under the operation of the Fugitive Slave Law." To
Powell's chagrin, the Mayor had refused to answer his letter and thus
left him with no choice but to urge his brethren to resist the law. He
did not explicitly urge violent resistance, but many blacks at the
meeting were able to read between the lines. A number of resolutions
were drawn up denouncing the law. One declared that if "any attempt
to execute its provisions on any one of us either by invading our homes
or arresting us on the street, we will treat such an one as assaulting our
persons with intent to kill, and, God being our helper, will use such
means as will repel the aggressor and defend our lives and liberties."
Another resolution called upon Chairman Powell to set up a secret
committee to receive the names of those fugitives who wanted help
and aid them to escape. Powell was also called upon to appoint a
committee to advise fugitives to remain, and if any attempt were made
to capture them, that they be rescued as an example to the community
This plan of action was approved.
Before the meeting adjourned, Jeremiah Powers, a member of the
Committee of Thirteen, arose to make a few remarks. He contended
that the black man had fought side by side with his white American
brethren and had just as much a right to this country as whites. He
was chary of the efficacy of speeches and resolutions because he feared
that the resistance would begin and end right there—in speeches. He
insisted that the only argument that could be used against the Fugitive
Slave Law would be the "bowie knife and the revolver."[31]
The Hamlet case was the first in the city to come under the
operation of the Fugitive Slave Law of 1850. On September 20, 1850,

---

[30] *North Star*, October 24, 1850.
[31] *Ibid.*, October 24, 1850.

George Hamlet of New York was claimed to be the slave of Mary Brown of Baltimore. About thirty years of age, he had been a resident of New York City for three years and had a wife and family.[32]

Thomas J. Clare, agent for the claimant, brought the case before Commissioner John Gardiner, clerk of the Circuit Court of New York. who, upon a cursory examination of the affidavit presented by the claimant. issued a warrant for Hamlet's arrest. Hamlet was at his work as a porter when he was seized by a United States Marshal. He was then taken to City Hall. and the commissioner without even assigning an Attorney or rendering any kind of assistance whatever, accepted *ex parte* the testimony of Clare and Gustavus Brown, son of the alleged claiment.[33] By accident, a man of anti-slave sympathies heard of these proceedings and obtained an attorney for Hamlet. At the hearing, Hamlet testified that his mother was a free black, and that therefore he was entitled to his freedom. But since the Fugitive Slave Law prohibited the testimony of an alleged fugitive, this statement was not received into evidence. The commissioner then ordered Hamlet remanded to slavery.

Preparations were made by the marshal to have Hamlet returned immediately to the South. He was not even allowed to say farewell to his wife and children. After arriving in Baltimore, he was put in prison until he could be sold farther South.

The reaction of the Negro community to this affair was swift, united and firm. The New York *Journal of Commerce* launched a vigorous campaign to have Hamlet ransomed from slavery.[34] In response to this drive 1500 blacks gathered at a church and subscribed $500. One African-American contributed $100. Hamlet was brought back to New York, and 5,000 people, white and black, assembled to greet him. Overwhelmed by emotion, he stood by the chairman of the

---

[32] *Liberator*, October 4, 1850.

[33] *The Fugitive Slave Bill: Its History and Unconstitutionality with an Account of the Seizure and Enslavement of James Hamlet, and his Subsequent Restoration to Liberty* (New York, 1850), 5. (Hereafter cited as *Fugitive Slave Bill*)

[34] Samuel J. May, *The Fugitive Slave Law and Its Victims* (New York, 1856), 11.

meeting "tears rolling down his cheeks." Later, Hamlet was escorted home "amid great cheering, shouting and rejoicing."[35]

A most unusual situation involving the Fugitive Slave Law occurred in April 1852 when George T. Downing wrote to *Frederick Douglass Paper* pointing out to his horror that the (white) pastor of the influential St. Philip's Church openly avowed his refusal to support those who were seeking to circumvent the law. In his letter, Downing made reference to Dr. James McCune Smith, a member of St. Philip's, who sought to interview his pastor to see if the charges made against the minister were true. He did. But as a result, to use the graphic expression of one of the vestrymen of that church, "the Doctor came and raised the devil." Downing concurred in this opinion by saying, "yes, his satanic majesty was in the very body of the sanctuary *in robes.*" Smith was upset because when he asked the pastor flatly whether he would sanction disobedience to that law, the Reverend gentleman made clear that the Fugitive Slave Law was the law of the land and that every Christian was bound to obey it.[36]

Yet by 1859 opposition to the Fugitive Slave Law by blacks and their white friends had become so great that the New York State Legislature was forced to deal with the situation, Early in February 1860, a select committee of the New York Assembly voted in favor of a Personal Liberty Bill, It provided that "every person who shall be brought into, or be in the state shall be free, and whoever captures or holds a person as a Fugitive Slave, in the state, shall be imprisoned in the state penitentiary, and fined $1,000, to go to the party agrieved." Despite the pressures for its final passage by anti-slavery groups, the bill was defeated.[37]

---

[35] *Fugitive Slave Bill,* 36. See also *Liberator,* October 11 and 18, 1850; *North Star,* October 3, 1850; *National Anti-Slavery Standard,* October 17, 1850; Wilson, *Rise and Fall of the Slave Power,* 2:304; American and Foreign Anti-Slavery Society, *Eleventh Annual Report* (New York, 1851),23-24.

[36] *Frederick Douglass Paper,* April 29, 1852. (Italics in the original.)

[37] American Anti-Slavery Society, *Twenty-Seventh Annual Report* (New York, 1861) 261-262; *Douglass' Monthly,* April 1860. It was not until 1864 that the Fugitive Slave Law of 1850 was repealed. For a greater discussion of this whole issue see George Walker's,

When Louis Kossuth, the Hungarian Revolutionary hero, came to the United States in 1851, seeking American financial and moral support to free his country from the yoke of Austrian tyranny, he was lionized everywhere went.   While in this country, Kossuth found himself face to face with the Abolition movement, similar in many respects to the cause which he was promoting. He was immediately called upon by antislavery groups to speak out against the institution. It was clear, however, that to do so would have doomed his mission to failure. By his silence, he incurred the displeasure and invited the attacks of the friends of freedom.[38]

Blacks in New York City, through the Committee of Thirteen, welcomed Kossuth, however, read to him a moving address, and pledged their moral and financial aid to his cause.[39] But William G. Allen, a black leader from McGrawville, New York, attacked the Committee of Thirteen for its cowardly surrender to the cause of universal freedom and justice. In a letter to *Frederick Douglass*, he said:

> You have seen the address of the colored people of New York City to Kossuth. What a stupendously foolish thing! Not a word of their own wrongs—their sufferings—their enslavement;—no point, no directness, no nothing, except the rhetoric. Palaver, the whole of it; and to cap the climax of absurdities, the address winds up with the assurance to the Hungarian, that on the day of giving, they (the colored people) will be on hand with at least the 'widow's mite,' if no more.

"Black Resistance to the Fugitive Slave Law of 1850, 1850-1856" (Unpublished Master's Thesis), Columbia University, 1971.

[38] Woodson, *The Mind of the Negro*, 287-288.

[39] In the *Address*, the Committee noted: ". . . The attention of the nations is fixed upon you! At the mention of your name, tyrants tremble, the oppressed rejoice! There is not a principle advocated by you, not a word that escapes your lips but is caught up and wafted to every civilized nation. And deep and wide-spread is the joy felt through Europe, when you proclaim the thrilling and trumpet-toned annunciation, "Ye oppressed nations of Europe, be of good cheer and courage." Quoted in the *National Anti-Slavery Standard*, December 18, 1851.

. . . Kossuth is not asked to turn anti-slavery lecturer. . . .He is not asked to turn aside from the Hungarian cause, or to divide his energies between the cause of the American slave, and that of the Hungarian oppressed. Nobody but a fool would ask that. He is simply asked to do nothing while here, which would imply that he regarded the liberty of the American black man as less sacred than that of the Hungarian white man. . . .[40]

The anti-slavery movement among blacks in the city reached a new high with the formation of the Abolition Society of New York City and Vicinity in March 1855. This group was characterized as "political" abolitionism because it declared that slavery was contrary to the "Constitution of the United States, and therefore it is the duty of the people through the Federal Government or otherwise, immediately to abolish the whole system." The officers of the Society included prominent New Yorkers Lewis Tappan was president, James McCune Smith, vice-president and William Goodell, secretary. The executive committee included such staunch anti-slavery advocates as Simeon S. Jocelyn and Charles B. Ray.[41]

After 1855 evidence is somewhat scanty concerning the role which blacks played in the Abolition movement of New York City. But from available sources it is known that Henry Highland Garnet emerged as perhaps the leading spokesman for black people in the city For it was in 1855 that Garnet became pastor of the Shiloh Presbyterian Church, a congregation whose pulpit could boast of having had such distinguished and influential black ministers as Samuel E. Cornish, Theodore S. Wright, and James W.C. Pennington.

Garnet, however, was not above criticism, as was seen earlier with his African Civilization Society scheme. On another occasion, even his militant anti-slavery stance was questioned by fellow abolitionists. The *National Anti Slavery Standard* once remarked:

THE REV. HENRY HIGHLAND GARNET, the Coloured minister of the Shiloh Presbyterian Church, has long

---

[40] Woodson, *The Mind of the Negro*, 289. See also *Liberator*, January 9, 1852.

[41] *Frederick Douglass Paper*, April 27, 1855.

professed to be a thorough-going Abolitionist; and yet he consented to receive the installation, on Tuesday last, at the hands of a pro-slavery Presbytery, that unmitigated old hunker, Dr. Prentiss, of the Mercer Street church, preaching the sermon!   When educated coloured men thus stultify themselves, we need not wonder that white men so often find their sectarianism overmastering their consistency as abolitionists.[42]

Despite these shortcomings, Garnet had played a prominent role in the meetings which were called by blacks in the city following John Brown's capture for his attack on the federal arsenal at Harpers Ferry, Virginia, in October 1859.   Brown, a zealous abolitionist, whose relationships with blacks had been "close, continuous, and on a peer basis,"[43] sought to strike at the institution of slavery by driving the bondmen off the Southern plantations into the Allegheny mountains and thence northwards into Canada.[44]   Brown was convicted for his part in the insurrection on October 31, 1859, Two days later a judge pronounced a sentence of death by hanging.[45]

During the thirty-day interval between sentence and execution, Brown bore himself with such fortitude and serenity that he won the universal admiration and respect of blacks, While he remained in jail, "innumerable prayer and sympathy meetings were held throughout the North." But as Benjamin Quarles has pointed out, "none were more fervent than those called by Negroes."[46]

In New York City, the Reverend James W.C. Pennington wrote a guest editorial which was carried in the *Weekly Anglo-African* entitled, "Pray for John Brown."[47] Later, on November 26, 1859, the Negro women of Brooklyn sent the following letter to Brown:

Dear Sir: We, a portion of the American people, would fain offer you our sincere and heartfelt sympathies in the cause

---

[42] *National Anti-Slavery Standard*, November 7, 1857.

[43] Quarles, *Black Abolitionists*, 235.

[44] Fjoner, Life and Writings of Frederick Douglass, 2:86.

[45] Stephen B. Oates, *To Purge this Land with Blood, A Biography of John Brown* (New York, 1970), 325-327.

[46] Quarles, *Black Abolitionists*, 240.

[47] *Weekly Anglo-African*, November 5, 1859.

you have so nobly espoused, and that you so firmly adhere to. We truly appreciate your most noble and humane effort, and recognize in you a Savior commissioned to redeem us, the American people, from the great National Sin of Slavery; and though you have apparently failed in the object of your desires, yet the influence that we believe it will eventually exert, will accomplish all your intentions. . . .We rejoice in the consciousness of your perfect resignation. We shall ever hold you dear in our remembrance, and shall infuse the same feelings in our posterity.

. . .And now, in view of the coming crisis which is to terminate all your labors of love for this life, our mortal nature fails to sustain us under the trying affliction; but when we view it from our religious standpoint, we feel that earth is not worthy of you, and that your spirit yearneth for a higher and holier existence. Therefore we willingly give you up, and submit to His will "who doeth all things well."[48]

Finally on Friday, December 2, 1859, the day of Brown's execution, a solemn service of sympathy was held in Shiloh Church where the Reverend Henry Highland Garnet presided. The service began at ten o'clock in the morning with the singing of a hymn beginning,

Dear Father, to Thy mercy seat,
My soul for shelter flies

after which a prayer was offered by the Reverend Charles B. Ray, who asked that the sacrifice of "this dear old friend of freedom may mark the downfall of this sinful system of bondage." Before the conclusion of the meeting, the Reverend Garnet spoke and declared that "henceforth the Second of December will be called 'Martyr Day.'"[49]

With John Brown's death a critical turning point had been reached in the Abolition movement of New York City. Heretofore, moral suasion had been a strong prop in the anti-slavery crusade. Brown's

---

[48] Woodson, *The Mind of the Negro*, 509-510.
[49] *Weekly Ango-African*, December 10, 1859. See also New York *Tribune*, December 16, 1859.

raid, more than anything else, brought that approach under sharp challenge. Frederick Douglass spoke for a growing number of fellow abolitionists, when he declared that "moral considerations have long since been exhausted upon slaveholders. It is in vain to reason with them. . . .Slavery is a system of brute force. It shields itself behind might, rather than right. It must be met with its own weapons."[50] And met it would be. Few there were in 1859 who could confidently foresee that Brown's actions, had in many ways, tolled the death-knell of slavery.

---

[50] *Douglass' Monthly*, November 1859. (Italics in the original.)

In Retrospect

The history of the African-American in New York City as developed in this study of his condition during the period of General Emancipation offers strong testimony to his enduring attributes. Despite repeated rebuffs and discouragements on almost every hand, free blacks nevertheless continued their struggle to obtain the full rights and privileges of citizenship.

Closely linked with this struggle by blacks was the emergence during these years of an aroused community "self-consciousness" among them out of which grew the tactics and strategies for liberation. While it is difficult to gauge accurately the intensity and depth of this consciousness, one can make valid generalizations based on the *statements* and *actions* of black leaders and institutions which sought to mold and channel community thought.

There were at least three powerful institutional structures operative in the black community life of the city which served to give it cohesion and "consciousness." These were the societies, the press, and the church.

The societies, both benevolent and literary, reflected a deepening concern on the part of some in the black community for the mental and moral uplift of their people.

The societies, by their very nature, were manifestations or extensions of that very "self-consciousness" which leads a people to begin an assessment of their overall condition.

In a day when public welfare, social security, unemployment insurance, and other supportive social programs did not exist, blacks, who occupied a status in American Society even lower than that of immigrants, felt impelled to shelter and support those of their race who for some reason or another had lost the means or ability to care for themselves. The mutual aid societies are an excellent example of that sense of brotherhood and concern even in a day when the vast majority of blacks lived in abject poverty. Even though their privileges and benefits were limited to members and their immediate families, the aid societies performed invaluable roles in caring for those blacks who were sick, homeless, and destitute.

What philanthropic society could have provided clearer witness of the self-consciousness and burgeoning maturity of the black community than the African Dorcas Association? This group, formed by women connected with the African Free Schools, for the specific purpose of providing clothing for the destitute black children of the city to enable them to attend school, performed a service of incalculable importance.

The more structured benevolent organizations, such as the Colored Orphan Asylum, the Home for Aged and Indigent Colored People, and the Colored Sailors' Home, provide proof that the black community included devoted individuals with the requisite vision and intelligence to deal with some of the more vexing problems confronting their people.

The Colored Orphan Asylum, in particular, stands as a tribute to the relentless struggle of the African-Americans to overcome the effects of the soul-crushing poverty and instability which wreaked havoc on so many families and condemned their children to a future filled with hopelessness and insecurity. Even though the Asylum received funds from both public and private sources, its value lay in the fact that it grew out of a heightened "self-conscious" concern on the part of some in the black community to deal constructively with the problem of orphan children, and to seek ways to ameliorate their general condition.

The literary societies established by blacks exemplify a clear tendency among these people to improve and cultivate their minds. While it is true that schools for blacks existed in the city, the objective of the literary societies was to allow for a more general diffusion of knowledge within the community Thus, they did not limit their activities to those within a certain age bracket, but opened their doors to all who sought the means of mental elevation.

The Phoenix Society, for example, founded to promote the improvement of blacks in morals, literature, and the mechanic arts, offered a broad and diversified range of opportunities. It sponsored lectures, essays, and poetic recitations, and later established a library, reading rooms and museum where black youth and adults could go to make constructive use of their time.

The literary societies underline a significant trend among blacks in the city. They show that a surprising degree of individual and group interaction did take place, which lends further support to the view that this was a dynamic and self-conscious community, keenly aware of its needs, and determined somehow to meet them.

As an institutional mechanism for unity, change, and self-consciousness the Black Press in New York City played a decisive role in presenting the issues and debating the themes which impinged on the well-being of the community. Beginning with the appearance of *Freedom's Journal* in 1827, followed by such other papers as the *Rights of All* and the *Colored American*, a forum was offered for a spectrum of opinion touching many subjects.

Even though popular and anti-slavery newspapers existed and often touched at length upon the vital concerns of the African-American people, these organs could not, like the Black Press, devote their columns *exclusively* to the *special* and *peculiar* needs of the black community. Since their situation in America was unlike that of any other group, blacks needed an instrumentality separate and apart from the general population to plead their own cause.

As an agency in the molding of self-consciousness, the Black Press stands unparalleled during the prolonged and arduous suffrage and political struggles of blacks in New York City. Particularly during the active years of the late 1830's, it was the *Colored American* that spoke out persistently and consistently on the suffrage issue. Week after week, it hammered away on this theme, convinced of the immediate necessity for blacks to obtain their voting rights. Even in 1841, when the State Legislature refused to take quick action on this question after blacks had bombarded the Capitol with petitions, it was the *Colored American* that remained in the front ranks of the battle and urged blacks not to lose heart in their determination to reverse majority legislative sentiment in favor of this objective.

In addition to this, the *Colored American* sought to clarify to its readers the many other issues which confronted the free black community, hoping that a consensus could be formed to effect desirable goals. On the political front, for example, the Black Press performed a remarkable job in keeping the African-American people well-informed of the various candidates, parties, and platforms which affected their interests. Even though that press generally spoke with conviction its advice was not always heeded. During the New York gubernatorial contest of 1838, as we have seen, the *Colored American* came out flatly against the election of William H. Seward, because that Whig candidate would not commit himself to support a law granting jury trials to fugitive slaves. Yet, in spite of this, a convention of blacks in the city gave him their unqualified endorsement. This incident, though unusual, demonstrates that there existed enough self-conscious awareness in the black community to perceive when its avowed mouthpiece had miscalculated. For Seward, as we know, later went on to become one of the staunchest champions of black rights.

When the Liberty Party came into prominence after 1840, it was the *Colored American* that undertook the task of encouraging a shift in black political allegiances from the Whigs to this third party. While the paper at first hedged on the practicality of supporting a third party, owing mainly to doubts concerning its vote-drawing abilities, it nevertheless saw merit in the platform of a group dedicated to "equal rights for all."

Since the *Colored American* ceased to publish after 1841, and no other major black newspaper appeared in the city until 1859, one can legitimately ask if a case can be made for the effectiveness of the black press during the pre-Civil War years. While it is obviously true that the careers of these organs were ephemeral, they did lay the groundwork for a tradition of *agitation* and *protest* which remained within the black community and helped to sharpen the general consciousness of these people.

As an institution whose influence touched a multiplicity of black concerns in New York City the Black Church stands preeminent as a force in welding a greater sense of group and community self-consciousness. Comprising a variety of denominational units, collectively the church enjoyed the allegiance of a considerable cross-section of the city's black population and its ministers numbered in their ranks some of the most brilliant and influential of the community's leaders.

The Black Church played a unique role among these people because it can be said to be the one institution whose roots were embedded in a common shared tradition. It organized its approach around a program which entailed not only the fulfillment of spiritual needs but also a deep interest in the resolution of worldly problems.

Politically, the black Church was indirectly involved, through its ministers, in a number of activities. The Reverend Charles B. Ray, pastor of the Bethesda Congregational Church, and the Reverend Henry Highland Garnet, who later ministered at Shiloh, were each strong supporters of the Liberty Party. Ray, in particular, through his editorship of the *Colored American*, vigorously sought to rally blacks under that party's banner. He, along with Garnet, later became the first blacks to actively participate in a political convention, when in 1843, the Liberty Party, meeting at Buffalo, nominated both men to serve as its officers.

The social condition of the free black community did not escape the attention of the church. It sought to maintain the viability and integrity of the black family unit by encouraging parents to bring up their children under a strict moral regimen and by seeking to impress upon them the necessity of keeping their young in school. The church also participated, as will be recalled, in the Temperance campaign, and made some headway among blacks in this endeavor.

The Black Church can then be said to be the institution from which that community derived much of its leadership, consciousness, and inspiration as a people. It militantly struggled against social injustice and was the radiating point from which programs for action frequently occurred. Shiloh, to cite an example, served as a center not only for religious activity, but for political and cultural gatherings as well. The church which could accommodate 1,600 people in the building at Prince and Marion Streets, was considered to be "eminently suited as a meeting hall."[1]

Despite the substantive gains made by blacks toward racial self-consciousness and solidarity, their fundamental social, economic and political condition in New Work underwent little change. We have seen that from a social point unfortunate effect of making the free Afro-American's color the symbol of his own degradation. This operated to limit harshly the full advance of blacks within American society.

From a housing standpoint, the black man, like his immigrant counterpart, was forced to live in tenements totally unfit for human habitation. The high rents and overcrowded conditions of some of these dwellings in many cases militated against the acquisition of those traits deemed conducive to one's physical and mental well-being.

The Afro-American's health, for reasons often connected with the appalling conditions within his environment, suffered throughout this period. As the reader will recall, the ravages of disease and the high mortality rate exacted a disproportionately greater toll among his people than among whites, thus underlining the glaring social disparities between these two groups.

---

[1] New York *Tribune*, December 14, 1859.

While vice and crime among blacks posed an ever-present danger to the social health and stability of their community, the problem by no means assumed such ominous proportions as the larger society was inclined to attribute to it. The black man appears to have possessed a propensity for these activities no greater than his white counterparts. Factual evidence has shown that blacks generally attempted to check the more virulent forms of vice and by no means tenanted the prison houses proportionately to the extent widely believed at the time.

While social discrimination was experienced by all classes of black people, and took its psychic toll accordingly, its effects did not completely stifle black aspirations. While the African-American was denied access to travel, recreational, and other sublets enjoyed by the white community, he still hoped, at no distant day, to be judged and treated on the basis of his character as an individual rather than by the irrational and artificial criterion of color.

Economically, the black man found himself in a depressed condition. From the beginning he was systematically barred from many of the skilled trades which alone could have led to greater upward social mobility. We have observed how the intense competition of the Irish and other immigrant groups precluded his achieving economic parity.

While it is true that some blacks achieved an unusual degree of comfort and security in their own private enterprises, the vast majority of these people, having been cut off from skilled and remunerative positions, were forced to scrounge a livelihood as best they could. Thus relegated to such menial pursuits as waiters, barbers, servants, and laborers, few blacks possessed the wherewithal or spirit to diversify their occupations.

Even in unskilled jobs, blacks found themselves being gradually nudged out by immigrant groups. And among the professional and business class, who generally fared better, discrimination and lack of capital sometimes reduced the chance for their economic security.

Yet despite these drawbacks, one must not overlook the fact that a feeble start was made toward group economic independence. We have seen that some blacks did make gains in the accumulation of real and personal property. And a substantial amount of money was deposited by these people in the savings banks during the same period.

While the acquisition of land, particularly the huge tracts distributed by Gerrit Smith, seemed at first to hold out the opportunity for visible economic improvement, projects of this sort failed owing to a number of problems, and the African-American would experience no meaningful alteration of his economic predicament until well after the Civil War.

On the educational front, the prospects of the African-American community appeared hopeful. From the establishment of the African Free Schools in 1787, on through the administration of the Public School Society, and later of the New York Board of Education, blacks resolutely struggled to secure an avenue for their children's intellectual advancement. While it is true that the quality of instruction and buildings in the public schools were not at all that they might have been in comparison with those provided for white children, still some progress was achieved.

Although black attendance in the public school system often fell far short of the levels attained in the former African Free Schools, it would be precipitous to condemn black parents for want of proper concern in this regard, for as Rhoda G. Freeman noted, "white parents were no more conscientious. . . .Attendance was not compulsory, child labor abounded, and poverty took its toll in many ways."[2]

On the whole, despite the debilitating factors which tended at times to circumscribe the full educational potentialities of these people, blacks remained steadfast in their determination to overcome the many disadvantages to which their community was subject. The efforts of the Society for the Promotion of Education Among Colored Children testifies to the active and tireless leadership of this community in increasing the opportunities for black children.

While attendance at the Society's schools generally remained small, due largely to competition from the public system, the group nevertheless performed a praise-worthy activity. It frequently monitored the progress made by Negro children in the public schools and published vital statistics relating to differences in financial expenditures and educational quality between white and black schools.

Thus education, while by no means a panacea for the deep-rooted problems of the Afro-American community, did function to expand black horizons, and in so doing operated to raise the day-to-day expectations of these people. These expectations would gain greater relevance and immediacy after the end of slavery.

---

[2] Freeman, "The Free Negro in New York City," 374.

In their struggle to regain the suffrage, blacks in New York displayed a level of sophistication and intensity of purpose which seemed to dwarf many of their other activities. As we have seen, the franchise question touched such a deep and sensitive chord in this community that its spokesmen in both the press and pulpit rallied in solid phalanx to make the acquisition of the vote an overriding priority.

The endless procession of meetings and conventions which were called from the middle 1830's up to the eve of the Civil War testify to the searing discontent and frustration which blacks felt with respect to this question. Unlike any other issue, the suffrage controversy had direct and practical consequences for every black person in New York City. Denied the suffrage by an unfair $250 property qualification, the majority of African-Americans were deprived of one retaliatory weapon capable of protecting their interests from the inroads of hostile elements.

Even when repeated petition campaigns and convention resolutions failed to move white majority opinion in the state to granting blacks the suffrage, they did not quit the field altogether on this issue. Inherent in their fight for the vote was the strong belief that Americans could not in good conscience extend political rights to one section of the people while withholding them from another. In this sense, blacks were the true exponents of democracy, for they sought to unmask the hypocritical pretensions of a nation whose political orientation was based in part on the ideology of caste. It was in the area of the suffrage alone that blacks tried repeatedly to achieve the leverage and influence necessary to improve their conditions. Thus, they threw their support first to the Whig Party, then to the Liberty Party, followed by the Free Soil and Republican Parties.

It will be remembered that blacks shunned almost to a man the Democratic Party, because that body had remained adamant in its hostility toward black rights. It was the same party which had championed, at the 1821 New York State Constitutional Convention, the imposition of a $250 property qualification for blacks, and in 1826, as was noted earlier, voted to remove the few remaining suffrage restrictions on whites, while simultaneously voting to retain them for blacks. One thing was clear to blacks: the Democratic party and slavery were the twin engines of their oppression, and thus, only by aligning themselves with a party whose position on race was not so blatantly reactionary and racist could they even hope to surmount some of the difficulties they faced. So we see that the African-American came out in support of the Whig Party, not because the platform of that party declared itself to be in favor of an extension of black legal and political rights, which it at no time explicitly did, but because it contained such progressive spokesmen as William H. Seward and Horace Greeley, who saw no conflict in their party finding an accommodation to these black objectives.

The story was the same for the Liberty Party, founded in 1840. Here, however, was the appearance of a totally new party, dedicated altogether to the overthrow of slavery and a policy of equality for all, While this party was essentially abolitionist in character, and had little chance of achieving controlling status in the nation, blacks supported it because that group was willing to advocate and proclaim the *principle* of political equality. This fact marked a sharp break with the two traditional parties, which feared that such an openly avowed concession would upset public sensibilities.

Finally, with the advent of the Free Soil and Republican Parties, blacks came out strongly in support of them, not because they were free of racist propensities, which they clearly were not, but because, like the Whig Party before them, they included some leaders who expressed favor toward an unqualified extension of black rights.

Thus, while it must be conceded that the voting strength of blacks was not commensurate with their numbers in the general population, the participation of this minority in politics had the welcome result of producing a greater awareness and sophistication on the part of this community. Further, participation in political activity impressed upon this group the necessity of striving unceasingly for the attainment of those goals deemed essential to the continued viability of black community life.

The opposition of blacks to the colonization scheme demonstrated the degree to which an entire community could be mobilized, almost within hours, to express its deeply held sentiments with regard to this issue. With the single exception of slavery, no other question was capable of evoking such an intense and widespread emotional response as colonization.

We have seen that this program, especially the approach endorsed by the American Colonization Society, elicited the almost unanimous resistance by the black community of New York City. The reason was that colonization, in whatever guise presented, could not free itself from the grave implication that the black man was incapable of advancing within American society. The American Colonization Society publicly expressed this belief, and Robert Goodloe Harper, one of the founders of that organization, stated flatly on one occasion: "You may manumit the slave, but you cannot make him a white man; he still remains a negro or a mulatto"[3]

Thus blacks could not in good conscious support a movement whose obvious tendency was to increase racial prejudice against them.[4] Moreover, they felt doubly betrayed when prominent black persons, operating outside of the auspices of the American Colonization Society, formed their own groups with this objective in mind. Thus it is not difficult to understand the vehement protests generated in the Negro community by such black organizations as the Liberian Agricultural and Emigration Society and the African Civilization Society.

---

[3] Quoted in Pease and Pease, *The Antislavery Argument*, 20. In the *Fifteenth Annual Report* of the American Colonization Society, it was stated: "*Causes behond the control of the human will* must prevent their [blacks] ever rising to equality with the whites. The managers consider it clear, that causes exist, and are operating, to prevent their improvemnet and elevation to any consideratble extent, as a class, in this country, which are fixed, not only beyond the of the friends of humanity, *BUT OF ANY HUMAN POWER*. . . .This is not the fault of the colored man, *nor of the white man, nor of Christianity*; but it is AN ORDINATION OF PROVIDENCE, *and no more to be changed than the laws of nature.*" Quoted in Lewis Tappan, *Life of Arthur Tappan,* 137. (Italics in the original.)

[4] Yet the American Colonization Society remained increasingly on the defensive after 1830. To the charges that it was not eliminating slavery, combating prejudice nor improving the condition of free blacks, the Society could only cling to its official proclamation of 1831 that such was not its business: "The emancipation of slaves, or the amelioration of their condition, with the moral, intellectual, and political impovement of the people of color within the United States, are subjects foreign to the powers of this society . . . but it does not follow, because the Society does not direct or encourage these objects, that it is either hostile to them or that it exercises any deleterious influence in regard to them." Quoted in Charles I. Foster, "The Colonization of Free Negroes in Liberia, 1816-35," *Journal of Negro History,* 38 (1953): 65.

The latter group, founded by Henry Highland Garnet, sought to destroy slavery in America by producing cotton in Africa. Yet Frederick Douglass, an opponent of this Society, contended that the most effective organization against slavery, must be where slavery actually was—in America, not in Africa.

So with the exception of Canada, and to a small degree, even of Haiti, no consensus could be formed among blacks in New York for an emigration to Africa. Because that continent had been so closely linked with the plans of the American Colonization Society, and since blacks viewed colonization itself as an extension of slavery, it was doomed to failure.

The Abolition movement in New York City offered blacks the greatest opportunity to strike a blow against slavery. For as was outlined above, blacks played active roles in the organization and proceedings of anti-slavery societies.

If blacks expressed apprehension toward colonization, and various other movements which sprang up at this time, the abolition crusade was not one of these. For whatever differences existed among its co-workers as to tactics and strategies, all believed themselves to be engaged in a common struggle against slavery.

Thus from the 1830's onward, with the advent of militant abolitionism, blacks would become increasingly vocal in the anti-slavery ranks. In addition to participation in predominantly white anti-slavery bodies, blacks would also increasingly rely on their own community instrumentalities to effect change. The *Colored American*, for example, railed repeatedly in its columns against the excesses of the peculiar institution, not only in its treatment of the slaves in the South, but also for its baneful influence on the status of free blacks in the North.

The Black Church, too, was enlisted in the fight. Its doors remained open at all times to groups who sought through meetings and conventions a forum to express their opposition to slavery.

Perhaps the New York Committee of Vigilance, founded by David Ruggles and others, marked a high point in black abolition activity. For this group had refined the technique of protecting fugitive slaves, securing them legal assistance when necessary, and preventing, if possible, the kidnapping of free blacks.

This organization engendered a tremendous degree of hostility among certain elements in the white community, yet its value lay in the fact that a sufficient number of black people in New York felt impelled, when danger threatened, to protect the integrity and inviolability of their community against designing and nefarious individuals.

Although the New York Vigilance Committee had passed out of existence by the middle 1840's, blacks in the city did not relax their activity in this area. All through the 1850's, when a new Fugitive Slave Law was in force, the African-American community united militantly around a program of resistance and gradually was able to win considerable white support to their cause. By early 1860, even with the heart-rending John Brown episode of the previous year, the morale of the black anti slavery apostles in the city was high. Events in the nation were signaling the approach of a mighty contest that would terminate either in the continued existence or in the destruction of slavery. Black abolitionists had made no small contribution to bringing about the results.

In concluding this history of the Afro-American in New York City, we have traced the many avenues through which black people sought to achieve their full liberation. Yet, overall, while it must be admitted that the African-American made notable strides in the areas of education, the church, and through his press and societies, he failed in his attempt to move into the mainstream of American life. Perhaps the majority of his white countrymen never really took too seriously the statement in the Declaration of Independence that all men were created equal. Certainly, many whites felt that this formulation did not include the black people in their midst. Thus, while the status of New York City blacks consistently showed a downward trend in the three decades before the Civil War, their dogged determination to be free, notwithstanding the formidable obstacles against them, constitutes a significant chapter in the story of the American people.

I. Primary Sources

Unpublished Manuscripts

African Free School Papers. 4 vols. New York Historical Society.

New York County, Religious Incorporations, 1784-1886. 2 vols. Register's Office, Hall of Records, New York City.

New York State, Census of 1855. 22 vols. New York County Clerk's Office, Hall of Records, New York City.

Lewis Tappan. Papers. 15 boxes. Library of Congress.

Federal Documents

Statutes at Large of the United States . . . 1789-1873. 17 vols., Boston: Little, Brown and Company, 1845-1837.

U.S. Census Office. *Fifth Census or Enumeration of the Inhabitants of the United States . . . 1830.* Washington: Duff Green, 1832.

U.S. Census Office. *Heads of Families at the First Census of the United States in the Year 1790.* Washington: Government Printing Office, 1908

U.S. Census Office. *Population of the United States in 1860; Compiled from the Original Returns of the Eighth Census. . .* Washington: Government Printing Office, 1864.

U.S. Census Office. *Sixth Census or Enumeration of the Inhabitants of the United States . . . 1840.* Washington: Blair and Rives, 1841.

U.S. Census Office. *Statistical View of the United States . . . Being a Compendium of the Seventh Census. . . .* Washington: B. Tucker, Senate Printer, 1854.

U.S.W.P.A. *Calendar of the Gerrit Smith Papers in the Syracuse University Library.* 2 vols. Albany: Historical Records Survey, 1941.

U.S.W.P.A. *Inventory of the Church Archives of New York City.* The Methodist Church. The Presbyterian Church. The Protestant Episcopal Church in the United States Diocese of New York. Reformed Churches. Roman Catholic Church. Protestant Episcopal Church. Prepared by the Historical Records Survey. . . New York: The Historical Records Survey, 1940-1941.

State and City Documents

*Census of the State of New York for 1835. . . .*Albany: Printed by Croswell, Van Benthuysen & Burt, 1836.

*Census of the State of New York for 1845. . . .*Albany: Carroll Cook, 1846.

*Census of the State of New York for 1855. . . .*Albany: C. Van Benthuysen, 1857.

Constitution of the State of New York, Adopted in Convention, November 10th, 1821. Hudson: William E. Norman, 1822.

Debates and Proceedings in the New York State Convention for the Revision of the Constitution. Albany: Office of the Albany Argus, 1846.

N.Y.C. *Annual Report of the Alms House Commissioner, Comprising Reports from the Several departments Embraced in the Institution, etc., etc., For the Year Ending December 31, 1847.*

New York: *Board of Aldermen.* Printed by William B. Townsend, 1848.

N.Y.C. City Inspector. *Annual Reports,* 1842, 1857.

N.Y.C. *First Annual Report of the Governors of the Alms House, New York, For the Year 1849.* New York: George F. Nesbitt, Stationer and Printer, 1850.

N.Y.C. *Report of the Commissioner of the Alms House in Answer to Certain Resolutions of Enquiry, Adopted by the Board of Aldermen, Document No. 23.* New York: Printed by Levi. D. Slamm, 1843.

New York (State) Legislature. *Journal of the Assembly of the State of New York, at their Sixty-Fourth Session, Begun and Held at the Capitol, the City of Albany, on the Fifth Day of January, 1841.* Albany: Printed by Thurlow Weed, Printer to the State, 1841.

"Report of the Committee on Charitable and Religious Societies on the Memorial of the Colored Home in the City of New York, and the Memorials etc., in Relation to the State Hospital in Said City." New York State Senate. *Documents.* 68th Sess., 1845, 3:112.

"Report of the Committee on Charitable and Religious Societies on the Petition of the Managers of the Association for the Benefit of Colored Orphans, in the City of New York." New York State Assembly. *Documents.* 74th Sess., 1851. 2:43.

"Report of the Committee on the Judiciary, on a Resolution Introduced by Mr. Duer, Relative to the Right of Suffrage." New York state Assembly. *Documents.* 64th Sess., 1841, 5:181.

"Report of the Select Committee Appointed to Examine into the Condition of Tenement Houses in New York and Brooklyn." New York State Assembly. *Documents.* 80th Sess., 1857, 3:205.

Selections from the Revised Statutes of the Sate of New York: Containing All the Laws of the State Relative to Slaves, and the Laws Relative to the Offence of Kidnapping, which Several Laws

Commenced and Took Effect January 1, 1830. Together with Extracts from the Laws of the United States, Respecting Slaves. Published in behalf of the New York Manumission Society, by direction of the Standing Committee. New York: Vanderpool & Cole, 1830.

Newspapers

African Repository, 1846. Schomburg Collection.

Anglo-African Magazine, 1859. Schomburg Collection.

Colored American, 1837-1841. Schomburg Collection.

Douglass' Monthly, 1859-1860. Schomburg Collection.

Emancipator, 1837-1841. New York Public Library.

Frederick Douglass Paper, 1851-1855. Schomburg Collection.

Freedom's Journal, 1827-1829. Schomburg Collection.

Liberator, 1841-1850. New York Public Library.

National Anti-Slavery Standard, 1841-1858. New York Public Library.

New York Evangelist, 1831-1853. New York Public Library.

New York Tribune, 1850-1858. New York Public Library.

New York Weekly Tribune, 1851. New York Public Library.

North Star, 1848-1850. Schomburg Collection.

Radical Abolitionist, 1858. Columbia University Library.

Ram's Horn, 1847. Schomburg Collection.

Rights of All, 1829. Schomburg Collection.

Weekly Advocate, 1837. Schomburg Collection.

Weekly Anglo-African, 1859-1860. Schomburg Collection.

Contemporary books, convention proceedings and pamphlets

Address to the People of Color, in the City of New York, by Members of the Executive Committee of the American Anti-Slavery Society. New York: S.W. Benedict Printer, 1834. Schomburg Collection.

American and Foreign Anti-Slavery Society. *Annual Reports* (1850-1851). Schomburg Collection.

American Anti-Slavery Society. *Annual Reports* (1834-1840; 1855-1861). [No reports published between 1841 and 1855.] Schomburg Collection.

Andrews, Charles C. *The History of the New York African Free Schools, from their Establishment in 1787 to the Present Time; Embracing a Period of More then Forty Years: Also a Brief Account of the Successful Labors of the New York Manumission Society.* New York: Mahlon Day and Co., 1830. Schomburg Collection.

Association for the Benefit of Colored Orphans, *Annual Reports* (1837-1838). New York Historical Society.

Boyd, W.H. *New York City Tax Book, being a List of Persons, Corporations and Co-Partnerships, Resident and Non-Resident, who were Taxed, According to the Assessors Books, 1856 and 1857.* New York: Wm. H. Boyd, 1857. New York Public Library.

Clark, Rev. James Freeman, *Present Condition of the Free Colored People of the United States.* New York: American Anti-Slavery Society, 1859. Schomburg Collection

Cornish, Samuel E. and Wright, Theodore S. *The Colonization Scheme Considered in Its Rejection by the Colored People—in Its Tendency to Uphold Caste—in Its Unfitness for Christianizing and Civilizing the Aborigines of Africa and for Putting a Stop to the African Slave Trade; in a Letter to the Hon. Theodore Freylinghuysen and Hon. Benjamin F. Butler.* Newark: Aaron Guest, 1840. Schomburg Collection.

Delany, Martin R. *The Condition, Elevation, Emigration and Destiny of the Colored People of the United States. Politically Considered.* Philadelphia: Published by the Author, 1852. Schomburg Collection.

Fifth Annual Report of the New York Committee of Vigilance, for the Year 1842, With Interesting Facts Relative to Their Proceedings. New York: n.p., 1842. Schomburg Collection.

The First Annual Report of the American Society for Colonizing the Free People of Color, of the United States; at Their Annual Meeting in the City of Washington, on the First Day of January, 1818. Washington City: American Colonization Society, 1818. Schomburg Collection.

The First Annual Report of the New York Committee of Vigilance for the Year 1837 Together With Important Facts Relative to their Proceedings. New York: Piercy and Reed, 1837. Schomburg Collection.

Foner, Philip S. and George E. Walker, eds. *Proceedings of the Black National and State Conventions, 1865-1900.* Philadelphia: Temple University Press, 1986.

Foner, Philip S. and George E. Walker, eds. *Proceedings of the Black State Conventions, 1840-1865.* Philadelphia: Temple University Press, 1979-1980 (2 vols.)

The Fugitive Slave Bill: Its History and Unconstitutionality with an Account of the Seizure and Enslavement of James Hamlet, and his Subsequent Restoration to Liberty. New York: William Harned, 1850. Schomburg Collection.

Goodell, William. *Slavery and Anti-Slavery; A History of the Great Struggle in Both Hemispheres; With a View of the Slavery Question in the United States.* New York: William Goodell, 1855. Third edition. Schomburg Collection.

Greenleaf, Jonathen. *A History of the Churches of All Denominations in the City of New York, from the First Settlement to the Year 1846.* New York: E. French, 1846. First Edition. Schomburg Collection.

Hamilton, William. *An Oration Delivered in the African Zion Church, on the fourth of July 1827, in commemoration of the abolition of domestic slavery in the state.* New York: Printed by Gray & Bunce, 1827. Schomburg Collection.

Jackson, Lewis Evans. *Walks About New York. Facts and Figures Gathered from Various Sources.* New York: Published for the (City Mission) Society, 1865. New York Public Library.

Jay, John. *An Address in Behalf of the Colored Orphan Asylum Delivered at their Seventh Anniversary, December 11, 1843.* New York: Mahlon Day and Co., 1844. Schomburg Collection.

Jay, John. *Caste and Slavery in the American Church.* New York: Wiley and Putnam, 1843.

Journal of the Proceedings of the Sixty-Second Convention of the Protestant Episcopal Church in the Diocese of New York, Held in St. John's Chapel in the city of New York, Wednesday, Sept. 30 to Saturday, Oct. 3. Inclusive, A. D. 1846. New York: Henry Onderonk, 1846. Schomburg Collection.

Minutes and Proceedings of the First Annual Convention of the People of Colour, Held by Adjournment in the City of Philadelphia, from the sixth to the eleventh of June, Inclusive,

1831.   Philadelphia: Published by order of the Committee of Arrangement, 1831. Schomburg Collection.

Minutes and Proceedings of the Second Annual Convention, for the Improvement of the Free People of Colour in the United States, Held by Adjournment in the City of Philadelphia, from the Fourth to the Thirteenth of June Inclusive, 1832. Philadelphia: Martin and Boden Printers, 1832. Schomburg Collection.

Minutes of the Fifth Annual Convention for the Improvement of the Free People of Colour in the United States, Held by Adjournment in the Wesley Church, Philadelphia, from the First to the Fifth of June, Inclusive, 1835. Philadelphia: Printed by William P. Gibbon, 1835. Schomburg Collection.

Minutes of the National Convention of Colored Citizens: Held at Buffalo, on the 15th, 16th, 17th, 18th and 19th of August, 1843, for the Purpose of Considering Their Moral and Political Condition as American Citizens. New York: Piercy and Reed, 1843. Schomburg Collection.

Minutes of the State Convention of Colored Citizens, Held at Albany, on the 18th, 19th and 20th of August, 1840, for the Purpose of Considering Their Political Condition. New York: Piercy and Reed, 1840. Schomburg Collection.

May, Samuel Joseph. *The Fugitive Slave Law and Its Victims.* New York: American Anti Slavery Society, 1861. Schomburg Collection.

Proceedings of the Colored National Convention held in Rochester, July 6th, 7th and 8th, 1853. Rochester, NY.: Printed at the Office of Frederick Douglass Paper, 1853. Schomburg Collection.

Proceedings of the National Convention of Colored People And Their Friends, held in Troy, NY., on the 6th, 7th, 8th, and 9th October, 1847. Troy, NY.: Steampress of J. C. Kneeland and Co., 1847. Schomburg Collection.

Rush, Christopher. *A Short Account of the Rise and Progress of the African Methodist Episcopal Church in America. Also, A Concise View of Church Order or Government, From Scripture and from the Best Authors on the Subject of Church Government, Relative to Episcopacy.* New York: Published by the Author, 1843. Schomburg Collection.

Sixth Annual Report of the Colonization Society, of the City of New York, etc. New York: Marcein & Post's Press, 1838. Schomburg Collection.

Thompson, Mary W. *Sketches of the History, Character, And Dying Testimony of the Colored Home, in the City of New York.* New York: John F. Trow, Printer, 1851. Schomburg Collection.

Williams, Edwin ed. *New York Register* (1834-1840).

Wright, Theodore S., Ray, Charles B., and Smith, James McCune. *An Address to the Three Thousand Colored Citizens of New York, Who are the Owners of One Hundred and Twenty Thousand Acres of Land in the State of New York, Given to Them by Gerrit Smith Esq. of Peterboro.* New York: n.p., 1846. Schomburg Collection.

Yates, William. *Rights of Colored Men to Suffrage, Citizenship and Trial by Jury: Being A Book of Facts, Arguments and Authorities, Historical Notices and Sketches of Debates—With Notes.* Philadelphia: Pr. by Merrihew and Gunn, 1838. Schomburg Collection.

Collected source manuscripts

Foner, Philip Sheldon. *The Life and Writings of Frederick Douglass.* 4 vols. New York: International Publishers, 1950-55.

Woodson, Carter G. *The Mind of the Negro as Reflected in Letters Written During the Crises: 1800-1860.* Washington: Association for the Study of Negro Life and History, 1926.

Collected source documents

Baker, George E. ed. *The Works of William H. Seward.* 3 vols. New York: Redfield, 1853.

Travel Accounts

Abdy, Edward Strutt. *Journal of a Residence and Tour in the United states of North America, from April, 1833 to October, 1834.* 3 vols. London: John Murray, 1835.

Dickens, Charles. *American Notes for General Circulation.* Boston, Mass.: Estes & Laurint, 1892.

Duncan, Mary Lundie. *America as I Found It.* New York: Robert Carter & Brothers, 1852.

Playfair, Robert esq. *Recollections of a Visit to the United States and British Provinces of North America in the Years, 1847, 1848, 1849.* Edinburgh: Thomas Constable and Co., 1856.

II. SECONDARY WORKS

General

Boese, Thomas. *Public Education in the City of New York, Its History, Condition, and Statistics, an Official Report of the Board of Education.* New York: Harper and Bros., 1869.

Bourne, William Oland, A.M. *History of the Public School Society of the City of New York With Portraits of the Presidents of the Society.* New York: G.P. Putnam's Sons, 1873.

Dann, Martin E. ed. *The Black Press, 1827-1890: The Quest for National Identity.* New York: Capricorn Books, 1972.

Davis, Thomas J. "Slavery in Colonial New York City," (unpublished Ph.D. dissertation), Columbia University, 1974.

De Costa, Rev. B.F., D.D. *Three Score and Ten: The Story of St. Philip's Church New York City.* New York: Printed for the Parish, 1889.

Field, Phyllis J. The Politics of Race in New York: the Struggle for Black Suffrage in the Civil War Era, Ithaca, NY: Cornell University Press, 1982.

Foner, Philip S. ed. T*he Voice of Black America: Major Speeches by Negroes in the United States, 1797-1971.* New York: Simon and Schuster, 1972.

Franklin, John Hope. *From Slavery to Freedom: A History of Negro Americans.* 3rd edition. New York: Alfred A. Knopf, 1967.

Hood, Bishop J.W., D.D. LL.D. *One Hundred Years of the African Methodist Episcopal Zion Church.* New York: A.M.E. Zion Book Concern, 1895.

Hough, Franklin. *Statistics of Population of the City and County of New York as Shown by the State census of 1865, with Comparative Results of this and Previous Enumerations and other Statistics, given by the State and Federal Census from the Earliest Period. Prepared at the Request of the Committee on Annual Taxes of the Board of Supervisors.* New York: New York Printing Company, 1866.

Lincoln, Charles Z. *The Constitutional History of New York From the Beginning of the Colonial Period to the Year 1905, Showing the Origins, Development and Judicial Construction of the Constitution.* 5 vols. Rochester, NY.: The Lawyers Co-operative Publishing Company, 1906.

Nash, Gary B. *Forging Freedom: The Formation of Philadelphia's Black Community, 1720-1840.* Cambridge, MA: Harvard University Press, 1988.

Meier, August and Rudwick, Elliott, eds. *The Making of Black America.* 2 vols. New York: Atheneum, 1969.

Payne, Daniel A., D.D. LL. D. *History of the African Methodist Episcopal Church.* Nashville, TN: Publishing House of the A.M.E. Sunday School Union, 1891.

Payne, Daniel A., D.D. LL. D. *Recollections of Seventy Years.* New York: Arno Press, 1968. Reprint of 1888 edition.

Pease, William H., and Jane H., eds. *The Antislavery Argument.* New York: Bobbs-Merrill Company, Inc., 1965.

Porter, Kirk H. and Johnson, Donald Bruce, eds. *National Party Platforms, 1840-1956.* Urbana, IL.: The University of Illinois Press, 1956.

(Ray, Mrs. C.A.B.). *Sketch of the Life of Rev. Charles R. Ray.* New York: J.J. Little and Co., 1887.

Richmond, J.R. (Rev.). *New York and Its Institutions, 1609-1872.* New York: E.B. Treat, 1872.

White, Shane. *Somewhat More Important: The End of Slavery in New York City, 1770-1818.* Athens, GA: The University of Georgia Press, 1991

Wilson, Henry. *History of the Rise and Fall of the Slave Power in America.* 3 vols. Boston: J.R. Osgood and Company, 1872-77.

Woodson, Carter G. *The Education of the Negro Prior to 1861.* New York: G.P. Putnam's Sons, 1915.

Woodson, Carter G. *The History of the Negro Church.* Washington, D.C.: Associated Publishers, 1921.

Monographs and special studies

Bell, Howard. "A Survey of the Negro Convention Movement, 1830-1860." Unpublished Ph.D. Dissertation, Northwestern University, 1953.

Dumond, Dwight Lowell. *Antislavery: The Crusade for Freedom in America*. New York: W.W. Norton & Company, Inc. 1961.

Ernst, Robert. *Immigrant Life in New York City, 1825-1863*. Port Washington, NY: Ira J. Friedman, Inc., 1949.

Foner, Eric. *Free Soil, Free Labor, Free Men: The Ideology of the Republican Party Before the Civil War*. New York: Oxford University Press, 1970.

Freeman, Rhoda G. "The Free Negro in New York City in the Era Before the Civil War." Unpublished Ph.D. Dissertation, Columbia University, 1966.

George, Carol V.R. *Segregated Sabbaths: Richard Allen and the Emergence of Independent Black Churches, 1760-1840*. New York: Oxford University Press, 1973.

Groisser, Philmore L. "The Free Negro in New York State, 1850-1860." Unpublished M.A. dissertation, Columbia University, 1939.

Haynes, George E. *The Negro at Work in New York City: A Study in Economic Progress* ("Columbia University Studies in History, Economic and Public Law," No. 124). New York: Columbia University, 1912.

McManus, Edgar J. "Negro Slavery in New York." Unpublished Ph.D. Dissertation, Columbia University, 1959.

Olson, Edwin. "Negro Slavery in New York, 1627-1827." Unpublished Ph.D. Dissertation, New York University, 1938.

Ovington, Mary White. *Half A Man: The Status of the Negro in New York*. New York: Longmans, Green & Co., 1911.

Pease, Jane H. and William H. *Bound With Them in Chains: A Biographical History of the Antislavery Movement*. Westport, CT: Greenwood Press, Inc., 1972.

Quarles, Benjamin. *Black Abolitionists*. New York: Oxford University Press, 1972.

Sorin, Gerald. *Abolitionism, A New Perspective*. New York: Praeger Publishers, 1972.

Sorin, Gerald. *The New York Abolitionists: A Case Study of Political Radicalism*. Westport, CT. Greenwood Publishing Corporation, 1971.

Williamson, Chilton. *American Suffrage from Property to Democracy*. Princton, NJ,: Princton University Press, 1960.

Woodson, Carter G. *The Free Negro Heads of Families in the United States in 1830 together with a Brief Treatment of the Free Negro*. Washington, D.C.: Association for the Study of the Negro Life and History, Inc., 1925.

Biographies

Brown, Clarence Winthrop. *Arthur and Lewis Tappan*. New York: n.p., 1883.

Frothingham, Octavious B. *Gerrit Smith, A Biography*. New York: G.P. Putnam's Sons, 1909.

Harlow, Ralph V. *Gerrit Smith: Philanthropist and Reformer*. New York: Henry Holt and Company, 1939.

Oates, Stephen B. *To Purge this Land with Blood, a Biography of John Brown.* New York: Harper Torchbooks, 1970.

Ofari, Earl. *"Let Your Motto Be Resistance" The Live and Thought of Henry Highland Garnet.* Boston: Beacon Press, 1972.

Tappan, Lewis. *The Life of Arthur Tappan.* New York: Hurd & Houghton, 1870.

Wyatt-Brown, Bertram. *Lewis Tappan and the Evangelical War Against Slavery.* Cleveland: The Press of Case Western Reserve University, 1969.

Periodical Articles

Barnett, Enid Vivian. "Educational Activities By and In Behalf of the Negroes in New York, 1800-1830," *The Negro History Bulletin,* 14 (February 1951):99-114.

Boardman, Helen. "David Ruggles," *The Negro History Bulletin,* 5 (November 1941):39-40.

Brewer, William M. "John B. Russwurm," *Journal of Negro History,* 13, No. 4 (October 1928):413-422.

Clarke, James Freeman. "Conditions of the Free Colored People of the United Sates," *The Christian Examiner,* 66 (March 1859):246-265.

David, C.W.A. "The Fugitive Slave Law of 1793 and Its Antecedents," *Journal of Negro History,* 9 (January 1924):18-25.

Dyson, Zita. "Gerrit Smith's Efforts in Behalf of the Negroes in New York," *Journal of Negro History,* 3 (October 1918):354-359.

Foner, Eric. "Racial Attitudes of the New York Free Soilers," *New York History,* 4-6, No. 4 (October 1965):311-329.

Foster, Charles I. "The Colonization of Free Negroes in Liberia, 1816-35," *Journal of Negro History*, 38 (January 1953):41-66.

Fox, Dixon Ryan. "The Negro Vote in Old New York," *Political Science Quarterly*, 32, No. 2 (June 1917):252-275.

Gross, Bella. "Freedom's Journal and the Rights of All," *Journal of Negro History*, 17, No. 3 (June 1932):241-286.

Harmon, J.H. Jr. "The Negro as Local Business Man," *Journal of Negro History*, 14, No. 2 (April 1929):117-155.

Hirsch, Leo H. Jr. "New York and the Negro, from 1783 to 1865," *Journal of Negro History*, 16 (October 1931):382-473.

Lindsay, Arnett G. "The Economic Condition of the Negroes of New York Prior to 1861," *Journal of Negro History*, 6 (April 1921):190-199.

Lindsay, Arnett G. "The Negro in Banking," *Journal of Negro History*, 14, No. 2 (April 1929):156-200.

Mehlinger, Louis H. "The Attitude of the Free Negro Toward African Colonization," *Journal of Negro History*, 1, No. 3 (June 1916):276-301.

Myers, John L. "American Antislavery Society Agents and the Free Negro, 1833-1838," *Journal of Negro History*, 52, No. 3 (July 1967):200-219.

Olbrich, Emil. "The Development of Sentiment on Negro Suffrage to 1860," *Bulletin of the University of Wisconsin*, 3, No. 477 (1912):1-135.

Payne, A.A. "The Negro in New York Prior to 1860," *Howard Review*, 1, (June 1923):1-64.

Perlman, Daniel. "Organizations of the Free Negro in New York City, 1800-1860," *Journal of Negro History*, 56, No. 3 (July 1971):181-197.

Quarles, Benjamin. "Letters from Negro Leaders to Gerrit Smith," *Journal of Negro History*, 27 (October 1942):432-453.

Reddick, Lawrence D. "Samuel E. Cornish," *The Negro History Bulletin*, 5 (November 1941):38.

Thurston, Eve. "Ethiopia Unshackled: A Brief History of the Education of Negro Children in New York City," *Bulletin of the New York Public Library*, 69 (April 1965):211-231.

Wesley, Charles H. "Negro Suffrage in the Period of Constitution-Making, 1787-1865," *Journal of Negro History*, 32, No. 2 (April 1947):143-168.

Wesley, Charles H. "The Negroes of New York in the Emancipation Movement," *Journal of Negro History*, 24 (January 1939):35-103.

Wesley, Charles H. "The Participation of Negroes in Anti-Slavery Political Parties," *Journal of Negro History*, 29 (January 1944):33-74.

Table 1

The number of free blacks in New York City who were untaxed, taxed, and qualified to vote in 1835

Ward	# of persons of color in same town who are *not* taxed	# of persons of color in same town who *are* taxed
First	581	1
Second	297	14
Third	599	1
Fourth	180	19
Fifth	1,999	1
Sixth	1,797	3
Seventh	820	—
Eighth	2,773	—
Ninth	296	—
Tenth	990	10
Eleventh	792	2
Twelfth	1,238	19
Thirteenth	694	3
Fourteenth	992	11
Fifteenth	929	—
Total	**14,977**	**84**

Table 1
continued

Wards	# of persons of color in the same town who are taxed, and entitled by the constitution of this state to vote for all officers by the people
First	1
Second	1
Third	2
Fourth	11
Fifth	3
Sixth	5
Seventh	—
Eighth	3
Ninth	—
Tenth	—
Eleventh	4
Twelfth	19
Thirteenth	2
Fourteenth	6
Fifteenth	11
Total	**68**

Source: New York State, *Census for 1835* (Albany, 1836), Double Leaf, No. 26.

Table 2

*The number of free blacks in New York City who were untaxed, taxed,
and qualified to vote in 1845*

Ward New York City	Total population	# of persons of color in the County not taxed
First	12,230	179
Second	6,962	273
Third	11,900	525
Fourth	21,000	178
Fifth	20,362	2406
Sixth	19,343	1060
Seventh	25,556	357
Eighth	30,900	1809
Ninth	30,907	363
Tenth	20,993	443
Eleventh	27,259	537
Twelfth	13,378	459
Thirteenth	22,411	663
Fourteenth	21,103	1236
Fifteenth	19,422	697
Sixteenth	40,350	1073
Seventeenth	27,147	391
Total	**371,147**	**12,658**

Table 2
continued

Ward New York City	# of persons of color in the County who are taxed	# of persons of color in the County who are legal voters
First	13	5
Second	4	2
Third	5	4
Fourth	3	22
Fifth	27	6
Sixth	13	—
Seventh	11	6
Eighth	32	3
Ninth	4	2
Tenth	2	3
Eleventh	3	15
Twelfth	100	2
Thirteenth	4	5
Fourteenth	7	6
Fifteenth	15	6
Sixteenth	6	2
Seventeenth	6	2
Total	**255**	**91**

Source: New York State, *Census for 1845* (Albany, 1845), Double Leaf, No. 29-1

Index

217

George E. Walker is an Associate Professor of History at George Mason University. He received his B.A. degree from Lincoln University, Pennsylvania, and his M.A., M.Phil., and Ph.D. degrees from Columbia University. In 1989, he received a law degree from Georgetown University and is currently a member of the Pennsylvania bar.

Dr. Walker has held the Woodrow Wilson Fellowship (1970–71), Columbia University Fellowship (1970–73), Ford Foundation Fellowship (1971–75), John Hay Whitney Fellowship (1971–72), and research grants from the Ford Foundation (1978), American Philosophical Society (1977, 1980), American Historical Association's Albert J. Beveridge Research Grant (1982), and the National Endowment for the Humanities (1984).

He is currently at work on a book entitled, *The First Black Congressmen, 1870–1901: Spokesmen for Freedom*, to be published by Garland Publishing Company in 1994.